HUMANITARIAN CHALLENGES AND INTERVENTION

DILEMMAS IN WORLD POLITICS

Series Editor

George A. Lopez, University of Notre Dame

Dilemmas in World Politics offers teachers and students of international relations a series of quality books on critical issues, trends, and regions in international politics. Each text examines a "real world" dilemma and is structured to cover the historical, theoretical, practical, and projected dimensions of its subject.

EDITORIAL BOARD

FORTHCOMING TITLES

James A. Caporaso
Challenges and Dilemmas of European Union

□ □ □

Janice Love
Southern Africa in World Politics

HUMANITARIAN CHALLENGES AND INTERVENTION

■ ■ ■

World Politics and the Dilemmas of Help

Thomas G. Weiss
and Cindy Collins

WestviewPress

A Division of HarperCollinsPublishers

Dilemmas in World Politics Series

Copyright © 1996 by Westview Press, A Division of HarperCollins Publishers, Inc.

Published in 1996 in the United States of America by Westview Press, 5500 Central Avenue, Boulder, Colorado 80301-2877, and in the United Kingdom by Westview Press, 12 Hid's Copse Road, Cumnor Hill, Oxford OX2 9JJ

Library of Congress Cataloging-in-Publication Data
Weiss, Thomas George.
   Humanitarian challenges and intervention : world politics and the
dilemmas of help / Thomas G. Weiss and Cindy Collins.
      p.   cm.—(Dilemmas in world politics)
   Includes bibliographical references and index.
   ISBN 0-8133-2844-6.—ISBN 0-8133-2845-4 (pbk.)
   1. International relief.   2. War victims—Services for.   3. World
politics—1989–   I. Collins, Cindy.   II. Title.   III. Series.
HV553.W425   1996
362.87'0526—dc20   96-32664
                                                                              CIP

This book was typeset by Letra Libre, 1705 14th Street, Suite 391, Boulder, Colorado, 80302.

The paper used in this publication meets the requirements of the American National Standard for Permanence of Paper for Printed Library Materials Z39.48-1984.

10   9   8   7   6   5   4   3   2   1

Contents

□ □ □

Illustrations

Tables

Figures

Boxes

□ □ □

Preface and Acknowledgments

I was initially quite pleased when Jennifer Knerr, a former political science editor at Westview, and George A. Lopez, the editor of the series "Dilemmas in World Politics," approached me about writing a much-needed addition to their series, one dealing with humanitarian intervention. After working on humanitarian issues at Brown University's Watson Institute for International Studies, I welcomed the chance to synthesize for student readers the insights that I have gained through field research in war zones in recent years.

I then began to balk in front of what was clearly an overwhelming assignment not only in terms of information but also in terms of the distressing feelings that arose in me from such extensive encounters with such depressing subject matter. The first problem was overcome by my asking Cindy Collins, a graduate student in the Department of Political Science at Brown, to give me a hand at researching the book. As we proceeded, she added her own perspectives and insights. In the end, she became a coauthor; this book would not have taken its present form and been published in such a timely fashion without her able helping hands.

The second problem was more difficult to address. I asked myself, Would students be overcome with a sense of powerlessness in the face of horror? I was buoyed by rereading *La peste* (The plague), by Albert Camus, which for me is ultimately uplifting, rather than depressing, in spite of the tragedy in its pages. Even with the pain throughout this novel, I was able to find new meaning in a concluding passage that is every bit as poignant in translation as in the original: "He knew that the tale he had to tell could not be one of a final victory. It could be only the record of what had to be done, and what assuredly would have to be done again in the neverending fight against terror and its onslaughts . . . by all who, while unable to be saints but refusing to bow down to pestilence, strive their utmost to be healers."

In the preface to a book, it is customary to express gratitude. This task is particularly necessary here because of the number of persons responsible for the evolution in my own ideas in the last few years. I wish to thank the program officers in the foundations and the governmental, intergovernmental, and nongovernmental humanitarian agencies who have seen fit to support the work of the Humanitarianism and War Project. This book benefits from the applied research done under the auspices of the project since 1991 and from the project's openness to considering the lessons of recent experience. This book is unusual in that it is targeted at a younger generation of readers, who are different from the scholars and practitioners for whom I normally write.

I also wish to acknowledge the friendship of Larry Minear since the early 1970s; I have worked intensely with him on humanitarian issues since 1990. It is often difficult to trace accurately the origins of one's arguments and prose, particularly in the kind of partnership that we have enjoyed. Rather than adding one giant endnote, I prefer to acknowledge my intellectual debt at the outset. Larry inevitably pushes me to break new ground, and I hope that the product here reflects well on our efforts to plow the analytical fields of humanitarian action in war zones over the last half decade. His comments on the draft manuscript, as always, were helpful in clarifying my thinking. He is very much present in many of the following pages.

Two other colleagues, Antonio Donini and Giles Whitcomb, have contributed personally to humanitarian efforts through their own fieldwork and analyses over the years. They have also helped immensely through their constructive criticisms of the draft manuscript. I am grateful to them for their comments and also to two other readers, unknown to me, who were given the manuscript by Westview and whose critiques strengthened this final version.

I also wish to thank specifically five members of the Watson Institute staff who retyped, edited, and helped shape various versions of this book. Special thanks are in order to Fred Fullerton, Richard Gann, Gregory Kazarian, Amy Langlais, and Jennifer Patrick.

If students can get a better idea of the dynamics of humanitarian action in war zones and if there are some insights about what has been done and could be done better in the future to help victims, then I will have succeeded in this endeavor.

Thomas G. Weiss

Acronyms

ADRA	International Adventist Development and Relief Agency
AICF	International Action Against Hunger
AIDAB	Australian International Development Assistance Bureau
CIS	Commonwealth of Independent States
CISP	International Committee for the Development of Peoples
CMOCS	Civil-Military Operations Centres
COMECON	Council for Mutual Economic Assistance
CRS	Catholic Relief Services
CRS	Congressional Research Service
DHA	Department of Humanitarian Affairs [U.N.]
DRI	Direct Relief International
EC	European Community
ECHO	European Commission Humanitarian Office
ECOSOC	Economic and Social Council [U.N.]
ECOWAS	Economic Community of West African States
EU	European Union
FAO	Food and Agriculture Organization [U.N.]
GNP	gross national product
HUMPROFOR	Humanitarian Protection Force
ICJ	International Court of Justice
ICRC	International Committee of the Red Cross
ICVA	International Council for Voluntary Agencies
IDP	internally displaced person
IFOR	Implementation Force (in the former Yugoslavia)
IFRC	International Federation of Red Cross and Red Crescent Societies
IGO	intergovernmental organization
IMC	International Medical Corps
IMF	International Monetary Fund
INMED	International Medical Services for Health
IRC	International Rescue Committee
JNA	Yugoslav People's Army
MDM	Médecins du Monde

MSF	Médecins sans Frontières [Doctors Without Borders]
NATO	North Atlantic Treaty Organization
NGO	nongovernmental organization
NRC	Norwegian Refugee Council
OAS	Organization of American States
OAU	Organization of African Unity
ODA	Overseas Development Administration [U.K.]
OFDA	Office of Foreign Disaster Assistance [U.S.]
ONUCA	U.N. Observer Group in Central America
ONUSAL	U.N. Observer Mission in El Salvador
PDD	presidential decision directive
RPF	Rwandan Patriotic Front
SCF/NZ	Save the Children Foundation/New Zealand
SPLA	Sudan People's Liberation Army
SRSG	special representative of the secretary-general [U.N.]
SST	Swedish Support Team
UNAMIR	U.N. Assistance Mission in Rwanda
UNDP	U.N. Development Programme
UNDRO	U.N. Disaster Relief Office
UNHCR	U.N. High Commissioner for Refugees
UNICEF	U.N. Children's Emergency Fund
UNITAF	Unified Task Force
UNOSOM	U.N. Operation in Somalia (I and II)
UNPA	U.N. Protected Area
UNPROFOR	U.N. Protection Force (in the former Yugoslavia)
USAID	U.S. Agency for International Development
WFP	World Food Programme
WHO	World Health Organization

□ □ □

Introduction

A steady stream of gruesome images assaults your senses. Within a
few short years, the media have loaded your visual memory bank
with pallid Bosnian faces behind barbed wire in concentration camps;
corpses floating on Lake Victoria after Rwanda's genocide; adolescent
warriors riding Jeeps with machine guns and contributing to Somalia's
failed statehood and starvation; and waves of freezing Kurds fleeing Saddam Hussein into mountain passes. There are probably fifty wars with
accompanying human suffering going on across the globe today. In the
past decade, war has taken the lives of 2 million children. Every fifteen
minutes, someone steps on a land mine.

This is the world of humanitarian action. Although you may feel removed
from such nightmarish events, this is your world, too. Some 6 billion people
share it with you. One to 2 billion lack clean water or sanitation. Some 50 million of your global neighbors are homeless tonight because of war or famine;
millions of others are displaced or in fear of homelessness because of the
more subtle violence of chronic poverty. More people with fewer resources
and less hope result in environmental degradation; massive migration; the
quick spread of diseases not adequately addressed or quickly identified, such
as acquired immune deficiency syndrome; and increased conflict, with its accompanying proliferation of light and conventional weapons.

For humanitarian specialists whose business it is to track and intercede in
these matters, witnessing and administering to the needs of those steeped in
human tragedy carry their own elements of suffering and vulnerability. Victims of war and humanitarians have been physically and emotionally tossed
about in varying degrees by armed political struggles and an unpredictable
international political will to end the tragedies that are the media's daily bill
of fare. The ethical, legal, and operational challenges and dilemmas that
occur in war zones present tortuous trade-offs to policymakers and to those
working directly with victims. If you worked in such a position, your decisions would bear life-affecting consequences. Would you choose to move
noncombatants out of the country, lead them to food distribution points
within country, or designate an area as a safe haven? Would you focus solely
on delivering food and medical supplies and turn a blind eye to blatant vio-

1

lations of human rights such as rape and torture? Would you throw your hands up or sit on them, claiming that the suffering of those whom you cannot see and most probably will never meet are not your problem? In contemplating your alternatives, you would also have to consider the agenda of your organizational employer as well as your own. Would dead peacekeepers cost you votes in the next election? Would donors support your using funds in crises that do not receive media attention? These and other thorny problems are addressed directly in the pages that follow.

This book is about the challenges facing the humanitarian actors who make up the global safety net that lessens the life-threatening suffering of civilians in war zones. It concerns two types of war-related **humanitarian action**—the provision of **relief** to civilian populations and the **protection** of their basic **human rights**—within the capacity of the present international humanitarian system. Characteristics unique to conflicts and to each actor in the humanitarian system present the challenges and dilemmas of humanitarian action.

The international humanitarian system comprises governmental, institutional, and individual actors who respond to war-related human tragedy. This system is often called the international humanitarian *community*. But this idealistic term hides the diversity of interests and characteristics among institutional actors—a diversity that cannot be wished away as we try to understand the nature of dilemmas in humanitarian operations and how to address them. The moral and practical reasoning that supports each actor's participation in collective humanitarian action may differ dramatically from that of others and will be reflected in the choices that each actor "sees" when deciding upon courses of action (or in some cases, inaction). For these reasons, "system" is more useful than "community" for the purpose of examining challenges.

Humanitarian tasks include gathering data about the severity of the crisis, negotiating a framework with the warring parties for providing aid, mobilizing the necessary resources, orchestrating the aid effort, delivering the goods, staffing the operation, and assuring appropriate accountability. When war becomes a barrier to providing noncombatants with relief, traditional forms of humanitarian assistance may be augmented by a military presence. Human rights action during conflicts also involves data gathering and negotiations but focuses more specifically on efforts to document and expose abuses and to mobilize international pressure and policy to halt violations against human dignity. Postconflict war crimes tribunals are also part of the humanitarian and human rights agendas.

Humanitarian action in war zones shares similarities with assistance provided after natural disasters and with noncrisis reconstruction and development projects. However, when armed conflict rages, humanitarians face challenges that are far more acute. In a war zone, for example, a relief agency responsible for emergency relief or coordination may be unable to maintain **impartiality** or political **neutrality**, equal access to all noncombatants, or adequate communications with belligerents. Impartiality means helping without discrimination as to ethnic or national criteria, religious beliefs, or political opinion. In principle, humanitarian efforts made to relieve the suffering of individuals are guided solely by the victims' needs, and priority is given to the most urgent cases of distress. Neutrality means not taking sides in hostilities or engaging at any time in controversies linked to an armed conflict. Neutrality excludes advocacy in favor of a party to the conflict and public accusation. But neutrality does not mean keeping silent in defending the victims' rights, especially when those rights are grossly disregarded by the belligerents. A dilemma emerges for humanitarians between maintaining the principle of impartiality and neutrality when noncombatants are clearly being targeted by a warring party and making public the violations and taking the chance that the belligerents will withdraw their consent for a humanitarian presence.

The purpose here is to address specifically the operational, ethical, and legal problems faced by humanitarians working amid active armed conflicts, such as choosing between the provision of humanitarian relief and the protection of human rights. Solutions to various dilemmas of war-related involvement may, in fact, hold fruitful lessons for organizations preoccupied with natural disasters or longer-term development as well.

THE CONCEPT OF HUMANITARIANISM

Disagreements flourish regarding the legitimacy of various actions labeled "humanitarian," fueled in part by the absence of an unambiguous and universally accepted definition of the word. If by humanitarian we include "apolitical" as a characteristic, we may need to discard from the humanitarian roster a number of relief organizations, state agencies, and donations. For example, the food, telecommunications equipment, and uniforms funneled to the Nicaraguan insurgents (contras) in 1985 by the U.S. government were labeled "humanitarian." In 1995, with a U.S. trade embargo still in place against the Castro regime, a U.S. citizen received permission from Washington to donate thirty pianos to Cuba under the semantic umbrella of "humanitarian aid" after promising that the pianos would not be used for political purposes. On a less humorous note, following the 1977–1978 Ogaden War between Ethiopia and Somalia, some food aid providers followed a path of action that roamed from humanitarian to self-serving and back to humanitarian again. The donors, motivated by organizational survival and politics, continued to provide free or heavily subsidized food to the Somali people long after famine and refugee flows had subsided. Local farmers, unable to compete with free agricultural commodities, lost the incentive to work the land and maintain self-sufficiency. Resulting cycles of famine and mass urbanization were exacerbated by war, and all of these factors contributed to the **complex emergency** in Somalia in 1992. Part of the humanitarian response to the new crisis was to deliver free food again.

A complex emergency combines internal conflicts with large-scale displacements of people and fragile or failing economic, political, and social institutions. Other symptoms include noncombatant death, starvation, or malnutrition; disease and mental illness; random and systematic violence against noncombatants; infrastructure collapse; widespread lawlessness; and interrupted food production and trade. Table I.1 illustrates the number of countries experiencing complex emergencies in 1995 and describes the political environments that can impede humanitarian efforts. The root causes of complex emergencies are a combination of political power struggles, ethnic or religious tension, economic or territorial disputes, a perceived sense of widespread injustice, and/or natural disasters such as drought or flooding. Because different actors conceive humanitarianism as limited to the provision of emergency relief, the symptoms rather than the root causes of complex emergencies usually receive attention. Limited resources are thus allocated to relief operations instead of reconstruction and development, sometimes in the midst of external military involvement. The absence of a standard definition or principles for humanitarianism intensifies the challenges already posed by the motivations and actions of warring parties as well as by those of humanitarian actors.

Within various organizational forms, from states to grassroots groups, concepts related to humanitarianism take on different meanings. They are then reflected in a course of action that may not be truly humanitarian in the eyes of others, even of recipients. As detailed in subsequent chapters, a variety of perceptions and organizational forms greatly affect the coordination and implementation of efforts in war zones and contribute to the fuzziness of "humanitarian" as an operational concept.

Even the dictionary offers minimal insight beyond the commonsensical. "A person actively engaged in promoting human welfare" is a humanitarian.[1] That is, each person is free to determine what promotes human welfare. For some, human welfare is enhanced by adherence to a particular religious or political dogma; for others, by the building of an irrigation system or the education of women. Some humanitarians have an irresistible impulse and philosophical commitment to help wherever suffering exists; others are more calculating in trying to determine where their efforts would make a difference. Some humanitarians seem to fit images of naïveté and bleeding hearts; others, of hardened heads and hearts capable of practicing **triage**—that is, calculating who can be helped and who cannot and then making judgments about who should be.

The International Court of Justice (ICJ) missed an opportunity for clarification in a 1986 decision that ruled in favor of Nicaragua and against the United States, which had laid mines in Nicaraguan territorial waters. The

TABLE I.1 Complex Humanitarian Emergencies, 1995

Country	Population at Risk[a]	Political Environment
Afghanistan	4.2 million Includes over 3.2 million refugees, primarily in Iran and Pakistan	Escalated fighting 1994 Little government control Land mines
Algeria	N.A.	Insurgency Government consent to relief unlikely
Angola	3.7 million Includes 300,000 refugees in Congo, Zambia, and Zaire	Civil war Intensified hostilities Limited government ability to support relief operations Corruption in security forces Land mines
Armenia	300,000 Includes 250,000 refugees in Azerbaijan and Russia	Government support for relief limited to ethnic Armenians
Azerbaijan	1 million Includes 300,000 refugees in Armenia and Russia	Limited government control in west Resistance to relief for Armenians
Bosnia and Herzegovina	2.5 million Includes 1.1 million refugees, primarily in Croatia, Germany, and Serbia	Little government control All factions periodically oppose relief to other groups
Burma (Myanmar)	N.A. Estimated 200,000 refugees in Bangladesh and Thailand	Civil war
Burundi	900,000 Includes 300,000 refugees in Rwanda, Tanzania, and Zaire	Unstable Ethnic violence
Cambodia	300,000	Factional strife Land mines Government supports relief Theft, corruption
Croatia	650,000 Includes 300,000 refugees, primarily in Germany, Hungary, and Serbia	Government permits relief Ethnic strife Land mines
Eritrea	1.6 million Includes 400,000 in Sudan	
Ethiopia	4.3 million Includes 200,000 refugees, primarily in Sudan	Antigovernment activities in eastern, southern, western Ethiopia and Islamic Jihad antigovernment activites in Eritrea not a threat to regimes

(continues)

TABLE I.1 *(continued)*

Country	Population at Risk[a]	Political Environment
		Military could provide minimal support to relief operations
		Land mines
Georgia	1 million	Government supports relief
	Includes 150,000 refugees, primarily in Russia	Control of countryside doubtful
Haiti	1.3 million	Minimal government capability to support relief operations
Iraq	1.3 million	Government can deliver support throughout country
	Includes 8,000 refugees in Iran	Government hinders relief to Kurds and Shi'ites
		Land mines
Liberia	2.1 million	Civil war
	Includes over 800,000 refugees, primarily in Côte d'Ivoire, Ghana, and Guinea	
Former Yugoslavia Rep. of Macedonia	10,000	N.A.
Mozambique	1 million	Fragile security
	Includes 200,000 refugees, primarily in Malawi, South Africa, and Zimbabwe	Bandits
		Returning refugees
		Demobilized military
		Devastated economy
		Government welcomes aid
		Land mines
Russia (Chechnya)	N.A.	Government would support relief
		Some armed opposition
Rwanda	4 million	Ethnic warfare
	Includes 2 million refugees, primarily in Burundi, Tanzania, and Zaire	
Sierra Leone	1.5 million	Collapsed state
	Includes 300,000 refugees in Guinea and Liberia	Insurgents along Liberian border
Somalia	1.1 million	No local authority can assist relief
	Includes over 200,000 refugees, primarily in Ethiopia and Zaire	Opposition from clans, bandits, religious radicals
		Land mines
Sri Lanka	700,000	Ongoing insurgency
	Includes 100,000 refugees in India	Government can provide limited support for relief operations

(continues)

TABLE I.1   (*continued*)

Country	Population at Risk[a]	Political Environment
Sudan	3 million Includes 400,000 refugees, primarily in Ethiopia, Uganda, and Zaire	Ongoing insurgency All sides use relief as weapon Government opposes relief to south and to non-Muslims in north Land mines
Tajikistan	1 million Includes 300,000 refugees, primarily in Kazakhstan, Russia, and Uzbekistan	Government cannot assist relief in south Armed opposition
Zaire	600,000 Includes 75,000 refugees, primarily in Burundi, Tanzania, and Zambia	Government cannot assist relief Little or no civil authority Crime and extortion

Notes: N.A.—not available.

[a]The term *population at risk* indicates those people who are in need of or dependent on international aid to avoid large-scale malnutrition and deaths, including refugees, internally displaced persons, and others in need.

Source: U.S. Mission to the United Nations.

ICJ, the judicial organ of the United Nations, had the opportunity to define humanitarianism in legal terms but declined. Instead, the ICJ pointed to the principles held by one humanitarian actor, the International Committee of the Red Cross (ICRC), to demonstrate the actions, rather than define the concept, of what is indeed humanitarian. The principles of the ICRC state that humanitarian aid must be given without discrimination to all in need of assistance once belligerents have given their **consent** for the ICRC to do so. However, the belligerents' consent to the presence of humanitarian actors can be withdrawn if the warring parties no longer see a political or military benefit.

The ICJ decision may lead some observers to believe, perhaps hastily, that all activities undertaken by other actors under the rubric of humanitarian action that are *not* actions or principles condoned by the ICRC or clones of its model are *not* truly humanitarian. The ICRC principle of independence cannot be adhered to at all times by humanitarian actors with multiple functions and considerations, such as governments and **intergovernmental organizations (IGOs)**. The ICRC principle of independence demands that those providing assistance act without ulterior, mainly political or military, motives and instructions. If one were to eliminate all actors whose motives include political, military, or organizational considerations, in addition to their desire to relieve suffering, the ICRC might find itself operating alone and without the resources of its greatest benefactors—governments.

In addition to conceptual fuzziness, there have been other reasons for cynicism and criticism of humanitarian action. Just as there is scrutiny in the domestic arena about the legitimacy of welfare and the extent of its abuse and waste, there are opportunists who carry that dialogue into foreign policy and humanitarian arenas. As a result, impressions of how much the United States contributes to foreign aid or to U.N. peacekeeping operations are distorted. For instance, a January 1995 poll found that the average American respondent believed that 15 percent of the federal budget went to foreign aid, but the actual figure was approximately 1 percent. An April 1995 poll showed that Americans believed that U.S. troops accounted for 40 percent of U.N. peacekeepers worldwide instead of the actual 5 percent at that time. The perception that the American people are calling for isolationism is also erroneous, the prognostications of political pundits notwithstanding. Instead, polls indicate that the average American is returning to universalist ideals that call for distributing among all states the responsibility for upholding principles of humanity. It is multilateral cooperation, not isolationism, that Americans view as the best possible means for solving current conflicts with humanitarian consequences. The desire to stop being the "world's policeman" is not synonymous with the desire to withdraw from involvement altogether. A 1994 poll conducted by the Program on International Policy Attitudes revealed that only 14 percent of respondents believed that "the U.S. should not make sacrifices in an effort to help the world as a whole." And even when United Nations–bashing seemed a sport in media circles, 84 percent of respondents polled in late 1994 felt that strengthening the United Nations should be part of a U.S. foreign policy goal.[2]

Thus, although there is a profusion of misinformation as well as private and public debates over the efficacy and value of humanitarian action, the impulse to help remains strong and unyielding. Regardless of whether discussants are speaking positively or pejoratively, the increased attention to the mitigation of civilian suffering is indicative of a widening acceptance that humanitarian **norms** are firmly rooted in the psyche of international society. The belief that all of humanity—regardless of race, religion, age, or gender—deserves protection from unnecessary suffering is becoming a more universally accepted truth as well as a norm that occasionally guides the behavior of state-to-state and state-to-society relations.

It is worthwhile to spend a moment on the second noun in this book's title because clarity is often absent from considerations of "intervention." This term covers the spectrum of possible actions—from making telephone calls to dispatching military forces—that are intended to alter internal affairs in another country. As such, intervention is almost synonymous with the state practice of international relations, which in the post–Cold War period has witnessed more significant outside intrusions into domestic affairs for humanitarian reasons than previously.

The history of humanitarian military intervention is the history of accessing suffering civilians without the consent of the warring parties, under whose political control such victims live. Included in that history are the cross-border forays of **nongovernmental organizations (NGOs)** into Tigray and Afghanistan. Specifically what concerns us in this volume are **Chapter VII** decisions by the United Nations Security Council, which allow for the use of economic sanctions or military force to alter the behavior of belligerents. Talk-show hosts, academic conference participants, politicians, and the proverbial woman in the street are preoccupied with what the editor of *Foreign Affairs* described prematurely as the "Springtime for Interventionism."[3] These individuals are hesitating at a fork in the road about using military force in support of humanitarian objectives. One route leads back toward traditional peacekeeping and the other toward the measured application of superior military force in support of more ambitious international decisions, including the enforcement of human rights in northern Iraq and even of interrupted democratic processes in Haiti. (See Box I.1.)

The present balance of opinion, however, favors the return to traditional peacekeeping, and the Somalia and Bosnia experiences are critical. Reflecting the residue from Vietnam, military reticence about the prospects for involvement in **humanitarian intervention** ironically joins critics who see U.S. dominance in multilateral military efforts as a continuation of American hegemony.

Two unlikely apologists for outside military forces, Alex de Waal and Rakiya Omaar, have observed: "Humanitarian intervention demands a different set of military skills. It is akin to counterinsurgency."[4] Equating humanitarian intervention with counterinsurgency causes alarm to those in the U.S. Pentagon who are still recovering from the **Vietnam Syndrome**. The tremendous loss of U.S. lives in Vietnam has made policymakers skittish about intervening in civil wars, especially without an exit strategy for U.S. troops prior to entering a conflict zone. Moreover, humanitarian intervention often requires a longer-term commitment to assist in postconflict nation-building. Many states are unwilling to make such a commitment. Operation Desert Storm is illustrative of the desire by states to apply overwhelming force quickly, using high-tech weaponry, and then leave the area. Although the primary objective of removing Iraq from Kuwait was accomplished, the devastation to Baghdad was left to humanitarians to remedy. The United Kingdom's military intervention in Malaysia provides an interesting contrast. There, a relatively small number of well-trained soldiers with adequate political support at home were able to accomplish their objective without resorting to excessive force or pulling out before the region was fully stabilized.

Dissenters from "military humanitarianism" include many developing countries clinging to the notion that state **sovereignty** does not permit outside intervention.[5] Sovereignty is an abstraction that theoretically gives states an equal legal status. Each state has a monopoly over the control of the means of force within its boundaries, and no other actor has a right to interfere with a state's authority over its territory and people. Developing countries cling to the sanctity of sovereignty out of fear of renewed major

---

BOX I.1   Complex Humanitarian Emergencies, 1995

Peacemaking, also known as "conflict resolution," is action to bring hostile parties to agreement, essentially through such peaceful means as those foreseen in Chapter VII of the U.N. Charter, i.e., through negotiation, inquiry, mediation, conciliation, arbitration, judicial settlement, resort to regional agencies or arrangements, or other peaceful means. Military missions include military-to-military liaison, security assistance, preventive deployment, and show of force.

Peacekeeping is the deployment of a U.N. presence in the field, with the consent of all parties concerned, to allow contending forces that wish to stop fighting to separate with some confidence that they will not be attacked in order to create conditions conducive to a political settlement. Peacekeeping normally involves U.N. military and/or police personnel and frequently civilians as well. Military mission mandates include monitoring existing peace arrangements.

Peace enforcement refers to actions taken when traditional peacekeeping is not sufficient to keep the peace or when the safety of peacekeeping forces is threatened by actions of one or more parties to the conflict. Peace enforcement differs from peacekeeping in that it allows forces to use measured but sufficient force to restore peaceful conditions after peace has been broken or peacekeeping forces threatened. Peace enforcement measures are usually taken without the full consent of one or more parties to the conflict. Military involvement includes application of armed forces to compel compliance, forcible separation of belligerents, restore order, guarantee/deny mobility, establish protected zones, and protect humanitarian assistance.

Peace-building refers to actions taken to forestall future eruptions between the parties to the conflict. It includes disarming warring parties, controlling and destroying weapons, repatriating refugees, training and supporting security personnel, monitoring elections, promoting human rights practices, reforming or strengthening governmental institutions, and promoting political participation. Military mission statements include activities to restore civil authority and rebuild infrastructure.

Source: Congressional Research Service, *CRS Report for Congress* (Washington, D.C.: Congressional Research Service, June 29, 1995), Appendix I.

---

power bullying in the guise of protecting international peace. The Security Council's definition of what constitutes "threats" to international peace and security, on the one hand, is expanding to cover virtually any subject and, on the other hand, remains selective in application.

Developing countries are joined by others whose reasoning is less ideological and is based instead on a static interpretation of **international law**. In an anarchical world, one without a legitimate authority above the state, reciprocal rules among states are required to ease the inevitable competition. The presence of outside military forces makes more problematic the tasks of an affected country's own civilian authorities. If the principle of nonintervention was abandoned, further instability and weakened democratic tendencies and institutions might follow. Instead, international law represents a dynamic process that evolves as a result of changing contexts and interests.

International law exists only between states. It is that element that binds the members of the international system of states in their adherence to recognized values and standards. It is formulated primarily through international agreements that create rules binding upon the signatories and customary rules, which are basically state practices recognized by the community at large as laying down patterns of conduct requiring compliance. States make the laws, interpret them, and enforce them. For clarification, **international humanitarian law** seeks to regulate the conduct of hostilities during war, prohibiting certain methods of warfare and violations of human rights. A guiding principle is the requirement to protect civilians against the effects of hostilities.[6]

Other critics of robust intervention are civilian humanitarians working in the trenches. For them, what Oxford University's Adam Roberts has called "humanitarian war" is an oxymoron.[7] More numerous than Quakers or Mennonites, these civilian workers argue that humanitarian initiatives should be strictly consensual, premised on impartiality and neutrality. Political authorities in armed conflicts must be persuaded to meet their commitments—codified in international humanitarian law—for access to and respect of civilians. Intervention not only raises the levels of violence and complicates the lives of civilian humanitarians in the short run, argue some scholars, but also makes reconciliation more difficult in the longer run.

Yet with 1 in every 115 people on earth forced into flight from war, military involvement may sometimes be the only way to halt **genocide**, massive abuses of human rights, and starvation.[8] Genocide is the deliberate and systematic extermination of a national, racial, ethnic, or religious group. It is a crime under international law bearing individual responsibility by belligerents and a response by the Security Council to intervene on behalf of the victims. Thus, partisans of the other route at the fork in the road are open to the option of outside military forces intervening to assist civilians trapped in wars. When consent cannot be extracted, economic and military coercion can be justified in operational *and* ethical terms. The difficulty is knowing precisely when to wait for consent and when to act with coercive measures. When there is sufficient political will, an effective humanitarian response may include military backup that goes far beyond the minimalist use of force in self-defense by traditional U.N. peacekeepers. Rather than suspending relief and withdrawing, the international community can use enough force to guarantee access to civilians, protect aid workers, and keep thugs at bay.

Military intervention in support of humanitarian objectives is not an end in itself. Rather, it is a last-ditch effort to create enough breathing room for the reemergence of local stability and order, which ultimately are prerequisites for the conduct of negotiations that can lead to consent about humanitarian space and eventually about lasting peace as well. In order to be perfectly clear about the emergence of this new basis for intervention, the Commission on Global Governance proposed "an appropriate Charter amendment permitting such intervention but restricting it to cases that constitute a violation of the security of people so gross and extreme that it requires an international response on humanitarian grounds."[9]

Now that the United Nations has celebrated its fiftieth anniversary, it is worth recalling that the world organization was supposed to be different from its defunct predecessor, the League of Nations. There should be no illusion about the world organization's acting automatically as a fire brigade in humanitarian crises. But the provisions for enforcement in the U.N. Charter permit action to stop atrocities in such places as Somalia, Bosnia, Rwanda, northern Iraq, and Haiti when there is sufficient political will.

THE LAYOUT OF THIS BOOK

This book is structured to provide necessary building blocks for understanding the historical sources of the "humanitarian impulse." Chapter 1 outlines the evolution of humanitarian action from an idea, to its codification, to the creation of institutions to facilitate the international implementation of the idea. Chapter 2 introduces three types of external actors who make up the international humanitarian system. Chapter 2 also provides up-to-date sketches of the human and political dimensions of five war zones illustrative of complex emergencies and the responses of the international humanitarian system to those crises in the post–Cold War era. You can decide if, from crisis to crisis, any pattern of learning is emerging among the actors and if the lessons of one crisis have affected subsequent responses. Chapter 3 reflects on ethical, legal, and operational dilemmas that present daily challenges to the international humanitarian system. Discussion of four dilemmas draws in examples from the cases examined in Chapter 2 and culminates in an examination of a larger, more controversial dilemma: When does humanitarian action do more harm than good? When is doing nothing preferable to doing something? Chapter 4 presents policy debates that are currently being mulled over in the absence of clear international leadership, consistent will, and decisiveness. Chapter 5 attempts to lift you from the gloom that you may experience after reading the preceding chapters by showing the positive results of humanitarian action and the areas where improvements could be made.

At the end, you may find yourself unsure about the possibility for consistent, collective humanitarian responses. Rest assured that you have plenty of company. However, the challenges and dilemmas associated with providing relief and protection must not overshadow the reality that there are children, women, and men suffering from wars not of their making who depend upon outside sustenance for their survival. We would be surprised if most readers are not moved by the devotion and courage of the humanitarians who attempt to make a difference and if some readers do not choose to devote part of their professional careers to helping on the front lines.

ONE

□   □   □

Evolution of the Humanitarian Idea

Above all Nations—is Humanity.

—Creed of the Geneva Red Cross

On June 24, 1859, a summer storm and clashing armies had exhausted themselves by nightfall, leaving behind forty thousand dead Austrian and French soldiers scattered atop the battlefield near the Italian village of Solferino. Witness to the slaughter was a young Swiss pacifist and businessman, Henri Dunant, who was in Italy seeking the assistance of French emperor Napoleon III in remedying a problem Dunant was having with his mill in Algeria. Dunant, so the story goes, had been inspired by Harriet Beecher Stowe's accounts of slavery in the United States, Florence Nightingale's service to the wounded in the Crimean War, and Elizabeth Fry's efforts at prison reform. Without hesitation, he turned his attention toward assisting the wounded. The carnage on the battlefield was great; the magnitude of the casualties and the lack of sufficient medical personnel, facilities, and supplies were overwhelming. Within two months, forty thousand more would be dead from war-related wounds and insufficient attention.

Within a week of the battle, Dunant had convinced Napoleon III to render the first *official* proclamation regarding the rights of those suffering from war injuries. Napoleon III ordered the release of all Austrian doctors and surgeons so that they could return to their regiments and treat their own wounded. The morally inspired and politically astute actions of Dunant following the Battle of Solferino set into motion an advancement of the *idea* of international humanitarian action and the necessary *institutional form* to help ensure the actualization of the ideal in at least certain circumstances. Dunant would go on to found the Red Cross in Geneva in

13

1864. The precedent that he set—of seeking the approval of the sovereign authority so that politically neutral humanitarian succor could intercede on behalf of the suffering during war—is still the operating procedure of today's International Committee of the Red Cross. These principles were later codified in the 1864 Geneva Convention for the Amelioration of the Condition of the Wounded in Armies in the Field.

For some, the actions of Dunant in response to the Battle at Solferino mark the beginning of modern humanitarian action, even though charitable acts and religious organizations existed long before. The potency of that historical moment lies in the fortuitous convergence of four significant factors: the idea of humanitarian action, the codification of the idea through Napoleon's proclamation and the Geneva Convention, the institutionalization of the idea through the creation of the Red Cross, and the will of a powerful sovereign authority to place humanity before narrow sovereign self-interest. In studying a detailed history of humanitarian action, one can easily get lost in the number and meaning of various charters, conventions, **declarations,** and treaties and in the bureaucratic maze of institutions that seem, at times, to hinder a standard and predictable response to humanitarian crises associated with war. On a more general and abstract level, one need only remain mindful that the normative framework undergirding the written instruments and formalized institutions is the idea of humanitarian action or the humanitarian impulse, an idea that continues to evolve and manifest itself as international norms.

The historical evolution of the humanitarian idea is represented not by a steadily progressing line but by a zigzag. After great loss of life resulting from war, new laws and institutions are quickly established. The greater the distance in time away from cataclysms, the slower the pace of humanitarian evolution, until events occur that remind the world of the need for renewed restraint on inhumane behavior. This pattern cannot be explained by either idealist or realist perspectives. **Idealism** claims that war is not inevitable, that humankind is perfectible, and that state-to-state relations are moving progressively (and linearly) toward what political liberal Immanuel Kant called "Perpetual Peace" in the international system.[1] An idealist perspective does well in explaining the entrenchment of humanitarian ideals in largely democratic countries and the proliferation of nongovernmental humanitarian actors, but it is limited in its ability to explain the continual reemergence of war and the resistance to collective humanitarian action by states and nonstate actors.

In contrast, realism refutes claims to human perfectibility.[2] The motivations for behavior among individuals as well as among states are self-interest and domination. Realists do not see a linear progression toward harmony among individuals or states or a zigzag pattern to the evolution of humanitarian ideals; any appearance of humanitarianism in the actions of states is simply a smoke screen for self-interest. A cursory glance at Cold War politics seems to confirm this notion. However, realism cannot explain, for example, why Nordic countries have continually devoted a large percentage of their resources to humanitarian endeavors seemingly devoid of self-interest or why the liberal values that were international- ized as a result of U.S. hegemony since the end of World War II continue to influence states' behavior, both to resist their own aggressive inclina- tions and to respond to the call for humanitarian assistance . This phe- nomenon, often referred to as embedded liberalism,[3] is mirrored in the U.S. Constitution's Bill of Rights, expressed in Roosevelt's four freedoms, and codified in the United Nations' 1948 Universal Declaration of Human Rights and the Preamble to the Charter. Humanitarianism is a reflection of embedded liberalism. It dampens unequivocal acceptance of realists' overgeneralizations of what guides states' behavior toward other states and toward suffering populations.

The zigzag pattern of humanitarian evolution is best represented by **liberal institutionalism**, a theoretical compromise between idealism and realism. In agreement with realism, liberal institutionalism views states as the most important actors in the international system (al- though not the only significant ones) and defines power capabilities and self-interest as the most determinant factors for how states behave. However, according to this view there is a conflict-mitigating factor found in the creation of transnational institutions and **regimes,** which are "principles, norms, rules, and decision-making procedures around which actor expectations converge in a given issue area."[4] Regimes are consequential because they foster cooperation among states. Interna- tional humanitarian conventions and institutions with humanitarian agendas constrain, in various degrees, certain types of state behavior. States pursue their self-interests within successively narrower ranges of action as a result of increases in codification of international human- itarian law, increases in the number of humanitarian nonstate actors, increases in authority given to intergovernmental institutions such as the United Nations, and the embeddedness of liberal values in an ex- panding number of democratic societies.

In addition, turbulent conflicts that attract the attention of the interna- tional community because of gross violations of basic human rights are often followed by additional augmentation to humanitarian law and calls for changes in institutional forms and state action. For example, the atroc- ities of World War II prompted the Universal Declaration of Human Rights, the replacement of the League of Nations by the United Nations, and U.S. involvement in bringing the war to an end and assisting in West- ern Europe's reconstruction. As a result, the zigzag in the evolution of hu- manitarianism took another turn upward—the range of acceptable state behavior became more narrow, while acknowledgment of international responsibility to alleviate human suffering expanded.

THE EVOLUTION OF THE IDEA OF HUMANITARIAN ACTION

Political discourse, religion, and philosophy provide generous narratives to describe the genesis of the humanitarian impulse. In *Second Discourse*, political philosopher Jean-Jacques Rousseau (1712–1778) found the seeds for humanitarian action in the nature of humankind: "It is pity which carries us without reflection to the assistance of those we see suffer. . . . Commiseration is nothing but a sentiment that puts us in the place of him who suffers. . . . Commiseration will be all the more energetic in proportion as the Onlooking animal identifies more intimately with the suffering animal."[5]

All such social virtues as clemency, humanity, benevolence, and friendship find their origin in the virtue of pity. For Rousseau, pity stems from the intervener's identification with those in need of assistance. Rousseau might argue that if Westerners cannot "see" themselves in the hollowed and frightened faces of Rwandans or Sudanese, then the television channel will be changed, the newspaper page turned, and the aid withheld.

Grounded in Judaism, Christianity, and Islam are principles of human conduct that require a person to acknowledge his or her obligation toward the needy without consideration of self-interest or payoffs. The fourth chapter of Proverbs is illustrative: "Refuse no one the good on which he has a claim when it is in your power to do it for him. Say not to your neighbor, 'Go and come again, tomorrow I will give,' when you can give it at once."

Philosophy has left a trail of thought throughout history regarding similar obligations of the global community to intervene on humanitarian grounds.[6] Cicero (106–43 B.C.) suggested that assistance to suffering groups is a matter of justice, not morality. There are modern-day humanitarian scholars and practitioners who agree with Cicero that there is a **humanitarian imperative** rather than simply a humanitarian impulse. An impulse can allow other alternatives to prevail over the offering of assistance. A humanitarian imperative, which is held by individuals and many NGOs such as the ICRC, stifles any consideration other than providing assistance wherever it is needed, regardless of personal safety or negative potential consequences of involvement. In this we can find some explanation for varied responses by different actors in the international humanitarian system: Some are guided by the humanitarian imperative, while others are sensitive, although not always responsive, to the humanitarian impulse. Still others—and this is the reason for this book—are aware that yielding to an impulse or respecting an imperative can be problematic if more harm than good results from a particular humanitarian activity.

During the Middle Ages, the belief emerged that all people are internally connected as one universal, mystical body. To current scholars, this universal body, minus the mystification, is referred to as international society. St. Thomas Aquinas (1225–1274) laid the groundwork for challenging a sovereign authority's maltreatment of people. Human rights scholar Hersch Lauterpacht interprets Aquinas as believing that "justification of the state is in its service to the individual; a king who is unfaithful to his duty forfeits his claim to obedience."[7] Both statements—the recognition of one bond common to all humankind, with implied rights and obligations, and the justification for compromising the integrity of the sovereign authority should that authority fail to fulfill its duty to the welfare of its people—are integral to current debates about humanitarian action.

The Age of Enlightenment in the seventeenth and eighteenth centuries brought to open public discourse the long-standing rumblings against religious dogma and beliefs that justified the oppressive acts of religious and government authorities. The Age of Reason was ushered in. Hugo Grotius (1583–1645), an exiled Dutch statesmen who is now known as the father of public international law, synthesized Aquinas's call for civil disobedience toward a malevolent king and the idea of one common humanity. Grotius's 1625 *De Jure Belli ac Pacis* (On the Rights of War and Peace) "recognized as lawful the use of force by one or more states to stop the maltreatment by a state of its own nationals when that conduct was so brutal and large-scale as to shock the conscience of the community of nations."[8] Grotius's doctrine for humanitarian intervention is reflected in Chapter VII of the U.N. Charter.

Liberal thinker Immanuel Kant (1724–1804), who is believed to have provided the theoretical basis for the League of Nations, expanded on the notion of global solidarity by linking together the idea of national and international peace and security with the idea of promoting and protecting individual human dignity. To preach of democratic values and human rights within domestic politics without transferring those values to foreign politics is hypocritical, according to Kant and modern-day scholars of international ethics.

Throughout history these ideas of humanitarian action have been melded and transcended. Historical contexts have determined the pace of the evolution within various societies as well as among states. With colonization of "unclaimed" lands and peoples and the Industrial Revolution came an increase in the speed of transmission and the geographical coverage of the idea of humanitarian action. And ironically it was the spread of humanitarianism and human rights that led to the demise of slavery and **imperialism**. Codification and institutionalization of the idea were largely a Western product of the late nineteenth century. However, the West has not had a monopoly on humanitarian ideas; it has, however, codified more of its ideas and created more discernible institutions for their operationalization.[9] There is, according to many observers, ample evidence of the humanitarian idea in Africa, within Native American communities, and throughout much of the non-Western world.[10] Private journals, oral histories, traditional songs, and folklore chronicle repeated generosity in the presence of famine and disease. Buddhism and Hinduism accentuate the virtues of compassion and responsibility as much as do the faiths of the Western religious traditions. Islam, if anything, is even more explicit in this regard.

THE IDEA'S CODIFICATION AND INSTITUTIONALIZATION

Pre–World War I

The simultaneous rise of peace movements and more sophisticated war machines during the nineteenth century led Russia's minister of foreign affairs to call for a world conference to discuss international armament reduction in the interest of general peace. The work of pacifists such as Dunant and a more politically active and attentive world population, infused with information generated by capitalism and print media,[11] blended with sovereign authorities' concerns about the increasing costs of lives, property, and political legitimation associated with war. The First Hague Conference commenced on May 18, 1899 (the czar's birthday), with twenty-six governments attending. Although agreements to systematically disarm were never reached, three **conventions**, or legally binding documents, were negotiated and signed regarding the pacific settlement of international disputes. The idea that a large number of governments could negotiate in the collective humanitarian interest of a global community became a reality, and the snowball effect of conferences and conventions surrounding humanitarianism and human rights began its roll.

U.S. president Theodore Roosevelt called for a second "Peace Conference" at The Hague, which convened on June 15, 1907. Fifty-four governments were represented at this second conclave. The three conventions signed in 1899 were revised and ten new conventions adopted, including the Regulations for Land Warfare. More important, however, was the ability of an even greater number of states to discuss and negotiate matters involving humankind. The Law of The Hague sets out the rights and obligations of belligerents in the conduct of hostilities and limits the means to do harm to one's adversary. Embodied in The Hague Conventions of 1899, which were revised in 1907, international law continued to expand with the 1954 Convention for the Protection of Cultural Property in the Event of Armed Conflict and the 1980 Convention on Prohibitions or Restrictions on the Use of Certain Conventional Weapons Which May Be Deemed to Be Excessively Injurious or to Have Indiscriminate Effects—in recent years, referred to simply as the Conventional Weapons Convention. (See Table 1.1.)

In the process of negotiations among states in The Hague, the customary rules of international law in interstate matters were recognized and

TABLE 1.1   Key International Humanitarian and Human Rights Instruments

	Instrument
1928	Convention on Asylum
1933	Convention on Political Asylum
1946	Constitution of the International Refugee Organization (UNHCR)
1948	Universal Declaration of Human Rights
1949	Geneva Convention Relative to the Protection of Civilian Persons
1950	European Convention for the Protection of Human Rights and Fundamental Freedoms with 10 Additional Protocols (1952, 3 in 1963, 1966, 1983, 1984, 1985, 1990, 1992)
1951	Convention on the Prevention and Punishment of Genocide
1952	Convention on the Political Rights of Women; Declaration of the Rights of the Child
1954	Convention Relating to the Status of Refugees; Convention on Territorial Asylum; Convention on Diplomatic Asylum
1960	Convention Relating to the Status of Stateless Persons
1967	U.N. Declaration of Territorial Asylum
1969	International Convention on the Elimination of All Forms of Racial Discrimination; OAU Convention Governing the Specific Aspects of Refugee Problems
1970	Convention on the Non-Applicability of Statutory Limitations to War Crimes
1975	Convention on the Reduction of Statelessness
1976	International Covenant of Civil and Political Rights; International Covenant of Economic, Social and Cultural Rights; International Convention on the Suppression and Punishment
1978	Additional Protocol to the 1949 Geneva Convention; American Convention on Human Rights Pact of San Jose, Costa Rica, with Additional Protocol
1979	Convention on the Elimination of All Forms of Discrimination Against Women; International Convention Against the Taking of Hostages
1980	European Agreement on Transfer of Responsibility for Refugees
1981	African Chapter on Human and Peoples' Rights
1984	Convention Against Torture and Other Cruel, Inhuman, or Degrading Treatment or Punishment
1985	Declaration of the Human Rights of Individuals Who Are Not Nationals of the Country in Which They Live
1987	European Convention for the Prevention of Torture and Inhuman or Degrading Treatment or Punishment
1990	Convention on the Rights of the Child

legitimated. Provisions contained in the conventions of the two conferences were declaratory, not amendatory, of international law. Even if a state failed to ratify the conventions, it was merely rejecting the codified text. A country could not reject the principles of international law, which form the substance of the conventions, without also rejecting the basis of its own statehood.

As international law and codified texts expanded, the society of nations was expanding and expressing itself in a variety of ways other than state-to-state relations. The Hague conventions were manifestations of the "peace movement" or "internationalism" that grew in number and intensity from the 1850s onward. Other manifestations included the creation of the first truly functional international secretariats, the Expositions or World Fairs, the establishment of Alfred Nobel's Peace Prize in 1897, endowments for international peace, and political activism by religious groups such as the Quakers and Mennonites. The world was growing smaller with technological advances in communication and transportation, thereby facilitating a growing sense of common humanity and global responsibility. Private nongovernmental organizations increased in number and continued to meet the challenges of providing comfort to the oppressed, domestically and internationally, as they had done since the Middle Ages through hospitals, churches, schools, and care for the aged.[12]

World War I to World War II

The atrocities of World War I (1914–1919) led to increased codification of humanitarian law and the creation of the League of Nations. The representatives at the 1912 International Red Cross Conference in Washington, D.C., worked to formalize arrangements leading to standardized humane treatment of prisoners of war. Meanwhile across the ocean in Europe, the balance of power was shifting, offensive military tactics were being considered, and jingoistic nationalism was spreading. Advances in technology, communication, and transportation that fostered budding international organizations also produced the military means by which humanity could be torn apart. World War I mobilized 65 million soldiers, of whom approximately 8.5 million would die and 21 million would be wounded. An estimated 10 million civilians died from war-related causes—not just from armed attacks but also from starvation and disease. The creation of the League of Nations in 1919 was an effort toward collective security and global management by states repulsed by the war's human debris.[13] It is understandable, given the number of dead and dying, that the League of Nations would be cloaked in an aura of pacifism; however, the phrase *human rights* was never included in its governing legislation. With the exception of the Minorities Protection System and the endorsement of the Geneva Declaration of the Rights of the Child, the League of Nations was consumed by the regulation of state-to-state relations, with only the faintest glance of attention toward states' treatment of their own populations. Discussion of basic human rights was blocked by, among other things, the interests of states and individuals in continued imperialist holdings.

The League of Nations was incapacitated from the start. U.S. president Woodrow Wilson took the helm for drafting the League's Covenant, a kind of "constitution" for this organization. The sixty-sixth Congress refused to ratify U.S. membership, fearing a loss of control of foreign policy. By the 1930s, Germany, Japan, and Italy had left the League; by 1940 the Soviet Union had been expelled for invading Finland. Without any explicit mechanisms to punish transgressors and without the participation of all the great powers, the League was unable to enforce its mandates. The idealism concerning collective global security, which formed the basis of the League of Nations, was destroyed by World War II, along with much of Europe.

World War II to the End of the Cold War

Historically, new institutional responses or creations tend to follow conscience-shattering cataclysms as much as they follow transformations in the configuration of world power; the events following World War II (1939–1945) are not an exception. World War II became the next catalyst for propelling the humanitarian idea forward through increased codification of humanitarian law and the creation of the United Nations to manage the international system of states. Unlike in the guiding framework of the League of Nations, the rights of all persons and the duties of governments were explicitly, although not unambiguously, spelled out in the United Nations' Charter (rather than covenant). Much of the idealism found in the Preamble to the Charter would have to lie dormant for almost fifty years, however, as Cold War politics among the great powers of the Security Council placed a seemingly insurmountable barrier toward a collective response by states in alleviating human suffering and human rights violations. Nonpolitical humanitarian action was limited. As history reveals, even when ideas are codified, ratified, and institutionalized, their implementation is not guaranteed.

The United Nations is a complex institution with the unenviable task of trying to maintain order in the international system of states while facilitating change for those states and people for whom the status quo is a life sentence of impoverishment or injustice. This institutional schizophrenia is evident throughout the U.N. Charter, which was signed in 1945. (See Box 1.1.) The Charter's language is ambiguous in spots and therefore a source of competing interpretations of its intentions and procedural guidelines. The Preamble begins the list of misleading texts by explicitly stating that the authors of the Charter are "We the People." But the United Nations is an organization representing the interests and concerns of states. Individuals and groups have no recourse through the United Nations, nor is there a formal U.N. platform from which people can bring their concerns to the organization's attention. Although the Preamble is bathed in language supportive of human rights, equality, justice, and self-determination, other language within the Charter places a barrier between these ideals and their enforcement or protection. Specifically, Article 2(7) prevents any state from interfering in the "domestic matters" of another. Article 2(7) has been used, for example, to justify noninterference in China's documented human rights abuses against its own population and in Tibet. Only Chapter VII, which allows for the use of force to override the sovereignty of a targeted state, can override Article 2(7), and it does so on the grounds of grave threats to international peace and security. What is perceived as a threat is left to the subjective interpretation of U.N. Security Council members. Particularly during the **Cold War,** the perceived national interests of the five permanent members of the Security Council (the United States, the United Kingdom, China, France, and the Soviet Union) and the international context determined whether Chapter VII would be invoked or whether Article 2(7) would prevail. Each permanent member of the Security Council possesses veto power, and as such, resolutions require the approval, or at least the abstention, of all five countries. Interestingly, however, since the end of the Cold War, Article 2(7) has found less support, while Chapter VII has been increasingly invoked, more on humanitarian grounds than perceived national interest.

The contradictions and tension found in the text of the U.N. Charter—the primacy of the sanctity of state sovereignty versus (1) the collective defense against aggression and (2) the violation of norms for human rights and development—led to the creation of distinct and, at times, contradictory modes of power and concern within the U.N. system, that being its security, humanitarian, and development organs. Tensions between noninterference in internal affairs of sovereign states and an active concern for human dignity wherever it is at risk have played themselves out during the history of the United Nations and in international relations since World War II. The balance between the two has evolved toward a more circumspect embrace of sovereignty and a more integral relationship between sovereignty and respect for human rights and humane values. As a result, once-sacrosanct state sovereignty is no longer an acceptable justification for violations of the rights of civilians in zones of armed conflict, if it ever was. "How [a state] treats its own nationals on a range of issues is, in itself, now a proper subject of international law."[14]

Half a century of tension between the principle of sovereignty and the growing concerns with humanitarian access have led the United Nations itself to examine the need for articulating and implementing changing norms. The evolution is particularly evident in debates in recent years within the world's quintessential political forum, the General Assembly, where the political dynamics may be a more accurate barometer of world opinion than the views of the U.N. International Court of Justice or of academics. Recent U.N. resolutions defend a humanitarian and human rights agenda. They may influence the actual application of international humanitarian law as spelled out in the Geneva conventions and protocols. A few of the resolutions are worth elaborating.

In 1988, the General Assembly adopted Resolution 43/131, which recognized the rights of civilians to international assistance and the role of NGOs in humanitarian emergencies. Two years later, Resolution 45/100 reaffirmed these rights and specifically endorsed the concept of **corridors of tranquillity**, cross-border operations, and other devices to facilitate humanitarian access. In April 1991, Security Council Resolution 688 framed the plight of some 1.5 million Kurds as sufficiently threatening to international peace and security to authorize outside military intervention and create havens for them. Although contradictions in the U.N. Charter itself are just as glaring today as they were at its inception, the weight accorded state sovereignty in 1945 has lessened somewhat when measured against the recognition of basic human rights. It has been significant for the evolution of the ideals embodied in the Charter that they were further buttressed by another post–World War II instrument—the Universal Declaration of Human Rights.

The 1948 Universal Declaration, proclaimed by the General Assembly, was drafted as an ideal claiming legitimacy for the rights of individuals to human security—rights that superseded the rights of states against noninterference found in Article 2(7). With a U.S. delegation led by NGOs and Eleanor Roosevelt, this document replaced what had been impossible to negotiate in 1945, a kind of U.N. equivalent of the U.S. Bill of Rights as part of the Charter.[15] Declarations are not legally binding documents, but they are presented as an ideal that all ratifiers agree is worth approaching. The Universal Declaration of Human Rights challenges directly Article 2(7). It recognizes that all people have "the right to life, liberty and security of person" (Article 3); that "no one shall be subjected to torture or to cruel, inhuman or degrading treatment or punishment" (Article 5); that "everyone has the right to freedom of thought, conscience and religion" (Article 18) and "freedom of opinion and expression" (Article 19); and that everyone has "the right to a standard of living adequate for the health and well-being of himself and his family, including food, clothing, housing and medical care and necessary social services" (Article 25).

BOX 1.1   Key U.N. Charter Texts

PREAMBLE

WE THE PEOPLES OF THE UNITED NATIONS determined to save succeeding generations from the scourge of war, which twice in our lifetime has brought untold sorrow to mankind, and to reaffirm faith in fundamental human rights, in the dignity and worth of the human person, in the equal rights of men and women and of nations large and small, and to establish conditions under which justice and respect for the obligations arising from treaties and other sources of international law can be maintained, and to promote social progress and better standards of life in larger freedom, and for these ends to practice tolerance and live together in peace with one another as good neighbors, and to unite our strength to maintain international peace and security, and to employ international machinery for the promotion of the economic and social advancement of all peoples, have resolved to combine our efforts to accomplish these aims.

Accordingly, our respective Governments, through representatives assembled in the city of San Francisco, who have exhibited their full powers found to be in good and due form, have agreed to the present Charter of the United Nations and do hereby establish an international organization to be known as the United Nations.

ARTICLE 1

The Purposes of the United Nations are:

To maintain international peace and security, and to that end: to take effective collective measures for the prevention and removal of threats to the peace, and for the suppression of acts of aggression or other breaches of the peace, and to bring about by peaceful means, and in conformity with the principles of justice and international law, adjustment or settlement of international disputes or situations which might lead to a breach of the peace;

To develop friendly relations among nations based on respect for the principle of equal rights and self-determination of peoples, and to take other appropriate measures to strengthen universal peace;

To achieve international co-operation in solving international problems of an economic, social, cultural, or humanitarian character, and in promoting and encouraging respect for human rights and for fundamental freedoms for all without distinction as to race, sex, language, or religion; and

To be a centre for harmonizing the actions of nations in the attainment of these common ends.

ARTICLE 2(7)

Nothing contained in the present Charter shall authorize the United Nations to intervene in matters which are essentially within the domestic jurisdiction of any state or shall require the Members to submit such matters to settlement under the present Charter; but this principle shall not prejudice the application of enforcement measures under Chapter VII.

CHAPTER VI: PACIFIC SETTLEMENT OF DISPUTES

Article 33

The parties to any dispute, the continuance of which is likely to endanger the maintenance of international peace and security, shall, first of all, seek a solution by negotiations, enquiry, mediation, conciliation, arbitration, judicial settlement, resort to regional agencies or arrangements, or other peaceful means of their choice.

The Security Council shall, when it deems necessary, call upon the parties to settle their dispute by such means.

CHAPTER VII: ACTION WITH RESPECT TO THREATS TO PEACE, BREACHES OF THE PEACE, AND ACTS OF AGGRESSION

Article 39

The Security Council shall determine the existence of any threat to the peace, breach of the peace, or act of aggression and shall make recommendations, or decide what measures shall be taken in accordance with Articles 41 and 42, to maintain or restore international peace and security.

Article 40

In order to prevent an aggravation of the situation, the Security Council may, before making the recommendations or deciding upon the measures provided for in Article 39, call upon the parties concerned to comply with such provisional measures as it deems necessary or desirable. Such provisional measures shall be without prejudice to the rights, claims, or position of the parties concerned. The Security Council shall duly take account of failure to comply with such provisional measures.

Article 41

The Security Council may decide what measures not involving the use of armed force are to be employed to give effect to its decisions, and it may call upon the Members of the United Nations to apply such measures. These may include complete or partial interruption of economic relations and of rail, sea, air, postal, telegraphic, radio, and other means of communication, and the severance of diplomatic relations.

Article 42

Should the Security Council consider that measures provided for in Article 41 would be inadequate or have proved to be inadequate, it may take such action by air, sea, or land forces as may be necessary to maintain or restore international peace and security. Such action may include demonstrations, blockade, and other operations by air, sea, or land forces of Members of the United Nations.

Moreover, "everyone is entitled to a social and international order in which the rights and freedoms set forth in [the] Declaration can be fully realized" (Article 28).

However, with regard to humanitarian action, perhaps the Preamble contains the most significant paragraph: "Member States have pledged themselves to achieve, in cooperation with the United Nations, the promotion of universal respect for the observance of human rights and fundamental freedoms." Implied is the commitment that member states should take the necessary action, in conjunction with the United Nations, to nurture and protect basic human rights, freedoms of speech and belief (positive freedoms), and freedoms from fear and want (negative freedoms). Respect for Article 2(7) brashly confronts the respect of individual human rights found in the 1948 Universal Declaration of Human Rights and the application of humanitarian intervention to protect the collective rights of war victims.

The Universal Declaration of Human Rights contains principles that guided the French Revolution and that are considered by many scholars to represent three distinct generations of human rights. *Liberté, egalité,* and *fraternité* are codified in the Universal Declaration of Human Rights as the first generation of civil and political rights (Articles 2–21); the second generation of economic, social, and cultural rights (Articles 22–27); and the third generation of solidarity rights (Article 28), respectively. The first generation protects the rights of individuals from government interference; the second generation requests governments to interfere in order to foster minimal standards of welfare; and the third generation spawns a movement toward cooperative arrangements among states, regions, and peoples. The Organization of American States (OAS) is one such regional organization. The OAS demonstrated solidarity in recent years by being the first organization publicly to denounce the military overthrow of Haitian president Jean-Bertrand Aristide in 1991.

The term *generation* can be misleading. It conjures up an image of successive stages of development of the same organism; however, the generations of human rights outlined in the Universal Declaration were conceived simultaneously and are not without controversy and incongruity. The first generation, the negative rights, are largely a product of Western beliefs that private individuals in civil society should be protected from interference by public authorities. The second generation, the positive rights, are an outgrowth of largely anticapitalist ideas about the duty and obligations that public authority has for minimal standards of food, shelter, and health care. The second generation, while supported by the Nordic countries, was rejected by the U.S. administration of President Ronald Reagan because this group did not constitute basic human rights. The second generation flies in the face of rights of property and minimal government interference in the free market, whereas the first generation places individual liberties before the collective good. Depending on the culture of a society and the form of government and economics, the priority of one generation of rights over the other will vary.

The Universal Declaration of Human Rights is therefore instructive in that it points to a challenge created by the institutionalization and attempted universalization of an idea. The Universal Declaration does not specify under what conditions the rights of individuals justly supersede the rights of the collective. Moreover, it is left to philosophical debate what rights are inherent based on the fact of being human and what rights are constructed based on relative cultural, political, and economic systems. How states currently answer these questions correlates with their opinion about humanitarian intervention. During the three years that it took to finalize the draft of the Universal Declaration, these questions were points of contention among states with different political and social cultures. The sanctity of individual human rights is relative to one's country of origin, some opponents argue; therefore, the objective of humanitarian action is to nourish and protect communities of civilians trapped in a conflict zone, not to protect the abused rights of single individuals.

Although The Hague conventions had hardly inhibited the pursuit of war aims by the Third Reich or Japan during World War II, the widespread revulsion after the war—along with the momentum from war crimes trials in Nuremberg and in Japan—led to a call for improvements in international law relating to war. *Jus in bello* is law governing the resort to war, as codified in the two Hague peace conferences of 1899 and 1907. *Jus ad bellum* is law governing the conduct of belligerents once war has commenced and is codified in the Geneva conventions and additional protocols.

Picking up the pieces from war, as we have seen, has frequently provided an impetus to the codification of international humanitarian law. The aftermath of the Battle of Solferino motivated Henri Dunant. After World War I, a series of Geneva conventions attempted to address different aspects of combatants' conduct in war. The atrocities against civilians in World War II propelled the international community to address the specific needs of noncombatants. The 1949 Geneva conventions addressed the treatment of military personnel (the first three conventions) and the obligations of belligerents to the rights and needs of victims of war (the fourth convention). Article 59 of the Fourth Geneva Convention directs that if "the whole or part of the population of an occupied territory is inadequately supplied, the Occupying Power shall agree to relief schemes on behalf of the said population and shall facilitate them by all the means at its disposal." With the passage of time and the increasing suffering caused to civilians rather than soldiers, still more codification took place. Additional Protocol I of 1977 prohibits the "starvation of civilians as a method of combat." Additional Protocol II is particularly relevant in the post–Cold War era because it applies to the "protection of victims of noninternational armed conflicts,"[16] or what most people call **civil wars.**

The Geneva conventions of 1949 are widely accepted today; in 1996, 185 states were party to the conventions and between 125 to 135 to the two Additional Protocols of 1977. Although those "nonparties" are important—in particular, no major power has acceded to Protocol I—such international legislation nonetheless influences governmental decisions, even of the nonparties.

An Afghan man and boy use each other for support as they learn to walk with new artificial limbs. Land mines are excessively injurious and do not discriminate between combatants and noncombatants. One could argue that these weapons violate international law. UNICEF/5526/John Isaac.

The implementation of the rights outlined in the Geneva conventions and the two Additional Protocols of 1977 are monitored by the ICRC, the official custodian. Critics point out the documents' limited relevance to the increasing number of lethal civil wars; 530 articles apply to the conduct of international armed conflicts, whereas only 29 apply to civil wars. This limited scope is of consequence not only because of the growing number of intrastate wars but also because civilian casualties are now the main product of armed conflict. In the U.S. Civil War, for instance, 95 percent of the casualties were soldiers; in Bosnia, Rwanda, and Somalia, perhaps as many as 95 percent were noncombatants or civilians.

Currently more than one hundred conventions and covenants exist concerning humanitarian assistance and human rights. Adherence to them has been ad hoc and varies according to domestic politics and international contexts. Nonetheless, they represent the normative framework that ratifiers claim is worth universalizing. Collectively, in many respects they represent the "conscience" of the international system. Even if the international system does not actively and effectively respond to all transgressions of particular conventions, covenants, and international law—Serbian and Hutu immunity were preceded by that of white-minority South Africa—members of the international system feel compelled to take, as a minimum, rhetorical umbrage at transgressors. Although more feeble than proponents would like, verbal commitments are a necessary, if insufficient, condition for improved behavior and better compliance with stated norms. They also are a prelude to an effective system of enforcement.

Thus, the idea of humanitarian action was institutionalized in the form of the United Nations and other international organizations, such as the International Court of Justice, of which all U.N. members are parties as well as in the form of nongovernmental organizations, particularly the ICRC. Humanitarian obligations and rules of engagement are codified in the U.N. Charter, the Hague conventions, the Geneva conventions and additional protocols, and other binding conventions, such as the 1951 U.N. Refugee Convention and 1967 protocol, which defines the term **refugees** and sets out minimum standards for their treatment. Each new attempt by the international system and its institutions, norm-guided conventions, and declarations to address humanitarian concerns advances the idea of humanitarian action.

The possibilities for international military intervention vary as power relations among states change and a commitment to human rights strengthens. During the Cold War, there was a standard sequence of events in what came to be known as **peacekeeping**: The warring parties (normally states) would agree to a cease-fire, generally through **peace-making** efforts; then a militarized U.N. presence would appear to monitor the cease-fire and act as a buffer between belligerents. With the respite, negotiations about the peaceful settlement of the conflict could take place, although parties sometimes used the calm to avoid serious negotiations or to prepare for the next war. There is still no settlement in Cyprus in spite of a U.N. peacekeeping presence that began in 1964, and there are several peacekeeping operations in place arising from four Arab-Israeli wars.

Impartial "peacekeepers"—lightly armed and using force only in self-defense and as a last resort—were helpful tools of conflict management, but they hardly were the powerful enforcers originally imagined by the Charter's framers. With over forty years of U.N. history, the Security Council could not reach agreements that would satisfy the agendas of all five permanent members. In particular, Washington's and Moscow's ideological divide effectively prevented collective responses, with the exception of the narrow boundaries of peacekeeping and of Korea, where action was initially approved by the Security Council during a boycott by the Soviet Union and was continued by the General Assembly. Although limited in scope, peacekeeping did diffuse some international tension among states. Sir Anthony Parsons, a former British ambassador to the United Nations, has written that during this time the world organization's peacekeeping actions "help[ed] Great Powers descend a ladder from the backs of dangerously high horses that their national policies had led them to mount."[17]

The Aftermath of the Cold War

The recent flood of intrastate conflicts with high civilian casualties has been met with seemingly improvised international responses.[18] Asking whether these responses have pushed the idea of humanitarian action forward or to the left or right is premature. There is plenty of action on the humanitarian front—an abundance of Security Council resolutions specifically addressing humanitarian concerns, the blue helmets of peacekeepers seen on the nightly news, relief budgets expanding and then quickly drained by demand. Yet the action belies the paralysis of leadership and decisive, competent, and thoughtful decisionmaking in the international humanitarian system. The effectiveness of humanitarian action is being held captive by state actors unsure of whether to lead, follow, or get out of the way of collective responses to crises of inhumane proportions and by a United Nations treading water in a sea of complex emergencies. State governments individually and the member states collectively are currently receiving the brunt of criticism for their paralyses in action and in vision. There is a certain irony here as the idea of humanitarian obligations was one of the first to be taken out of Cold War storage.

The tectonic plates of international power relations began to shift shortly after Mikhail Gorbachev's 1985 ascension to power. The 1989 fall of the Berlin Wall and the collapse of the Soviet Union in 1991 changed the landscape of international relations. The decade began with a great deal of rethinking: States had to redefine their national interests, and the North Atlantic Treaty Organization (NATO) was forced to re-create itself since its mission—to contain Soviet threats to peace—vanished along with the Soviet Union. There was an element of renewed hope for global cooperation in the pursuit of world peace and the defense of the defenseless according to the spirit and the letter of the U.N. Charter. This new structure of power relations among states needed new ideas, and the Security Council requested the newly elected U.N. secretary-general, Boutros Boutros-Ghali, to offer suggestions for an enhanced U.N. role in international peace and security. In response, the secretary-general wrote *An Agenda for Peace*, outlining his ideas on issues of preventive diplomacy, peacemaking, peacekeeping, and **peace-building.**

An Agenda for Peace was an attempt to integrate the concerns of states for international order and the concerns of individuals and victimized groups for justice and quality of life. The tension and contradictions found in the U.N. Charter are no less evident in the secretary-general's more recent prose. The organization's executive head, the Secretariat, and other U.N. agencies tentatively straddle a conceptual and operational fence in their efforts toward preventive diplomacy, peacemaking, peacekeeping, and peace-building. The balancing act is, as the Preamble to the Charter specifies, between respecting the fundamental sovereignty and security of states to which the United Nations is a servant and reaffirming "faith in fundamental human rights, in the dignity and worth of the human person, in the equal rights of men and women and of nations large and small, and . . . to promote social progress and better standards of life in larger freedom." To further the commitment to human rights, intervention in domestic affairs must have teeth. To promote social progress and better standards of life, development policies must be integrated with peace and security policies for, more often than not, problems of development and justice lie at the root of intrastate conflict. "The authority of the United Nations system to act . . . would rest on the consensus that social peace is as important as strategic or political peace."[19]

Since *An Agenda for Peace* was published, the optimism for a unified response to human tragedies has diminished. The accelerated demand for humanitarian assistance and peacekeeping was unforeseen. The role of preventive diplomacy envisioned by the secretary-general—to act swiftly to contain conflicts and resolve their underlying causes rather than dealing after the fact with their consequences—became overwhelmed by an acceleration of the number and intensity of internal conflicts. During

FIGURE 1.1 Personnel Deployed in U.N. Peacekeeping Operations,
1990–1994 (year-end figures in thousands)

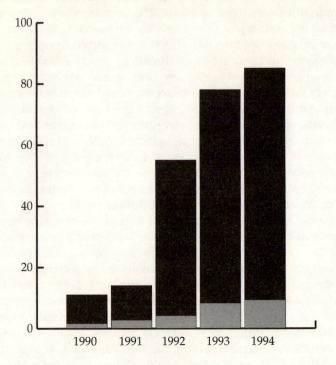

Source: United Nations.

1992, only some eleven thousand military personnel were deployed by the United Nations to address eleven peacekeeping operations; by December 1994, almost seventy-five thousand personnel were engaged in seventeen operations. (See Figure 1.1.)

The secretary-general noted with some anguish that the 1992 peacekeeping budget of $1,689.6 million had skyrocketed to $3,610.0 million by 1994. The increasing linkage of military force and humanitarian objectives is not an entirely new phenomenon, but scarcely was such frequent occurrence envisioned by the secretary-general in 1992. "This increased volume of activity would have strained the Organization even if the nature of the activity had remained unchanged."[20]

Peacekeeping began a metamorphosis to meet the new demands and the human consequences of war. Traditional U.N. peacekeeping missions between 1945 and 1988 normally involved separate military and diplomatic components. The purpose of the U.N. military was to interpose itself between belligerents and to monitor cease-fires after the warring parties had come to an agreement. Self-defense after an attack and as a last resort was the only legitimate cause for use of force by peacekeepers. The move away from Cold War political dynamics produced the opportunity for multidimensional peace operations, mixing together military, civil administration, and humanitarian components with an overlay of diplomacy. The military in multidimensional peacekeeping efforts, although still operating with the consent of the parties, has more freedom to squelch violence intended to impede implementation of its mandates.

The type of military intervention in support of humanitarian objectives that involves coercion (Chapter VII) goes beyond peacekeeping. It focuses more on relieving suffering civilian populations victimized by conflict than on securing consent from belligerents. Therefore, humanitarian intervention by military forces, unlike by peacekeepers, places human rights above the approval of the state. International efforts in Haiti, Somalia, the former Yugoslavia, Rwanda, and northern Iraq in some respects penetrate the sanctity of sovereignty to rescue what in political theory is the source of sovereign legitimacy—the people.

By the late 1980s, multifunctional operations were being adopted from a panoply of means for countries such as El Salvador, Cambodia, and Angola; and enforcement action was approved in 1990–1991 against Iraq for the first time in forty years. U.N. peacekeepers would assist in implementing negotiated settlements, thereby adding to the organization's menu of services, as the secretary-general outlined in 1995:

> The supervision of cease-fires, the regroupment and demobilization of forces, their reintegration into civilian life and the destruction of weapons; the design and implementation of demining programmes; the return of refugees and displaced persons; the provision of humanitarian assistance; the supervision of existing administrative structures; the establishment of new police forces; the verification of respect for human rights; the design and supervision of constitutional, judicial and electoral reforms; the observation, supervision and even organization and conduct of elections; and the coordination of support for economic rehabilitation and reconstruction.[21]

Multifunctional operations came about in direct response to the nature of the crises challenging international and individual security since 1990. These operations rely upon an international humanitarian system that is theoretically and operationally divided among those institutions that address the root causes of complex emergencies, those that provide relief of the symptoms, and those that employ force in the name of humanitarianism. Root causes include poverty and institutional weaknesses exacerbated by differences in the distribution of wealth and power, unresolved ethnic and religious animosity, and, in some cases, the withdrawal of **bilateral (or foreign) aid** and the removal of rivalry between the Cold War's superpowers. In 1993, representatives from the Organization of African Unity (OAU) and the United Nations as well as scholars and military experts listed specific root causes of African civil conflicts: uneven economic development and gross disparities in well-being between communities within the same country, a continuation of divide-and-rule governing strategies inherited from colonial eras, a lack of democratic practices, a widespread sense of systematic injustice, personal insecurity, and exogenous factors.[22]

Complex emergencies themselves are not new challenges for humanitarianism, but increased targeting of civilian populations and the widening range of options for dealing with them are. Unlike interstate wars, where governments are generally willing to respect the rights of their adversary's civilian population in exchange for the respect of the rights of their own, intrastate wars, which account for virtually all of the recent U.N. operations, are characterized by warring parties' blatant targeting of civilians and diversion of relief supplies for combatants. Humanitarian action on behalf of civilians caught in the crossfire often runs counter to the strategic military goals of belligerents. Institutions have met the challenges of post–Cold War complex emergencies by trial and error; and regardless of intent, institutions' actions carry negative consequences as well as positive gains for war victims.

An additional problem in responding to complex emergencies is that it is difficult to discern who, if anyone, controls the military forces of the belligerents and with whom peace negotiators and humanitarian groups should establish dialogue. Even in cases where political authorities have given humanitarian organizations permission to access vulnerable populations, local military or external mercenary groups may refuse to honor the permission granted by supposedly higher authorities. Fighting alongside uniformed soldiers are armed civilians and militias. Russian Cossacks were in Bosnia, joined in solidarity with their Serbian brothers, but were not necessarily under the control of the Bosnian Serb military command.

Humanitarians in the field are constantly confronted with operational and ethical challenges stemming from complex emergencies and must juggle resources to meet daunting demands. When displaced persons return to their homes, they are met with fields that cannot be plowed because land mines cover the countryside. In some countries,

Boy soldiers participate in a drill in Myanmar. UNICEF/4761/John Chiasson.

such as Cambodia, there are more land mines than people. Adult and child amputees flood temporary medical facilities in hope of receiving prosthetics. Governments and commerce cannot function because trained personnel—not always numerous in the first place—have been executed or forced to flee. Infrastructure has been destroyed by war or simple lack of maintenance over the extended period of the armed conflict. Demobilized combatants have difficulty finding work because of shattered production infrastructures and are often tempted to revert back to violence to achieve economic means of survival for themselves and their families. The demobilization and reintegration of combatants into civil society are further complicated because many entered the war, voluntarily or not, as children. The psychological implications for their involvement in organized lawlessness affects social and political stability for years

Other humanitarian challenges include parallel (or black) markets, often designed to circumvent international sanctions or simple scarcity. Black markets linger and obstruct the establishment of more formal market mechanisms and the construction of an adhered-to system of law and order. Economies have been distorted further by war and the presence of thousands of NGO and U.N. personnel, who may have been a formidable source of employment and of foreign exchange through their payments for housing, transportation, protection, and translators; but then these personnel leave. **Dependency** upon outside sources is a difficult and slow process from which to be weaned, and some argue that habits of dependency are virtually impossible to reverse.

In addition to the dramatically changed character of armed conflict, the costs of relief have escalated, affecting the political and humanitarian outcomes of disasters. Insurance companies require extremely high premium payments to cover relief workers who deliver food aid and medical supplies inside a war zone. If the premiums are too high, relief is limited. U.N. agencies are paying rising costs for charter trucks and airplanes from various governments to deliver food aid in addition to bearing the increased cost, because of increased need, of the food itself.

The changed character of intrastate conflicts requires a diversity of actors on the ground—for example, U.N. personnel coordinating policy, NGOs helping at the community level, and the military protecting the civilians who administer humanitarian relief and those who receive it. Within U.N., NGO, and military institutions, there are wide ranges of conflicting and contradictory perspectives on problems and solutions and a multiplicity of functional units. In addition to the increased number of relief and protection units, we must also factor in the continual rotation of personnel (generally six-month commitments and sometimes less) and the diversity of nationalities, which complicates communications and logistics. Directives for U.N. personnel emanate from headquarters in Geneva and New York. Peacekeepers receive often contradictory orders from the U.N. commander and their own governments. There is rarely a centralized coordinator of personnel, logistics, procurement, and administration.

Secretary-General Boutros-Ghali published in 1995 *An Agenda for Development,* a companion to the earlier *An Agenda for Peace*, at the request of countries that saw their concerns being overlooked because of the "obsession" with security and humanitarian relief. This document attempts to draw international attention back to the root causes of conflicts, which if addressed would prevent the extensive need for humanitarian relief in the wake of war. The government of Rwanda made a similar attempt to bring the focus back to issues of economic development and justice by calling for the termination of the presence of U.N. peacekeepers in 1996. So long as the peacekeepers remained, the government argued, the world would go on believing it was "doing something" and avoid assisting the country in long-term goals of sustainable development. The choice between providing relief or assisting development when funds are limited is an acute dilemma.

CHANGING LANGUAGE
AND EXPECTATIONS OF STATES

A glance at field operations is but one avenue for assessing the post–Cold War changes in humanitarian action and the advancement of human rights. Another is to look at what people are writing. One will find ideas that are new as well as old ideas framed in new language.

Inside most academic institutions, there are colloquiums, conferences, and conversations about the erosion of state sovereignty and the importance of international institutions in facilitating cooperation and advancing international norms. In the eloquent prose of Francis Deng, the U.N. secretary-general's special representative on **internally displaced persons (IDPs)**: "Sovereignty cannot be an amoral function of authority and control; respect for fundamental human rights must be among its most basic values."[23] Flourishing are debates about tensions between territorial integrity and self-determination, nonintervention and human rights, and relief and development. Within the Security Council, humanitarian concerns have been placed more frequently and higher on the agenda. Literature promoting a more people-centered world abounds. Ideas of "global governance," including a new journal with that title, are now more abundant than following World War I and World War II. Even visions of a "global neighborhood" are appropriately printed on recycled paper, with inputs from an array of culturally distinct scholars, unlike Cold War international relations literature, which is monopolized by Western (largely U.S.) minds. Old calls for a more representative Security Council are coupled with new ideas to allow individuals and groups to petition the United Nations for consideration of key issues of their concern. Privileges accorded to powerful states with primacy in 1945 are being scrutinized, and demands for greater transparency of action and accountability are voiced more strongly. Institutional reflection and reform are abundant as the twenty-first century approaches. The additional challenge for the international humanitarian system is to keep pace with the changes occurring within societies that will contribute to tomorrow's humanitarian crises.

The trends characterizing the shape of the planet at century's end are unsettling. Population growth in developing countries has mushroomed and continues to do so in an inverse relationship to the resources necessary to sustain life, while at the same time technology has facilitated an increase in social contact among diverse cultures. Environmental degradation, population movements, and intrastate conflicts are at least partial manifestations of the crises of expanding populations, limited resources, and a rise in the volume and intensity of social contact. Transitions in state behavior are no less dynamic.

Poor countries are often unwilling or unable to provide social services and have become more willing to accede to or are unable to prevent the transfer of some sovereign obligations to IGOs or international NGOs. "Increasingly, [some host] governing authorities are not fulfilling their responsibilities because they expect that international agencies will come in and do the job."[24] An example of the altered relationship between state and society can be found in foreign aid workers jokingly making reference to the "Donor Republic of Mozambique," where the presence of more than 250 NGOs has created an alternative and nonstate source of power and authority. One NGO, World Vision International, disbursed almost $90 million in both 1994 and 1995, which made it the single largest donor in this postconflict country.

Wealthy countries have also acceded some sovereign authority to various intergovernmental organizations and NGOs to act as their proxy in international humanitarian efforts. Because of the transformation of world politics, none of the large or medium powers seemingly has been in an economic or political position to act alone against transgressions of states against societies, yet most feel compelled by the acceptance of humanitarian norms to respond in some way, even if to regret noninterference in other states' domestic affairs. We see this in the case of Rwanda, where states and their representatives in the Security Council initially dodged usage of the term *genocide* to avoid Chapter VII intervention but could not ignore the crisis completely. Moreover, governments and intergovernmental organizations in the humanitarian arena, including members of the U.N. system and the European Commission Humanitarian Office (ECHO), increasingly subcontract for services to international NGOs, which often have preexisting relationships with vulnerable populations, local NGOs, and government institutions.

History has set the stage upon which, for better and for worse, the calls of the distressed are received and sometimes answered. In spite of spectacular lapses, there has been progress in the evolution of humanitarian ideals since the end of the Cold War. Political leaders are showing more respect for international law and are recognizing the link between providing humanitarian assistance and protecting human rights and securing international peace.[25] Impediments to further progress and implementation of ideals can be found in the nature of the international humanitarian system and in specific characteristics of each conflict.

TWO

□ □ □

Actors and Arenas

Not inexperienced in hardships,
I learn how to bring aid to the wretched.

—Virgil, *Aeneid*

Sometime in late 1995, a local health care worker in a Zairean refugee camp counseled a Rwandan mother about the health needs of her sick baby. He treated the infant with medical supplies donated by the U.N. International Children's Emergency Fund in a tent provided by the U.N. High Commissioner for Refugees (UNHCR). The local staff were part of a medical team put together by Médecins sans Frontières (MSF, or Doctors Without Borders), a nongovernmental organization that split from the International Committee of the Red Cross over two decades ago. An ICRC principle is to wait for the consent of local governments before providing assistance. MSF does not wait.

Money and politics merged a continent away, as the European Commission Humanitarian Office, an intergovernmental organization, contemplated its annual budget and recipient list, setting aside a substantial donation to MSF. The mood was somber, however, in Washington as personnel in the U.S. Agency for International Development (USAID) worried about their jobs and their relief and development programs.

In Paris, administrators of Médecins du Monde (Doctors of the World, or MDM), a relief and development NGO founded by former MSF staff, were troubled by their increasingly successful but seemingly unethical behavior in seducing the media so as to increase donations. A full-time public relations person gave guided tours of human tragedy in Goma to raise the $200,000 per day cost of emergency relief. Médecins du Monde was also worried that a government elsewhere was relying too heavily on MDM for the care of the poor without taking sufficient responsibility on itself. If MDM withdrew, those recovering and rebuilding from the last humanitarian crisis would become vulnerable again.

In Bosnia, a team of MSF medics treated the mentally and physically wounded in the besieged enclave of Gorazde. U.N. peacekeepers watched from a distance as the safe havens began to fall. NATO war planes sat on a runway in Italy.

And somewhere two journalists who covered the Rwandan massacre tried to come to terms with what they had witnessed and continued to witness, as all humanitarians in the field must, while the rest of the world seemed not to notice. "Do you think we did enough?" one journalist wondered. "Is it our fault that the world didn't react to the massacres?"[1]

The foregoing composite snapshot in time offers a glimpse of the complexity of humanitarian issues and the diversity of humanitarian actors that together present challenges to relieving human suffering caused or compounded by war. The entanglement of issues and actors can frustrate attempted analyses. Local humanitarians rely upon NGOs and the United Nations for supplies and salaries. Relief and development NGOs disagree over guiding codes of conduct in war zones. The missions of IGOs such as the United Nations are subject to the interests of states and party politics. The media have the ability to draw attention and donations toward or away from human tragedy. NGOs in the field continue to provide relief while the safety of their mission is either supported or compromised by military involvement.

Complex humanitarian emergencies require multiple responses from a variety of actors, none of whom is capable of responding alone. Yet few are willing to forfeit control of their operations to a centralized coordinating authority. The first half of this chapter presents the barriers to cooperative and consistent humanitarian relief and protection. The second half of the chapter provides thumbnail sketches of five different post–Cold War cases in which humanitarian operations were conducted. The challenges of cooperation among the actors in the humanitarian system and the case studies form the basis in subsequent chapters for in-depth treatments of dilemmas, policy options, and recommendations.

ACTORS

The most useful way to think about the bevy of outsiders who flock to the scene of a complex emergency is to place them into three categories: governments; intergovernmental organizations, most particularly the United Nations and ECHO; and nongovernmental organizations, such as CARE, the MSF, and the ICRC. The military, subsumed within the category of governments, is worthy of separate attention. Some might choose to leave the military out of the roster of humanitarian actors; however, a military presence in humanitarian action has rounded out (or distorted, depending on one's perspective) the entire architecture of humanitarian responses.

An actor's interests, resources, organizational structure, and functions affect its behavior and ability to cooperate with other actors in a complex emergency. As a result, it may act in concert or contention or somewhere in between. Conflicts of interest, competition for resources, incompatible organizational structures and cultures, and overlapping functions are the challenges that the actors themselves bring to humanitarian operations.

Interests

The interests of a humanitarian actor refer to that which motivates it to respond to a plea for help. Deciphering what is included in an actor's array of interests is a difficult task. What an actor states publicly to be its motivation for responding may not be the primary explanation for its participation. Concealed motivations or hidden agendas mean that an actor may pull out of a humanitarian mission or threaten to do so if its unexpressed interests are not being served.

For example, one of Italy's contributions in the former Yugoslavia was to allow use of its airfields for NATO planes. However, Italy threatened to discontinue open use of its landing strips if it was not made part of the multinational contact group mediating the peace agreement in Dayton, Ohio. Humanitarian concern was mixed with a desire to play a larger diplomatic role, which Italy perceived would increase its status as a player in international affairs.

Others may view Washington's involvement and later withdrawal of troops in Somalia as an example of changing priorities of interest. U.S. involvement may have served the perceived interests of decisionmakers, particularly a lame-duck president, to demonstrate to the international community pro-active American leadership. Somalia seemed relatively safe for such posturing, at least in comparison to Bosnia. As the bodies of dead U.S. servicemen were dragged through the streets of Mogadishu, the interest in demonstrating leadership paled in comparison with the public relations costs. And Washington's military resources for protecting relief delivery were withdrawn.

Government Interests. States are legal abstractions with institutions called governments, which ensure the state's control of a specified territory and its people. Primarily, governments have an interest in protecting the state against internal conflict or civil unrest and external inter-

Peace process negotiations for the former Yugoslavia are in session. U.N. Archives/181.958.

ference in that state's affairs or territory. External conflicts that yield immense human suffering touch upon the interests of states in different ways. Voluntary participation in humanitarian operations may reflect a reasoned national or material interest in the region of conflict, such as the protection of oil reserves in Kuwait; former colonial relations with the country in crisis, such as Belgium's and France's involvement in Rwanda and Italy's in Somalia; a national identity that considers humanitarian assistance a moral responsibility, such as that of Norway; a need to acquire foreign exchange currency through payment for peacekeepers, such as Bangladesh; or a desire to rekindle military honor, such as Argentina.

Governments also may participate in humanitarian operations as a strategy to avoid taking stronger political and military action, particularly if the government has difficulty determining its interest in a crisis or determines that a defined political or economic interest would be jeopardized by a stronger response. Humanitarian assistance allows a government to appease a public that morally demands that its government "do something" while avoiding the more substantial commitment of military resources.

Due to the nature of democratic societies, political leaders have an interest in satisfying the will of voters and special interest groups. Governments can be shamed into involvement in humanitarian operations or constrained from involvement by public protestation, particularly if soldiers' lives are at risk. Therefore, election years, the configuration of conservatives and liberals within a government, and the influence of politically or financially powerful minorities can have an impact on the contributions that governments are willing and able to make toward humanitarian action and related peacekeeping efforts. U.S. involvement in peacekeeping efforts in the Middle East since the 1960s has satisfied economic interests as well as the perceived views of the Jewish lobby in the United States. The military intervention in Haiti in 1994 ameliorated the influx of Haitian refugees onto Florida's southern shoreline and also satisfied extensive pressure by the Black Congressional Caucus and the Haitian diaspora.

On a more abstract level, governments also have an interest in maintaining the integrity of the international system of states, which hinges upon respect for state sovereignty and the principle of noninterference as codified in Article 2(7) of the U.N. Charter. Each time the U.N. Security Council invokes Chapter VII (the legitimate use of force) for humanitarian reasons, the legitimacy and sanctity of state sovereignty lose ground to basic human rights.

States are the most powerful actors in the humanitarian system and often the least predictable. Because the motivations for a state's involvement in a humanitarian crisis dramatically vary across time and among different governments as a result of their political, economic, social, and security issues, the other actors in the humanitarian system cannot rely upon states for consistent support or behavior.

Military Interests. Although armed forces are generally considered instruments of societies and governments, they have interests of their own. In fact, the armed forces should be considered a highly influential interest group in foreign policy making.[2] Budgets for defense must be justified, more so during times of relative peace. Armed forces commanders as well as politicians with home constituencies dependent upon naval yards, military bases, and industrial defense firms may have an interest in demonstrating the continued need for new weaponry and technology and for the maintenance of troop strength, and these interests can do so through humanitarian operations. Although there are those in Washington who prefer using Department of Defense funds for training exercises in a nonconflict arena, there are others with an interest in participating in multinational peacekeeping operations. Unilateral military actions are more expensive than joint operations. Learning to work with other military contingencies and civilian humanitarians, although an expensive lesson in the short term, may have long-term benefits for future security arrangements and the morale of the military.

As in other bureaucracies, career advancement is an interest of individual members of the armed forces. A number of U.S. enlisted soldiers involved in Somalia complained of the seeming overabundance of officers on the mission, whom they believed were using the Somalia operation as a career advancement strategy. Given the relative peace among industrial societies and the loss of the Soviet Union as an adversary, there are fewer opportunities for career-minded officers to demonstrate command expertise. For some, participation in military intervention for humanitarian reasons satisfies a field experience requirement for promotion.

Stereotypes of military personnel do not readily lend themselves to a humanitarian imaging, but there are soldiers who have a personal commitment to helping and thus volunteer for duty that allows them to express their individual humanitarian impulse. A number of U.S. soldiers who volunteered to provide humanitarian assistance in a hurricane-devastated Florida in 1991 also volunteered for the humanitarian mission in Somalia in 1992. Although U.S. soldiers involved in Somalia spent the majority of their time protecting themselves and their encampments (they were not allowed to distribute food), soldiers, particularly females and blacks, volunteered in orphanages during their off-hours.[3]

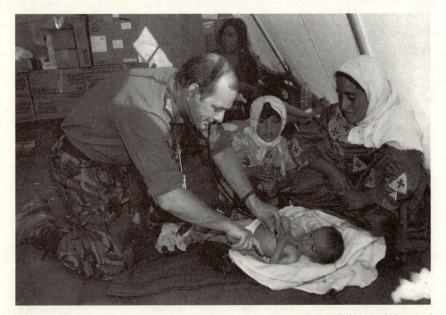

Returnees receive medical care at Zakho camp in Iraq. UNHCR/21006/05.1991/ A. Hollmann.

Careful observers can recognize the efforts that militaries are making to "fit" into humanitarian operations. For example, U.S. troops do not drink off-duty when operating in Muslim cultures. Manuals in military class-rooms explain the missions, operating procedures, and nature of non-governmental organizations and U.N. agencies. In the field, military units can be found holding informational meetings for all humanitarian actors operating in the same area. Technical expertise and sheer labor power have been offered to other actors who are short on both. Bright Star '95, conducted in Egypt, represented the largest coalition exercise since Desert Storm and brought together veterans of the Gulf War and interventions in Haiti and Somalia. According to a U.S. Army commander, "We demon-strate we can work together and we can fight together."[4] The mixture of political, military, and humanitarian interests is, needless to say, not al-ways as complementary as the actors would like. Interests can clash in the field, where the military can turn a relief operation into a militarized the-ater of engagement.

The civil war in Liberia offers one example. The Economic Community of West African States (ECOWAS) and its military Monitoring Group, with their own security concerns and economic interests in Liberia's civil strife, combined with a U.N. military observation effort. Also present in the field were humanitarian activities and imperatives carried out by U.N. humanitarian agencies and NGOs. In one instance, the regional peacekeeping troops bombed humanitarian personnel, and the United Nations itself tried to prohibit aid agencies from conducting programs in areas not controlled by the Liberian government. The political-military actors, anxious to secure a peace agreement, required the cooperation of the Liberian central authorities. The immediate humanitarian needs of those suffering from the conflict became subordinate to the peace process among the belligerents. Only those supporting the Liberian government received U.N. assistance. The logic in the discriminating distribution of relief was that the peace agreement itself, if successful, would have had positive humanitarian benefits.

IGO Interests. The United Nations is an example of an intergovern-mental organization—a multistate-created institution designed to fur-ther state interests on specific or broad-ranged issues. IGOs benefit states by serving as a forum for state-to-state dialogue, by reducing the cost of information gathering, and by setting forth guidelines for reciprocal state behavior. IGOs with humanitarian agendas, such as the United Nations itself or parts of the far-flung U.N. system, often find themselves in the impossible position of juggling the political in-terests of governmental elites with their own mandates to provide re-lief wherever there is suffering. And although IGOs conceptually represent the collective interests of *all* member states, those governments that are able and willing to pledge the most money to emergency budgets for individual crises also have the most to say about where and how money should be spent. Once a budget for a crisis is exceeded, the U.N. agencies with operations in the area make an appeal for additional funds. If state donors' interests have changed and pledges are therefore not made, the U.N. agencies are forced to withdraw their relief operations.

The larger the IGO is and more diverse its functions are, the more diverse are the interests among its internal organs and member states. The United Nations includes virtually all states (185 in 1996) and performs security, economic, social, and humanitarian functions. In contrast, the European Commission Humanitarian Office includes only the fifteen members of the European Union (EU); its function is largely to disburse humanitarian aid. NATO is an IGO with restricted membership and a security function that has recently become linked to humanitarian efforts. The OAS, the OAU, and the Commonwealth of Independent States (CIS) are examples of regional IGOs responding to regional security as well as economic, humanitarian, and social problems. The CIS has become a key player militarily in conflicts in the countries of the former Soviet Union where there are also significant humanitarian issues. The OAS and OAU have increased their involvement in conflict resolution in recent years, partly as a result of receding security interests of developed countries in Third World conflicts and partly as a barrier to future "imperial" military and economic intervention. Of the IGOs, ECHO and especially the United Nations are most relevant for understanding humanitarian action. Similar to governments and the armed forces, intergovernmental organizations are composed of officials whose promotions and careers can be enhanced by participation in a particularly visible way. As such, individual interests within a bureaucracy as large as the United Nations can affect coordination between agencies.

NGO Interests. Nongovernmental organizations are nonstate, nonprofit, private organizations whose principles, mandates, functions, and accountability in responding to civilians in crises defy any standard organizational form or predictable behavior. By definition, NGOs are not staffed by civil servants, although there is a career progression among NGO personnel, some of whom spend their entire active careers in the voluntary sector, while others assume U.N. positions. Many international NGOs are unfailing defenders of single issues, such as gender equality, humanitarian assistance, development, human rights, or the environment.

Some NGOs place empowerment of local NGOs as their primary goal. For example, when international NGOs were expelled from Ethiopia in 1988, the local NGOs they had supported were able to continue relief activities. But because a number of NGOs are dependent upon conditional funding from governments, the United Nations, other IGOs, and private citizens and organizations, subtle pressures bear down on NGOs to conform to the political will and interests of their supporters and may lead them to respect external, rather than internal, priorities.

A well-funded NGO, therefore, may not necessarily be a complement to a coordinated action in the field. What other humanitarian actors and war victims may need from an NGO may not be the desire or reflect the interests of the NGO's main financial contributors. Noncombatants in a safe area may need a rebuilt sewage system to stop the spread of disease, but NGO donors may restrict the NGO's activity to providing food. When one considers that there may be over two hundred NGOs in an area providing food and few working on water sanitation, it is easy to understand the need for a more centralized coordination of humanitarian activity. Staff experienced in field operations know the needs of the people through close work with local humanitarians and grassroots groups, but field staffs' missions can be held hostage by donors. Somalia represents an example of the need for NGO coordination. The Refugee Policy Group reported that CARE, Catholic Relief Services, World Vision, the ICRC, World Food Programme (WFP), and the UNHCR focused largely on food distributions, which were clearly needed, while other programs were "comparatively underrepresented—water, sanitation, essential drugs, case-finding, public health worker outreach, surveillance, and other health interventions."[5] In addition to donor constraints, NGOs' past activities dictated their activities in Somalia, whether they were needed or not.

International NGOs have grown rapidly in number, character, and influence. Some fifteen thousand NGOs operated in three or more countries and received their funding from sources in more than one country according to the 1993–1994 *Yearbook of International Associations*. The large number of NGOs is one indication of the broad range of interests that they bring to humanitarian operations. The list of major international NGOs that respond regularly to complex emergencies includes Catholic Relief Services, Lutheran Federation, OXFAM, World Vision, Médecins sans Frontières, and Save the Children Federation.

The International Committee of the Red Cross is a unique NGO worthy of special attention. Although it receives considerable funding from governments, and government representatives sit on the ICRC's board, the interests of the ICRC remain purely humanitarian. There may be political consequences as a result of its strict adherence to principles. Within the NGO community, the ICRC is the most coherent and perhaps has the most parsimonious list of interests that motivate its behavior during humanitarian missions: Where there is suffering, the ICRC will respond. Its interests are operationalized with strict adherence to apolitical principles, operational neutrality, and international humanitarian law. (It is, as noted earlier, the custodian of the Geneva conventions and additional protocols.) The national homogeneity of its Swiss staff, its internal code of conduct, and the safety of its personnel are also determinants of ICRC behavior. The ICRC philosophy is political neutrality, impartiality, and independence from the interests of other actors. Its Geneva-based staff employs a steadfast patience in waiting for the approval of host-state authorities before intervening in conflict zones. Because of an unwavering dedication to principles, the ICRC has an extraordinary role to play in the world of humanitarianism. It has observer status with the U.N. General Assembly—meaning it has the right to take the floor, to place documents before governments, and to suggest items for the agenda. In the last few years, the ICRC has held private, regularly scheduled monthly meetings with the president of the Security Council (a monthly rotating position) to exchange information regarding political-military conflicts and their humanitarian consequences and to offer recommendations.

Resources

The resources required for humanitarian missions include funds; medical, food, and housing supplies; transportation vehicles and communications equipment; staff experienced in relief, reconstruction, and development; diplomatic tools; and, when necessary, military personnel and equipment. Simultaneously occurring humanitarian crises result in a competition for limited resources and worldwide attention.

Government Resources. Governments, through taxation, have the most dependable source of revenue to fund humanitarian operations. Although government resources also include diplomacy and the provision of troops, food, equipment, supplies, or technical expertise, the primary channel for humanitarian assistance is bilateral aid. In theory, bilateral aid is given directly to another government; however, much of the aid is disbursed indirectly through U.N. agencies and NGOs. (See Figure 2.1.) Of the more than $6 billion spent on humanitarian emergencies in 1993, more than $4.5 billion originated from major donor governments.[6] Non-donor governments tend to be developing countries, whose major contribution to humanitarian operations has been peacekeepers.

FIGURE 2.1 International Flow of Financial and Other Resources to
Humanitarian Operations

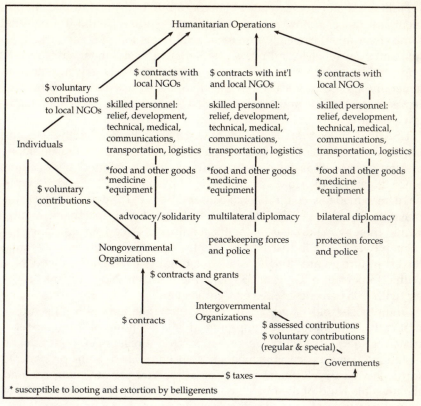

Credit: Cindy Collins

The limitations of bilateral aid agencies are normally that they reflect straightforwardly the political requirements and biases of contributing governments. Such agencies control more resources, but expenditures may be heavily conditioned by political, rather than developmental or humanitarian, concerns. The political relationships of a government and its history of involvement in a region may make it more or less welcome as a humanitarian resource when disaster strikes. Former colonial powers have historical and cultural links to many areas, which sometimes affects the acceptability of their involvement by countries in crisis—sometimes they are less acceptable, sometimes more. Because of resources, traditions, and influence, the United States normally plays a major contributing role—with food, funds, experts, and logistical support. Yet Washington is often more suspect than small countries such as Sweden or Austria, whose power and leverage are considerably less and whose past efforts at manipulation less visible.

Humanitarian or emergency aid is conceptually distinct from development assistance, although frequently they are administered through the same governmental agency. Emergency aid refers to funds earmarked for humanitarian relief for an unexpected crisis. Development assistance is budgeted by governments to foster economic and social advancement in generally less economically advanced countries that have traditionally represented some economic or security concern for a particular donor government.

USAID is an example of a government agency charged with distributing funds for development projects abroad in the form of development assistance as well as for disbursing funds for emergency relief action. Since the end of the Cold War, foreign aid has plummeted, and attempts have been made by congressional conservatives to dismantle USAID and place its functions under the control of the State Department, which would thereby make clear the political nature of American assistance. Of the top twenty-one industrialized countries, the United States now ranks lowest in foreign aid donations relative to gross national product (GNP) with 0.15 percent of GNP, or $38 per American, and Norway ranks highest, with 1.05 percent, or $236 per Norwegian.[7]

In the post–Cold War era, emergency humanitarian aid has risen dramatically, and foreign development aid has continued a longer-term trend and decreased. Populations supported by relief operations may be abandoned once peace agreements have been reached. Some proponents for decreased development assistance argue that private enterprise and the invisible hand of the free market will reach the previous objectives of foreign aid more efficiently and at less cost to donor governments. Whatever the logic in more economically advantaged societies, populations recovering from wars cannot rely upon the free market to pull the community out of crisis in a balanced and timely manner.

Military Resources. Armed forces receive all of their resources from their own governments. For involvement in peacekeeping operations, the United Nations reimburses each contributing government approximately $1,000 per month per soldier. Individual governments then determine how much to pay their soldiers. For less developed countries, the U.N. reimbursement usually leaves the country with a surplus of foreign exchange. For the more industrialized countries of the North, $1,000 per month per soldier only partially covers the cost of the peacekeeping effort.

Morale is a resource to the armed forces, and there are several scenarios that deplete morale in an international operation. National contingencies compare their wages with others in the field; morale can drop if one group finds its remuneration lower than that of other soldiers. Swedish troops in Bosnia complained that other Nordic counterparts in NATO were receiving one-third more cash, prompting the Swedish government to allow volunteers the choice to go home rather than proceed with their demining activities.[8] Another source of friction occurs when troops compare their levels of risk with those of other contingents that appear positioned in less dangerous situations. Fortunately, soldiers who are placed in the most demanding situations tend to be the best trained, best equipped, and best paid.

Less developed countries obviously are less able to provide their troops with all that is needed in a multinational peacekeeping operation, including appropriate clothing and equipment. In the middle of Croatia's winter, Pakistani troops arrived in summer uniforms. In Bihac, four Bangladeshi soldiers shared a single rifle. Bringing contingents from developing countries to the point of being functional often requires financial support from better-off countries.

The militaries from developed countries tend to be resource rich in human capital and equipment. Their training and material wealth allow them to readily render state-of-the-art skills in potable water production, bridge construction, crowd control, trauma care, and airlifting. France, for example, through Opération Turquoise in Rwanda, assisted the UNHCR in providing air traffic control, cargo handling, runway repair and security at Goma airport, water transport to the refugee camps, earthmoving work at burial sites, and food; France also provided general support to UNHCR and other agencies.[9]

IGO Resources. Intergovernmental organizations receive financial resources from their member states in the form of annual dues and voluntary contributions for particular crises. An IGO such as the United Nations uses a portion of financial resources to pay for overhead and staff. Another portion is used to hire nongovernmental organizations to implement programs in the field and to pay for transportation and communication equipment rentals. Still another portion is converted into humanitarian supplies. IGOs become vulnerable if governments choose not to pay their dues, a situation that plagues the United Nations itself. For example, as of early 1996, U.S. accrued debt to the United Nations had reached $1.2 billion. Assessed contributions are based roughly on a country's contribution to the world economy.

The special financial contributions that IGOs receive for particular crises tend to reflect the perceived national interests and, some might even argue, xenophobia of member states rather than the actual need of war victims. This donor bias is partially revealed in governments' responses to appeals for humanitarian assistance by the U.N. Department of Humanitarian Affairs (DHA). For example, 94 percent of requested funds for the former Yugoslavia were pledged by governments, whereas only 13 percent of the funds requested for the Rwandan refugee crisis in Zaire were met with concrete donor pledges in spring 1995.[10] Another explanation for the reduction in U.N. contributions is that a number of governments are now funneling more humanitarian assistance through nongovernmental organizations or doing so on a bilateral basis. By late 1995, a U.N. interagency appeal for donations to support humanitarian efforts in northern Iraq had netted only $39 million (28 percent of the $139 million needed). NGOs and other programs collected roughly $69 million.[11]

Once intergovernmental organizations have pledges in hand, the manner in which the money is allocated can be determined by war victims' needs. The benefit of **multilateral aid** is that it can, in principle, dilute some political bias commonly present in bilateral aid and grant the IGO more flexibility in distributing relief and development assistance.

The European Commission Humanitarian Office is an intergovernmental organization that has grown to be one of the most generous contributors to humanitarian relief. ECHO is not field operational; it serves only as a funding channel to NGOs and U.N. agencies. ECHO's 1993 and 1994 budgets were more than $700 million. The member states of the European Union fund ECHO in addition to their individual bilateral assistance programs. As complex emergencies have become the norm in recent years, ECHO has expanded its projects beyond the provision of food, its original focus and one that reflected the massive food surpluses resulting from the Common Agricultural Policy of the members. Since the crisis in Somalia, ECHO has funded water supply projects, medical aid, medical training for local personnel, nutritional supervision, mine clearance, and shelters. ECHO finances the work of the International Committee of the Red Cross and approximately thirty other nongovernmental organizations in the field.

NGO Resources. In terms of total resources in the mid-1990s, NGOs surpassed the resources of the U.N. system (excluding the International Monetary Fund [IMF] and World Bank) in the disbursement of total official development assistance. The largest NGOs have budgets of several hundred million dollars; however, most are reputed to be more responsive and manageable bureaucracies than their intergovernmental counterparts. As stated earlier, NGOs are dependent upon funds from governments and intergovernmental organizations such as the United Nations as well as donations from private individuals and foundations. Although some NGOs vehemently refuse any government contributions or limit them to a small percentage of the overall budget, the majority of NGOs are not so discriminating about contributors to their organizational well-being.

NGO dependency on voluntary donations and government and U.N. contracts can also produce another negative effect. To maintain contribution levels, NGOs must demonstrate to donors that their presence and inputs into a humanitarian mission were valuable; there is thus an incentive for an NGO to "do it all" and ignore the inputs and ideas of local groups. The creation and capture of **humanitarian space**—the breadth of operational freedom that humanitarian actors create or can find themselves— by NGOs can work to disempower local institutions and professionals and lead to prolonged dependency and stunted institutional growth— this is also a danger with U.N. assistance.

Humanitarian space expands and contracts as a conflict cools down or heats up. Some international NGOs, anxious to impress their donors and at times unwilling to trust local humanitarians and local coping mechanisms, can overpower local institutions and professionals. A problem occurs when local humanitarians are excluded from decisionmaking and program implementation processes and become involved in their own relief, rehabilitation, or reconstruction efforts only after powerful external actors have left the area, frequently taking needed resources with them. Amid a frenzied scramble to win government or U.N. contracts to implement humanitarian programs, NGOs have become more market efficient and business-wise. However, the clamor to acquire a market share in government and U.N. funding has also produced increased instances where war victims' needs are not thoughtfully assessed prior to the commencement of a relief program, nor is the impact of NGO activity adequately monitored or evaluated for effectiveness.

NGOs can also offer noncombatants a resource that is absent from the purse of IGOs and governments. Along with providing the same types of resources to missions as the United Nations, NGOs offer war victims advocacy and solidarity. In situations where the United Nations may be hesitant to publicly shame a warring party for human rights violations, some NGOs openly ignore the principle of political neutrality and advocate on behalf of noncombatants. In dangerous environments where the United Nations has been obliged for security conditions to shut down its field offices, NGOs have stayed to continue their services and provide comfort simply by their presence. NGO solidarity in Central America stimulated American public opinion against further U.S. intervention. In recent years, NGOs and the media have developed a symbiotic relationship whereby NGOs, such as Amnesty International, feed information to the press, the press moves public opinion, and public opinion (it is hoped) stimulates governments to act.

The ICRC's stature in the humanitarian community leads to a fund-raising position that is enviable. Some 90 percent of the ICRC's $800–900 million annual budget comes from states; and it has become a line item in many government budgets. Unlike the majority of NGOs, the ICRC has funds available before programs are in place and funding requirements are known. One ICRC staff member recalled, for instance, the organization being overwhelmed with funds to conduct food distribution in the rural areas of Somalia. But not all ICRC projects are so well funded. For instance, the ICRC has been working with very limited success to gather government and U.N. support to facilitate the release of nearly ten thousand Iraqi prisoners of war who, for more than fifteen years, have been held in subhuman conditions in Iranian prisons.

Organizational Structure and Functions

An actor's internal structure affects the manner in which and the speed with which it makes decisions and its capacity to pursue its interests. Organizational structure also affects an actor's ability and will to cooperate with other actors toward a common objective and its flexibility in adapting to unfamiliar cultures and rapid changes in the field. The structure and competing tendencies of large-scale bureaucracies, found within governments and the U.N. system, can prevent the formation of decisive and timely responses to calls for assistance. Multiple tiers of authority and competing interests within a bureaucracy dilute decisiveness. The policies that emerge from the bureaucratic maze are consolidated and compromised outcomes rather than clear, focused decisions that would provide the most efficient and effective responses to challenges. They are "outcomes in the sense that what happens is not chosen as a solution to a problem but rather results from compromise, coalition, competition and confusion" among key officials.[12]

Negotiations among external actors over how to act collectively, or at least in the same physical territory, produce yet another layer of political outcome, rather than decision, and reduce the potency of action to an even lower common denominator than was produced in the bureaucratic process within each organization. As such, it is difficult for an observer of a humanitarian crisis such as that in Bosnia to discern if inaction by the humanitarian actors is a calculated decision or if bureaucratic paralysis has set in. In addition to organizational structures, the functions of various humanitarian actors may not be complementary, or they may overlap with other actors' functions. At times this produces too little, and at other times too much, assistance.

Government Organization and Functions. Government bureaucracies are hierarchical organizational structures that yield multiple seats of authority and competition for power among different internal agencies, individuals, and political parties. Government agencies have varied and often competing agendas, and individuals within the bureaucracy hardly have uniform views. Members of the Bosnian desk of the U.S. State Department resigned over the political foot-dragging in Washington while war crimes flourished unopposed by governments, except rhetorically. In June 1995, Pentagon officials with long military careers jousted with young civilian White House aides over decisionmaking and statements to the press. One day the Pentagon publicly announced that it would be transplanting thirty-five hundred troops from Germany to Italy in preparation for a possible involvement on the ground in Bosnia. The next day, the Pentagon reduced the number to fifteen hundred and apologized for making statements without the approval of the White House or the NATO allies, including Italy, which was to receive the increased troop strength.[13]

In addition to internal power struggles, key information concerning a humanitarian crisis may not reach the appropriate decisionmakers before policy is formulated and action taken. Worse yet, misinformation may form as a result of multiple channels of communication. For humanitarianism, when information becomes hostage to bureaucratic haggling about power and resource allocation, high-sounding moral rhetoric flourishes, while action does not.

Military Organization and Functions. The organizational structure of armed forces is hierarchical, with a clear chain of command. Armed forces organizations are also bureaucratic in the sense that there are organs with specialized functions and clearly defined channels of authority and responsibility. As the establishers and stabilizers of order through the use or threat of force, armed forces tend to isolate themselves from nonmembers of the armed forces in living space and by uniform. "The isolation of armed force personnel means, among other things, that the interrelationships of armed force personnel and other members of the society [or humanitarian system] are periodic and delimited."[14] Whereas NGO and U.N. personnel rent residential and office space within the heart of a suffering community, armed forces establish a barbed-wire encampment immediately upon arrival. Isolation of armed forces personnel leads to solidarity with comrades but not with nonmilitary actors. The professional culture of armed forces is therefore conditioned by an isolation-solidarity process and by a regimented lifestyle with an overwhelming emphasis on training, planning, and hierarchical discipline.

It is not surprising that soldiers are having difficulty adjusting to humanitarian functions. Armed forces are capable of a wide range of activities, trained for and practiced repeatedly during times of peace. What is lost in this continual state of practiced preparation becomes evident in a field situation where flexibility in procedure and response as well as coordination with nonmilitary (unregimented) actors may be required. Soldiers' training prepares them to seek efficient functioning toward a well-defined end. Clear mission statements and well-defined standard operating procedures are essential for effective operations and maintenance of morale. Traditionally taught to identify an enemy, soldiers in peacekeeping missions frequently must practice a neutrality mentality. Yet as a female U.S. soldier remarked after participating in Somalia, "I have a hard time with the term *humanitarian* when I'm being shot at."[15] Her lament was born of an unclear mission statement in an unfamiliar environment.

The military can become frustrated by loosely organized NGOs and their young volunteers who resist attempts by the military to "protect" them or to have their operations guided by the military's agenda or operational procedures in a hostile environment. Military personnel that were interviewed following action in Somalia stated that there were no clear agreements between military forces and NGOs, nor did many NGOs have an understanding of military capabilities. The result was unnecessary confrontations between civilian and military personnel. The military was also frustrated with U.N. agencies that refused to provide incentives for belligerents to disarm. Without a clear mandate for the forces to begin widespread disarmament and without the economic incentives by the United Nations for warring parties to do so, the lives of peacekeepers were unnecessarily placed at high risk.

The military is trained to follow a regimented plan for disarmament: secure an agreement, establish and manage a cease-fire, withdraw and assemble belligerents, disarm belligerents, and disperse and rehabilitate belligerents. The military's resources, including its expertise, and its centralized command qualify it to perform multifunctions in the sequence of disarmament. Its frustration with the United Nations and NGOs stems from their not adhering to the military's standard operating procedures. In Somalia, cultures and agendas clashed, ending in the subsequent withdrawal of armed forces and government donations from the humanitarian mission.

Clearly, the expertise and resources of the military are invaluable in highly volatile environments, but the military's presence in humanitarian operations is not without a price. Armed forces involved in humanitarian operations can confuse the victims and belligerents alike, thereby moving the humanitarian effort away from neutrality and toward politicization.

As stated previously, soldiers who are professionally conditioned to operate in an environment that is cautious, hierarchical, and heavy-handed have difficulty coordinating with and understanding the organizational structure of relief and development agencies. The military is often a late arriver to humanitarian crises and an early departer. Yet while present, it has the power to take command and control away from humanitarian organizations that have developed important links of communication and services distribution with the civilian victims throughout the crisis. The armed forces can be disruptive to preexisting networks for delivery of assistance, or they can be essential players in assuring delivery. At times, the difference can be attributed to the personality and interpersonal skills of the military commander in the field.

IGO Organization and Functions. Similar to governments, the United Nations and other IGOs have problems associated with bureaucracies. The United Nations is hierarchically structured, with information gathering occurring at the base of the power structure, decisionmaking happening at the top, and strata of bureaucratic functions operating in between. The organization's multiple layers and agencies serve the political, sociocultural, economic, development, and humanitarian needs of member states, which are in theory equal entities—that is, Kiribati and China are supposedly on equal footing, which is clearly a fiction, although each has one vote in the General Assembly. The United Nations employs some sixty thousand people in various U.N. offices, which as Erskine Childers and Brian Urquhart note is about the same size as the civil service of the state of Wyoming for a population of just over half a million people. An even more striking observation about relative size was made by Foreign Minister of Australia Gareth Evans at the opening of the fiftieth session of the General Assembly: Four thousand fewer people work for the U.N. system than for the three Disney amusement parks, and over three times as many sell MacDonald's hamburgers worldwide.[16] The number of soldiers (eighty thousand in 1995) and temporary personnel would raise this figure considerably, but the United Nations' total budget (including peacekeeping) is scarcely more than the combined budgets of the police and fire departments of New York City. Agency infighting and contradictory agendas plague the United Nations as vigorously as they penetrate state-level decisionmaking. The Preamble and the 111 articles of the U.N. Charter are at odds with one another, and so are the institution's agencies. All in all, it would be erroneous to think of the U.N. system or the United Nations itself as monolithic or unified. Working out the problems associated with being a large bureaucracy, compounded by political demands from member states, presents a unique challenge to providing assistance to civilians trapped in a war zone.

The United Nations performs two distinct and oftentimes conflicting functions—one political, the other technical. It facilitates the maintenance of international peace and security via the Security Council, and it provides humanitarian and development assistance through a number of organizations that belong to what is sometimes familiarly called the "U.N. family." During the Cold War, peace and security were interpreted to mean the maintenance of the status quo without engagement in the superpowers' spheres of influence. In the absence of Cold War rivalry, governments are now finding it difficult to ascertain which worldwide conflicts constitute legitimate threats to the international system of states. The Security Council has the power of self-definition—that is, whatever it determines is "aggression" or a "threat to international peace and security" is, by definition, so considered. However, the lack of consistency in its decisionmaking makes the United Nations subject to the criticism of bias.

More particularly, the United Nations has come under criticism for its handling of humanitarian crises in three particular areas: (1) the poor coordination among U.N. agencies and between the United Nations and other external humanitarian agencies; (2) the organization's inability to link emergency relief with long-term development and to tie local groups and institutions more effectively to that process; and (3) "the difficulty of designing and implementing comprehensive programmes that combine peacemaking with measures that strengthen economic reconstruction, good governance and human rights."[17] A closer examination of the U.N.'s main functions and organizational structures helps to dispel the popular image of an internally united U.N.

Peace and security function: The Security Council is composed of fifteen members, five of which are permanent (the United States, Russia, China, France, and the United Kingdom). Whereas the agenda of the General Assembly is concerned with humanitarian and human rights issues as well as economic, social, legal, and financial concerns, the Security Council is the principal decisionmaker for matters regarding the maintenance of international peace and security. It is important to note, however, that "peace" and "security" are not synonymous; there are situations in which the Security Council will place security before peace and order before justice.

The Security Council rarely addressed directly humanitarian issues during the Cold War, yet in recent years humanitarianism has made more and more frequent appearances on the Security Council's agenda. The existing record for this mantra is the mention of "humanitarian" eighteen times in the resolution approving the U.S.-led intervention in Somalia in December 1992. Intervention in the affairs of other states had formerly been reserved for situations in which one state's sovereignty was jeopardized by aggressive acts of another, such as Iraq's invasion of Kuwait. However, the Security Council's decision to protect the Kurdish population of Iraq from its own central government was based not on issues of sovereignty but on international protestation against an "unjust" sovereign—one who had violated fundamental obligations to its people. It would be naive, however, to assume that an unequivocal precedent has been set by the Security Council's defense of the Kurds. For obvious political reasons, the council has done nothing to protect Tibetans against the inhumane treatment (to the point of genocidal acts) by the Chinese government or the Chechens against the leveling of Grozny by the Russian Army.

Humanitarian function: The primary organizations of the United Nations that are responsible for humanitarian action include the DHA, the UNHCR, the U.N. Children's Fund (UNICEF), and the WFP. Also involved are the U.N. Development Programme (UNDP), the Food and Agriculture Organization (FAO), and the World Health Organization (WHO).

The Department of Humanitarian Affairs is a creation of the post–Cold War era. It was established in response to the immense frustration of major donors over the inability of multiple U.N. agencies and NGOs to effectively coordinate humanitarian activities during the Gulf crises. The U.N. Disaster Relief Office (UNDRO) was the DHA's predecessor and is now subsumed within it. One of the major functions of the DHA is to launch consolidated appeals for funding. Though it has few funds of its own—it has a revolving emergency fund of only some $50 million—the DHA is a major source of information for the international community's response to natural and human-made disasters.

The Statute of the Office of the U.N. High Commissioner for Refugees (1950) "declares that UNHCR's work is humanitarian, social and of an entirely nonpolitical character."[18] The UNHCR is guardian of the 1951 Convention Relating to the Status of Refugees and the 1967 protocol. Its responsibilities include the protection and nurture of refugees, their **resettlement** into a recipient country when appropriate, and their **repatriation** back to their country of origin. The UNHCR also coordinates the actions of multiple relief organizations in the field that receive UNHCR funds to implement assistance projects to refugees. The UNHCR by design is not meant to be operational itself but provides the financial and material assistance necessary to carry out its strategies. Other U.N. agencies and NGOs routinely contract with the UNHCR to implement programs. When an emergency problem arises, such as the massive flow of refugees out of Rwanda, the UNHCR initially draws upon financial resources held in reserve in an emergency fund. Approximately $10 million are placed in the fund annually, and no more than $4 million are allowed for one emergency. But the main operating funds are raised from donor governments, increasingly orchestrated by a DHA-coordinated consolidated appeals process, for each emergency as it arises. In 1995, the commission's total budget was about $1.3 billion, about $500 million of which was devoted to the former Yugoslavia and another $300 million to Rwanda.

UNICEF was established in 1946 to provide immediate relief to the child victims of World War II. With headquarters in New York at Forty-fourth Street on the other side of First Avenue from the United Nations itself, UNICEF provides material assistance such as food, clothing, and medical supplies in emergency relief operations with an eye toward long-term development. UNICEF, like the UNHCR, draws upon an emergency fund for humanitarian crises in war zones. It, too, is financed almost exclusively by voluntary contributions from governments, although funds are also received through various UNICEF fund-raising activities. Many readers may remember receiving a Christmas or greeting card produced by UNICEF or trick-or-treating for UNICEF as a child without fully understanding that the fund-raising directly supported a U.N. agency. A growing percentage (now about 25) of UNICEF's almost $1 billion budget is devoted to emergency relief. In 1994, UNICEF provided $216 million of emergency assistance to sixty-three countries.

The funding source for the UNDP's development projects is voluntary contributions from governments. The UNDP was established as the central source of funding for technical cooperation and prefeasibility projects for the U.N. system as a whole. Its annual budget is now about $1 billion. The senior UNDP official in recipient countries (called the UNDP resident representative) acts during nonviolent times as the U.N. resident coordinator for all development activities by the members of the U.N. system. He or she also acts as the DHA country representative in case of natural disasters. When war erupts, sometimes this official remains to help with the coordination of humanitarian aid. Sometimes, however, this official (usually with a background in development and with a previous career in such a specialization) is inadequately qualified to assume such responsibilities; at other times U.N. security units force the preconflict U.N. personnel to be evacuated. In such situations, a special representative of the secretary-general (SRSG) may assume overall responsibility. Once violence is relatively under control, UNDP expertise generally focuses on reconstruction and development activities, and the UNDP's top official resumes overall coordination responsibilities.

Food insecurity following on the heels of World War II led to the establishment of the FAO in Rome. Its primary activity is agricultural development. It also deals with emergency food shortages brought on by natural or human-made disasters, and the organization is responsible for monitoring food insecurity situations and maintaining the International Emergency Food Reserve. Its work in field operations is crucial during the reconstruction phase of a war-torn society, when a gap exists between the time conflict is resolved or contained and the first viable harvest is brought in.

The WFP, also based in Rome, is a food surplus disposal body jointly established by the United Nations and the FAO. Originally intended as a development (food for work) organization, the WFP is now a mainstay of the U.N. system's response to emergencies. Part of the WFP's funding is derived from the FAO's International Emergency Food Reserve, but the remaining portion results from voluntary contributions in kind and in cash from bilateral relief donors. With a budget of over $1 billion, the WFP primarily provides emergency food, although it still pays attention to long-term issues of chronic malnutrition. In light of the growth recently in the number and intensity of armed conflicts, the WFP now devotes about 80 percent of its resources to emergency efforts rather than to longer-term development. The WFP closely coordinates food needs with other U.N. agencies and NGOs and has become the logistics specialist for emergency aid within the U.N. system.

The World Health Organization, based in Geneva, is another U.N. agency created after World War II. Its function in humanitarian operations is to coordinate the activities of health care providers in the field. The work of WHO is integral to attending to the health needs of noncombatants during a crisis and immediately thereafter. The agency has been seeking a longer and larger role in such assistance.

NGO Organization and Functions. Nongovernmental organizations are generally structured horizontally, meaning that there are fewer tiers of authority and those that exist are flat rather than top-down. Decisionmaking by consensus is more a norm in NGOs than elsewhere, particularly in smaller NGOs. NGO field operations are frequently staffed by younger volunteers, particularly as such agencies struggle to respond to more and more complex emergencies with larger numbers of victims. The age and inexperience of some NGO staff operating in conflict areas have become a problem in itself.

The organizational structure of NGOs often affords them the ability to mobilize quickly and to be flexible in field operations as conflicts evolve. A growing number of international NGOs perform both humanitarian and development functions and are therefore working in isolated areas long before and after most U.N. agencies and protection force contingents. However, given the diversity within the NGO universe, it is necessary, yet difficult, to distinguish among genuine humanitarians, on the one hand, and charlatans or loose cannons, on the other.

NGOs can complement U.N. efforts by their links to grassroots groups and their frequent expressions of solidarity with war victims. They are a key access point for first-source information. NGOs are often in-area assisting in humanitarian efforts before U.N. agencies arrive, remain long after the United Nations has discontinued its relief operations, and frequently continue with relief and development tasks in the midst of unfriendly fire. In Somalia, for example, the U.N. relief staff was evacuated for eleven months in 1991 due to increased hostilities, whereas Save the Children/UK was unstaffed for only seven days.[19]

The U.N. system and states increasingly depend upon NGOs to fulfill a variety of functions required in a comprehensive strategy to address humanitarian needs, from human rights monitoring, to the establishment of temporary hospitals and food distribution centers, to demining. Table 2.1 captures the diversity of NGO actors, functions, and degree of interaction with other humanitarian actors in Somalia from 1990 to 1994.

Clearly, NGO functions duplicate many IGO functions. And although diplomacy is generally a function of governments and IGOs, it is not entirely outside the range of NGO capabilities—an Italian Catholic NGO based in Rome, the Community of San Egidio, provided the venue and neutral mediation skills necessary to bring about a 1990 peace settlement between the Mozambican government and its challenger, Resistance Nationale Mozambique. Moreover, the advice of NGOs is sought by a number of U.N. agencies and at times by the Security Council. Article 71 of the U.N. Charter supports closer ties between IGOs and NGOs. It instructs the Economic and Social Council (ECOSOC) to "make arrangements for consultation with nongovernmental organizations which are concerned with matters within its competence."

Private advocacy NGOs typically make public statements, seek to produce documents that can be circulated among decisionmakers, and publicize widely the results of their research and monitoring. Targeting officials within governmental and intergovernmental institutions, these NGOs can be loud and theatrical or discreet and more subtle—Médecins sans Frontières or the International Committee of the Red Cross. Advocacy is a growing role, and deliberations about possible modifications of consultative status in U.N. forums are assuming growing salience. Consultative status can be useful in that it provides additional access to, and enhanced credibility in the eyes of, many governments and U.N. officials.

Unlike U.N. agencies, NGOs operate without regulation. With the exception of the host government, no one can expel an NGO from an area. And unlike U.N. agencies, because there is no duty to respond to a crisis, NGOs do not receive negative criticism when they choose not to be present (although their fund-raising may suffer). There is little profession-wide agreement on behavior in the field. NGOs have been known to

TABLE 2.1   Select NGO/Relief Agency Contributions to Somalia Relief Effort, 1990–1994

Agency	Involved in Food Delivery	Other Activities	Collaborating Agencies
ADRA		Health, water, training, orphans, Somali NGOs	CARE, IRC, WFP, ICRC
Africare	Logistics adviser to NRC	Pharmaceuticals, wells	IMC
AICF/USA		Health, sanitation	UNICEF
AirServe International	Transportation	Air transportation of relief teams and supplies, including to refugees in Kenya	UNICEF, international NGOs
American Jewish World Service		Health	DRI
American Refugee Committee		Medicine, health, education, and training	UNHCR, UNICEF, OFDA
CARE	Direct feeding, monetization, transportation	Agricultural, rehabilitation, vet services, water, health, environmental sanitation	WFP, OFDA, ODA, AIDAB, EC, Austrian and Norwegian governments, international NGOs
CISP/Italy	Direct feeding	Medical, sanitation, animal husbandry	OFDA, Italian government
Concern Worldwide	Monetization, feeding centers	Immunization, latrines, schools, agricultural projects	
CRS	Direct feeding, cross-border	Agricultural, rehabilitation, water, nutrition, health	
Direct Relief International		Medical supplies/equipment	Somali NGOs
International Aid (Sweden)	Direct feeding and food supplements	Reconstruction of primary schools	
INMED		Health	ADRA
International Rescue Committee	During 1992 only	Health, sanitation/water, vet services, monetization, garbage collection, income generation	UNHCR, UNICEF, WFP, CARE, JDC, international and Somali NGOs
Mercy Corps International		Medical	World Concern
Operation USA		Medical supplies/equipment	IMC
Oxfam-America	Provided through ICRC	Water, vocational training	Somali NGOs, ICRC

(*continues*)

TABLE 2.1 (*continued*)

Agency	Involved in Food Delivery	Other Activities	Collaborating Agencies
Save the Children/U.S.		Health posts, irrigation, training, sanitation, agricultural rehabilitation	OFDA, UNDP, UNICEF, MSF, ICRC
Save the Children/U.K.	Direct feeding, transportation, feeding centers	Health, water, agricultural rehabilitation, NGO coordination, education, nutrition, displaced persons	ODA, EU, OFDA, Cafod, UNICEF, SCF/NZ, Redd Barna, GOAL, Caritas-Switzerland
World Vision RD	Direct feeding, supplies, local purchase	Medical training, income generation, building	CRS, GOAL, ICRC, MSF, OFDA

Source: John G. Sommer, *Hope Restored? Humanitarian Aid in Somalia, 1990–1994* (Washington, D.C.: Refugee Policy Group, November 1994), Table C-9.

make "deals" with belligerents that control roads and border crossings to gain access to suffering civilians. Such actions often have political ramifications. For example, during fighting in the Afghan war, a number of the 150 or so NGOs present succumbed to the pressures from Afghan leaders and Pakistani authorities on where to go and what to do. Humanitarianism in this scenario transcends apolitical behavior by strengthening the position of one of the warring parties at the expense of the other and by doing so, possibly prolonging the conflict and the vulnerable position of those being "helped."

As with all humanitarians, NGOs bring strengths and weaknesses to complex emergencies. Nongovernmental organizations have earned a reputation for being more flexible, forthcoming, and responsive than other members of the international humanitarian system. Their customized or "retail" efforts at the grass roots can be legitimately distinguished for the most part from the "wholesale" efforts of governments and U.N. agencies. Yet NGOs are hardly without fault; their energy may lend frenzy and confusion. Careful planning and evaluation are rarer than they should be—the desire to get on with the next emergency contributes to a lack of attention to institutional learning. Impatience with bureaucracy can lead to naïveté and manipulation. Independence is guarded so jealously that opportunities for collaboration are missed. In response to criticism of questionable NGO behavior in the field, NGOs are rethinking what it means to be "political" and are attempting to broaden their understanding of the inevitable political repercussions of certain humanitarian strategies.[20] The 1995 annual meeting of InterAction, a professional association of U.S. NGOs, provided workshops on democracy and development, refugee reintegration, the impacts of trade liberalization on women, sustainable energy choices, and more broad issues such as advocacy, influence, and power. It was followed by a specialized forum to discuss the "certification" of NGOs capable of professional activity in complex emergencies. Given the complexity of recent humanitarian actions, NGOs are also forming permanent and temporary NGO coalitions to achieve efficiency in the division of labor and costs in certain field operations. Of the NGOs, the ICRC has gained a reputation for efficiency and effectiveness in the functions it performs.

The ICRC pallet of humanitarianism includes, but is not limited to, building and staffing hospitals and health posts for the war wounded, delivering food and medical supplies, and working toward humanizing the treatment of prisoners of war. Although traditionally the ICRC has chosen limited spheres in which to work—it addresses specific needs, such as a hospital here or food distribution there, rather than broad countrywide operations—in recent years the ICRC has been called upon by U.N. agencies and governments to expand its operations because of its logistical expertise and well-deserved reputation for professionalism. In fact, one former head of a major U.N. agency— James Ingram, the former executive director of the World Food Programme—has even proposed that the ICRC be expanded and "internationalized" (that is, lose its purely Swiss character) to provide in a more centralized fashion the types of help in war zones that are presently delivered by the host of U.N. agencies and NGOs described earlier.[21]

Currently, there is an identity crisis within the ICRC. For some, its strictly humanitarian agenda is being compromised by its association with the peace and security operations of governments and the United Nations; these critics call for a return to the essence of the ICRC—purely impartial and neutral humanitarianism. For others, it is unrealistic and impossible to keep the humanitarian sphere from colliding and merging with that of politics. For example, even the ICRC resorted to hiring armed guards in "technicals" (pickup trucks with mounted machine guns) for protection in Somalia. It is virtually impossible to insulate humanitarian efforts within the same arena as military and political activities, such as in the former Yugoslavia. Indeed, the ICRC is having difficulty maintaining an appearance of political neutrality; the introduction of outside peacekeeping forces has often cast an unwelcome hue upon ICRC activities in spite of protestations to the contrary by ICRC staff.

The ICRC is one organizational component of the International Red Cross and Red Crescent Movement. Other organizations under the movement's umbrella include the International Federation of Red Cross and Red Crescent Societies (IFRC) and National Red Cross or Red Crescent Societies, which exist in almost all countries. The fundamental principles of the movement must be stringently followed by ICRC member organizations. Although various ICRC personnel may desire changes in ICRC behavior, the power of the movement pulls it back to adherence to principles. As noted earlier, MSF was formed by ICRC personnel who refused to abide by the movement's principle that requires consent of the warring parties.

It is worth emphasizing the extent to which some nongovernmental organizations have contributed more to international agenda-setting than have many IGOs or governments. For example, at the San Francisco Conference in April 1945, NGOs acted as "consultants" to the U.S. delegation and played a pivotal role in securing the inclusion of human rights language in the final draft of the U.N. Charter; and they continued in 1948 with the formulation and subsequent ratification of the Universal Declaration of Human Rights. In fact, NGOs have spurred action since the middle of the nineteenth century at each stage in the evolution of the human rights regime.

There is disagreement about the precise NGO influence on governmental responses to civil wars. There is inconsistency sometimes even within individual organizations, and certainly within the entire group, about the extent to which the best responses by governments should be political, military, humanitarian, or some combination. Yet NGO efforts can be pertinent for the timing and shape of international responses to internal conflicts. In the United States, for example, they helped contribute to a supportive climate for President George Bush's decisions to override Iraqi sovereignty on behalf of the Kurds and to respond to the **anarchy** of Somalia's lapsed sovereignty. Nongovernmental organizations were unable to move the Clinton administration to acknowledge genocide and act in Rwanda in April and May 1994; but they eventually were able to get the Pentagon to help with refugee camps in Zaire and Tanzania. For three years, many American NGOs encouraged a robust enough military invasion to restore the elected government of Reverend Jean-Bertrand Aristide in Haiti. In France, NGOs have launched and sustained an activist humanitarian policy, *le devoir* (the duty) or even *le droit d'ingérence* (the right to interfere), that became the official policy of the Mitterrand government and its visible Minister of Humanitarian Action, Bernard Kouchner, and that survives both of their departures.[22]

Summary of Actors. A review of actors' interests, resources, and organizational structures and functions clarifies why there is a collective action problem associated with humanitarian operations. Collective action, according to Charles Tilly, "is about power and politics; it inevitably raises questions of right and wrong, justice and injustice, hope and hopelessness; the very setting of the problem is likely to include judgments about who has the right to act, and what good it does."[23] Indeed, the process of collective action in humanitarian crises is extremely complicated. The attached illustration on resource flow attempts to convey the potential for overlap, duplication, waste, and confusion. Without attention to the components of collective action for each actor of the humanitarian system, it is easier to place the blame for failed humanitarian missions entirely upon the culture of the combatants, as some have done with crises in Africa, or upon one institution, such as the United Nations.

Local Humanitarians

The humanitarian picture would not be complete without acknowledgment of the role that local groups and individuals play in relieving human suffering. This is particularly the case during the early stages of population movements when U.N. agencies and NGOs have not yet received in-country the resources necessary to meet the needs of distressed groups. Local resources are often mobilized more quickly, prove more appropriate and cost-effective, and have greater staying power than those of external actors. By ignoring the capacity and will of local individuals and groups, external actors fall into the conceptual and operational trap of considering suffering populations solely as objects of assistance rather than as subjects of their own survival and recovery—an unfortunate but frequent occurrence in humanitarian operations.

The first safety net for vulnerable populations is the people or victims themselves. In the early stages of the Rwandan crisis when the slaughter of Tutsis flooded the country, moderate Hutus risked their lives to harbor Tutsi families. A Somali woman, realizing that looters did not steal cooked food, set up a soup kitchen to feed the starving; the ICRC augmented her efforts and used her soup kitchen as a national model. By the time U.N. agencies and Western donor governments turned their attention to the more than 1 million refugees who had made their way into Jordan following the invasion of Kuwait, their needs had been met first by locals who donated bread and tomatoes from their own tables and then by local NGOs that set up tents and gathered donated food from locals. The Jordanian government committed some $55 million of its own resources to purchase for the refugees food, shelter, and transportation until the international humanitarian system was able to make any decisions. In the former Yugoslavia, 95 percent of refugees pouring into Serbia, Montenegro, and Croatia in 1992 found food and shelter in private homes, initially without consideration of the refugees' ethnic background.

In addition, concerned individuals and groups safely outside a conflict area have formed solidarity with the suffering and acted, often without formal organizational structure or guidance, in response to their own humanitarian impulse. Western Europeans rented buses and drove through mined areas and sniper fire to rescue children in Bosnia. A Rhode Island firefighter entered the country to organize emergency fire-fighting efforts in besieged areas. In Africa, countless individuals from around the world have volunteered their health care skills. Human rights and election monitors in Central America are often volunteers from abroad who have taken temporary leaves of absence from varied jobs to respond to the human need of strangers and perhaps to a personal need to do something.

KEY POST–COLD WAR ARENAS OF HUMANITARIAN ACTION

The human and political dimensions of five war zones—Central America, northern Iraq, the former Yugoslavia, Somalia, and Rwanda—illustrate the challenges that humanitarian action faces in a post–Cold War world. Many of the factors that affect institutional actor decisionmaking are linked to the contexts in which humanitarian operations are carried out. These factors include topography; weather (season); the number of warring parties; the existence of a regional hegemon; the condition of the area's infrastructure (particularly with regard to roads, ports, airfields, communication); the number of local and international NGOs and U.N. agencies established in the area before the crisis; the presence of the ICRC; the enforcement of economic or military sanctions; the availability of local resources (human and otherwise); the military and political objectives of belligerents; and the territorial scope of the conflict.

Central America

The countries of Central America—Guatemala, Belize, Honduras, El Salvador, Nicaragua, Costa Rica, and Panama—cover an area of only 228,000 square miles (some 40,000 square miles smaller than the state of Texas).

MAP 2.1   Central America

One explanation for the turbulent history of most Central American countries is encapsulated in the well-worn regional lament "So far from God, so close to the United States." U.S. economic and military involvement is tightly woven into the historical fabric of Central American countries—from the United Fruit Company's establishment of banana plantations in Guatemala in the late 1880s (hence, the term *banana republic*), to the military invasion of Panama one hundred years later. The cry for humanitarian action in Nicaragua, El Salvador, and Guatemala in the 1980s is best understood through an analysis of the economic and political conditions that formed the basis for violent civil strife.

The 1960s were a period of economic and agricultural modernization for most of Central America. **Import substitution** and a Central American common market produced high growth rates for economic elites and pushed those living on the margins of society further below the poverty level. In El Salvador, for example, the rural landless labor force rose from 12 percent in 1960 to 41 percent in 1975. As small family-owned farms were consumed by powerful elites and modern agricultural machinery reduced the need for manual laborers, wages fell and caused widespread malnourishment and massive urban migration in pursuit of work.

In response to government neglect of social and development needs, scores of Peace Corps volunteers joined ranks with nongovernmental and religious groups, most notably the Roman Catholic Church, in providing assistance. Health and education services and development projects were implemented by the Peace Corps and development NGOs. The Roman Catholic Church, in its shift toward **liberation theology**, became increasingly involved in the establishment of Christian communities, peasant associations, production and savings cooperatives, and women's groups. It also purposefully began training selected indigenous people for leadership positions, those deemed capable of articulating the needs and desires of all politically and economically marginalized people. The creation of organizational structures and leadership in opposition to government and military oppression permanently altered the social fabric of many Central American countries. The voice of organized dissent grew louder.

The political elites and the military responded with violence rather than political reform. Torture, rape, assassinations, and arbitrary arrests targeted at community organizers, the Catholic Church, popular organizations, and reformist political parties became the strategy for dealing with political and social unrest. In the absence of democratic means of political participation, revolutionary politics became operative, with Cuba as the model. The Reagan administration grouped all movements geared toward **distributive justice** together under the rubric of "communist"; every revolutionary movement looked like Cuba and smelled of the Soviet Union. This image of a communist monolith led to covert U.S. support of conservative Central American regimes and insurgent groups deemed complementary to U.S. national and business interests. Legitimation was won by force, not consensus. Even in cases where elections were held and civilians took office, the military regimes, strengthened by U.S. financing and training, often held sway over the principles of democracy and popular representation.

The turning points from submission to revolution in El Salvador, Nicaragua, and Guatemala were linked to the people's frustration over access to political power blocked by political and military elites and by blatant violations of human rights, both individual and collective. In El Salvador, a coalition party of civilian reformist parties and the National Democratic Union (allied with the Salvadoran Community Party), in opposition to military rule, won the 1972 presidential election, but the military prevented their taking office. In the same year in Nicaragua, a tremendous earthquake struck the capital of Managua, killing over ten thousand people and leaving some forty thousand others homeless. The Somoza regime, in control of Nicaraguan politics and economics since the mid-1930s, diverted the humanitarian assistance from abroad for personal gain. In Guatemala, the CIA-assisted overthrow of democratically elected President Jacobo Arbenz in 1954 led to twelve years of military rule, followed by a civilian government subordinate to a military intent on ample application of repressive counterinsurgency measures. Human rights violations soared.

In all three cases, the regimes in power made no distinction between noncombatants and combatants in repressing dissent and nascent insurgent movements—noncombatants were deemed to be supporting revolutionaries by providing food and shelter to them. Fleeing from death and destruction, from 1981 to 1993 more than 1.8 million people from El Salvador, Nicaragua, and Guatemala were either forced to flee the country or internally displaced—a small enough number in absolute terms, but 10 percent of the total population. Every country harbored refugees, and every economy was disrupted by the region's collective and cumulative disarray.

U.S. foreign policy met with substantial opposition in many other Latin American countries—which feared future direct military intervention—and in the European Community (EC). In early 1983, Mexico, Venezuela, Panama, and Colombia began the Contadora Peace Process, which excluded the United States from participation. As one commentator noted, "Although Contadora was designed in large measure to structure the process of diplomatic bargaining between the U.S. and Sandinista Nicaragua, it had the effect of restricting Washington's freedom of maneuver in Central America."[24] European governments overtly advanced their opposition to Washington's foreign policy in Central America by funding humanitarian assistance, implemented by NGOs, on behalf of those parties not supported by the United States. Nordic governments, in particular, gave substantial economic and political support to the Sandinista government in Nicaragua (while U.S. "humanitarian" and military assistance went to the contras) and to the revolutionary coalition fighting the military regime in El Salvador (while U.S. public and private help was channeled mainly to the government). In 1988, the EC as a whole supplemented the Contadora political initiatives with an economic aid package.

As there were few clear distinctions between combatants and noncombatants, all civilians were suspected by the governing regime and guerrillas in the civil wars in El Salvador, Nicaragua, and Guatemala. Fear of violence permeated rural communities, urban centers, universities, and virtually all social organizations. Actual and anticipated violations of basic human rights prompted thousands of noncombatants to seek refuge in across-border countries, such as Honduras, Costa Rica, and Mexico, while others moved further up into the mountains or toward international relief sites administering to internally displaced persons. Movement across borders affected the social and political fabric of recipient countries; movement up the mountains made the delivery of relief assistance impossible; movement to internal relief sites led belligerents to their targets.

The terrain of Central America is largely rugged. Populations, particularly ethnic minorities, were often scattered and isolated. Indigenous populations, familiar only with cultural and institutional prejudice against them, were suspicious of external institutions, even those offering assistance. Government neglect of transportation and communication systems led to further isolation of vulnerable groups. The most valuable organizations for the provision of relief and protection, given the geographic difficulties and the suspicion of outsiders, were religious groups that had been present throughout the long periods of terror. These groups were instrumental in creating pro-active organizational forms in support of political and economic justice.

Church-related groups were not only the choice of noncombatants for administering humanitarian assistance; they were also the choice of private donors. One ecumenical organization operating in El Salvador received a total of some $65 million in relief donations, compared to USAID's spending of $75 million during the same ten-year period.[25]

Guatemala was less dependent on outside sources for financial support of its conflict than were El Salvador and Nicaragua, which received bilateral assistance from a number of governments with interests, both national and humanitarian, in support of a particular warring faction. The military in El Salvador was dependent on Washington. The Sandinistas in Nicaragua received assistance from the Eastern European Council for Mutual Economic Assistance (COMECON) and from Western Europe, most particularly the Nordic countries. Their assistance was a counterresponse to massive financial assistance from USAID and military training of the former Somoza National Guard, in exile and popularly known as the contra rebels. The United States also imposed a trade embargo on Nicaragua, which delayed humanitarian supplies being delivered to the Sandinistas and stimulated overall economic hardship on the new Sandinista government and its development efforts.

The United Nations had spent much of the 1970s and early 1980s on the sidelines. The UNHCR was not present prior to the massive refugee problem and had no mandate to lend assistance to internally displaced persons, an increasingly acute need. Its strength came primarily during the repatriation phase, when the UNHCR implemented quick impact projects to ease noncombatants back into the communities that they had fled. The UNDP had virtually no experience with complex emergencies, and its development-related efforts were increasingly inadequate to the nature of the real tasks at hand. Of all the U.N. agencies, only UNICEF had a significant in-country presence prior to the widespread disruption of warfare, including access to remote regions.

Intermediate NGOs, those receiving bilateral aid from governments or the United Nations to implement projects, had severe logistical problems reaching isolated populations because of the often impossible terrain and harassment by the military. External NGOs concentrated their work in urban areas, relying upon church groups to provide assistance to those either not geographically in reach or fearful of being identified and targeted by combatants at a concentrated distribution point for food and medical assistance. One could argue, however, that the NGO function with ultimately the biggest humanitarian impact had little to do with delivering assistance in-country. That function was advocacy on an international scale—NGOs lobbying governments and policymakers, encouraging media attention, and activating public opinion against human rights abuses in Central America. Church groups also assisted in creating solidarity between suffering communities and those in developed countries by establishing **sister-city programs**. The ICRC, given its mandate not to operate in an area without the approval of the warring parties, which was elusive, was often paralyzed in the polarized terrain of Central America. Although its efforts paid off after ten years in Nicaragua, its access was limited in El Salvador and nonexistent in Guatemala.

The Esquipulas Accords of 1987 were the culmination of a lengthy negotiating process that had begun with Contadora and had continued under the auspices of Costa Rican president Oscar Arias Sánchez, who was awarded the Nobel Peace Prize in 1987 for his efforts. Signed by combatants, it called for "cease-fires, national dialogues, amnesty, an end to external support for insurgent movements, democratization, and free elections."[26]

The United Nations Observer Group in Central America (ONUCA, 1989–1992) was present in Costa Rica, Nicaragua, Honduras, El Salvador, and Guatemala monitoring cease-fires and elections. The United Nations Observer Mission in El Salvador (ONUSAL, July 1991–1995) provided military and human rights observers and police monitors. Both ONUCA and ONUSAL were composed partially of military, police, and civilians. Humanitarians were able to work expeditiously and effectively. In this case, at least, the end of Moscow and Washington's rivalry had permitted a page to be turned on armed conflict and, once repatriation and reintegration had occurred, enabled reconstruction and development to begin. By 1995, some seventy thousand Nicaraguans, thirty-two thousand Salvadorians, and fifteen thousand Guatemalans had voluntarily returned to their countries. Another forty-five thousand Guatemalans are still in Mexico waiting for further evidence that peace has truly come to their homeland.

Northern Iraq and the Gulf Crisis

The Gulf War was the first international emergency to be addressed in the post–Cold War world and the first to be televised live each evening. From a humanitarian perspective, the Gulf crisis actually consisted of three distinct crises. The first occurred as some 850,000 third-country nationals and 300,000 Palestinians from both Iraq and Kuwait fled, primarily to Jordan, in August 1990. The second crisis was the clash between Iraqi forces and the U.S.-led allied coalition. On January 17, 1991, and in pursuit of Security Council Resolution 678—which had authorized the use of "all necessary means," including the use of Chapter VII military force—the United States and its allies began an air war against Iraqi forces. This entailed civilian deaths and considerable damage to the country's infrastructure, but it was considered necessary to reverse Iraqi aggression.

The third crisis, which is the principal focus of our attention, took place after the cease-fire on February 27 and the relinquishment of Kuwait after Saddam Hussein's defeat. Popular insurrections against the Iraqi government exploded in the north and in the south, and Iraq's Republican Guard responded with brutal force. Some 1.5 million Iraqi Kurds fled to the Turkish border and into Iran.[27] Within one month's time, that number would reach nearly 2.5 million. The focus here is the plight of the Kurdish

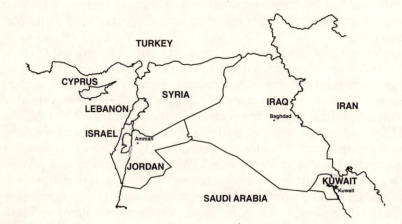

MAP 2.2   Iraq

population that sought protection in northern Iraq and received it through Operation Provide Comfort. The troop composition of that militarized humanitarian effort, without the consent of the sovereign authority, initially included elite units from the United States, the United Kingdom, France, and the Netherlands.

The Kurds are a substantial ethnic minority in Iraq, historically found in the northern mountainous region bordering Turkey. They constitute between 20 and 25 percent of the total Iraqi population. Since the creation of the Iraqi state in 1920, the Kurds have been fighting unsuccessfully for some form of political and territorial autonomy. Although Baghdad's constitution allows for political pluralism, certain opposition groups, such as the Kurds, have been violently repressed and prevented from participation. The fate of the Kurds has been, in fact, similar in all of the countries where they reside in substantial numbers—most particularly in Turkey and Iran.

Saddam Hussein, who became president of Iraq in 1979 as well as the primary wielder of military power and economic control over oil revenues, continued the practice of violent repression of opposition parties, including the documented gassing of civilian populations. Although the U.N. Commission on Human Rights was aware of Iraq's gassing of Kurds, human rights violations were largely ignored for political reasons: Hussein supplied the Western world with oil and received in return the means to build a large military complex. In 1980, Iraq's invasion of Iran, a true rogue state after its fundamentalist regime assumed power in 1970, permitted continued support for Hussein by much of the world throughout the 1980s. However, Hussein's unsatiated quest for regional supremacy led to Iraq's invasion of Kuwait in August 1990. Within moments, Hussein successfully shattered any state-level solidarity that he had created with the West in the preceding decades. The allied coalition, led by the United States and its five hundred thousand troops in the Gulf (Operation Desert Storm), acted swiftly to restore the status quo in the region.

Operation Provide Comfort resulted from Security Council Resolution 688 of April 5, 1991, which insisted "that Iraq allow immediate access by international humanitarian organizations to all those in need of assistance in all parts of Iraq." The operation also established a **no-fly zone** and banned the presence of any Iraqi military personnel in the protected area. This resolution is seen by many bullish observers to be a significant precedent in the steady progression toward humanitarian intervention. Operation Provide Comfort is illustrative of an unusually successful working relationship between the military forces that furnished protection and the NGOs that administered relief. The NGOs attended regular briefings held by commanders and had access to military telecommunications and transportation. The NGOs perceived the military as an ally in their efforts to assist a persecuted minority group. The NGOs also appreciated the fact that many of the military personnel involved in the operation were drawn from reserve and national guard units, with special competence in civil administration and engineering. The professional cultural divide that has stymied NGO-military relations in many joint relief ventures seemingly had narrowed. In addition, there was a clear, long-term political commitment by donor governments to maintain a ring of protection around the Kurds. It also did not hurt the operation that the party most likely to try breaking through the protection force had lost the war and was in no position to resist demands from the allied coalition. In contrast, the violation by Bosnian Serb forces of the so-called safe areas in Bosnia exemplified the difficulties inherent in protecting civilians when the conflict is still hot and the political will weak.

Inside the protection zone after Western military units had retreated and eventually returned to their country of origin, a poised hammer remained over the no-fly zone in the form of NATO aircraft. Inside the zone, order was facilitated by some five hundred U.N. security guards. Donning blue baseball caps and brandishing only pistols, these security guards gave the illusion of a U.N. presence without luring the United Nations into a situation where it did not have the genuine consent of the sovereign. At the time of this writing, the Kurds were still highly vulnerable but under the continued protection of NATO, while civilians elsewhere in Iraq continued to suffer from the seemingly indiscriminate bombing of Baghdad and more than five years of economic **sanctions**. In December 1995, a published study by the FAO stated that Iraqi children were suffering severe malnutrition and that U.N. economic sanctions against Iraq had been responsible for the death of more than 560,000 children since the end of the Gulf War in 1991. This is a clear illustration of how the agenda of the United Nations' humanitarian and human rights agencies confronts the security and political agenda of the Security Council.

The success of Operation Provide Comfort in addressing the third humanitarian crisis offers a sharp contrast to the melee that occurred in the coordination of humanitarian action in the first and second crises of the Gulf War. It was the failure of the United Nations as a system, especially in the first two crises, that led to the creation of the U.N. Department of Humanitarian Affairs. More particularly, U.N. organizations were unable to effectively coordinate their activities. UNICEF, the UNHCR, the WFP, the UNDRO, the UNDP, and WHO acted more as autonomous entities than as parts of what is deemed a "system." Mandates of organizations overlapped and contradicted one another, causing some activities to be overfunded and others to be relatively ignored. The UNHCR was designated the **lead agency**, responsible for coordinating the activities of other U.N. organizations as well as NGO activities and for ensuring that information was shared among actors.

In the field, response time was delayed as command and control of relief operations were directed from U.N. headquarters elsewhere. Different time zones between headquarters and the field exacerbated communications. In addition, there was no single contact point in Geneva empowered to provide guidance and take or authorize decisions. In other instances, junior staff in the field were wielding more authority than their experience qualified them to do. The level of inexperience in confronting emergency situations and in dealing with military personnel and strategy frustrated cooperation between those in the field providing relief and those rendering protection. In addition, U.N. agencies, with the exception of UNICEF, had difficulty in accelerating their procurement procedures to accommodate a quickly paced emergency. Roughly two months after refugees had begun appearing in Iran, the United Nations was able to provide only about 10 percent of the blankets and tents that were needed. Moreover, U.N. humanitarian aid seemed constrained by the political agendas of strong bilateral donor governments. As the minister of foreign affairs in Baghdad lamented: "Political considerations and interests were the prime motivation for the aid that was given, articulated, and implemented by the international community through the Gulf crisis. We welcome serious humanitarian and development activities and collaboration. However, if all the U.N. has to offer is what we have been receiving, I do not believe there is a humanitarian role for the United Nations in Iraq."[28]

Somalia

Somalia's history is generously peppered with colonial and Cold War interference in its government and military institutions and thereby its social cohesiveness. After more than two decades of authoritarian rule intent upon destroying the traditional clan system and authority of elders, 1991 ushered in the collapse of the functioning government, a civil war, drought, and strengthened warlords. Historic interference, a failed state, and famine proved a deadly brew for Somalia's 6 million inhabitants.

Since 1969, when General Mohammed Siad Barre's government eliminated Somalia's nascent democracy, four waves of light weapons have flooded the country and facilitated the development of a militarized society.[29] The first occurred upon Siad Barre's assumption of power, when he established a military alliance with the Soviet Union and received the first inundation of weapons, along with military advisers. The second wave of weapons entered Somalia after Siad Barre's failed attempt to claim the Ogaden region of Ethiopia (1977–1978). Some five hundred thousand Ogaden refugees and guerrillas fled into Somalia at that time, bringing with them the modern weapons they had received through U.S. support of Ethiopia. The Soviets and the United States changed partners during the Ogaden War. By 1978, the Soviets were supporting and supplying Ethiopia, and the United States had begun to provide Siad Barre's regime with the third wave of weapons (totaling $200 million in military aid in ten years) as well as economic aid (nearly $500 million dollars). After a coalition of warlords successfully ousted Siad Barre in January 1991, the coalition fragmented, and each warlord began his bid for territorial control.

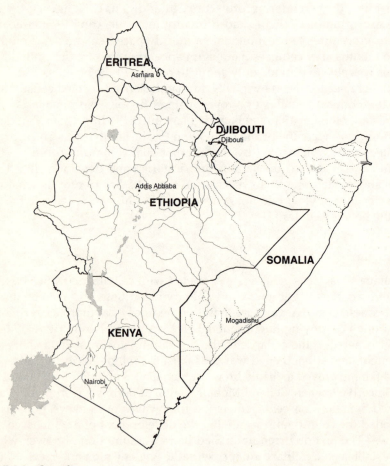

MAP 2.3   Somalia

Before a U.N.-brokered cease-fire began in March 1992, a year of intense fighting had laid much of Somalia's infrastructure to waste, and a fourth wave of weapons had found their way into the country through various channels (and still does to this day). At one point, a Greek freighter was caught delivering weapons to Somalia from Serbia. The Serbs were in need of cash because of U.N. economic sanctions but had a surplus of weapons to sell from a large arsenal stockpiled from the Cold War. Somalia's factions needed weapons because their Cold War supply was running low. They were receiving plenty of cash not only from wealthy local traders and Somalis living abroad, but also, and most surprisingly, from international relief agencies working in Somalia. From relief staff, militias collected payments for office and house rentals (house rents for modest accommodations often were $10,000 to $12,000 per month); armed escorts (approximately $2,000 per month per escort to protect workers, often from the escort's own faction); and transportation vehicles used in food distribution ($300 per day for "technical" cars, a $150 fee for landing a plane, a $10,000 fee for every boat brought into port). Militias also utilized and sold food and goods stolen from U.N. agencies and NGOs. Estimates claim that 40 to 80 percent of the nearly sixty thousand metric tons of emergency food rations per month that arrived Somalia in 1992 never reached the victims of the civil war and famine.[30]

In the midst of food insecurity and an abundance of weapons in 1992, the ICRC estimated that 95 percent of Somalis were suffering from malnutrition. This figure excluded about 350,000 who had already died from severe malnutrition and disease and the more than 1 million who had become refugees and were living in squalid relief camps in Ethiopia, Kenya, Djibouti, Yemen, and Saudi Arabia. Some 1,000 victims were dying daily in December 1992 when President George Bush, following a U.N. Security Council request authorizing the use of force to protect humanitarian relief efforts, committed almost 35,000 U.S. troops. France, Belgium, Saudi Arabia, Canada, Pakistan, and others also deployed troops. What was dubbed Operation Restore Hope in the United States and the Unified Task Force (UNITAF) by the United Nations took form. The strongest critics of humanitarian intervention in Somalia cite the excessive and unnecessary delay in U.N. response from the time Secretary-General Javier Pérez de Cuéllar called it "the most serious humanitarian crisis of our day" in January 1991 until Security Council Resolution 794 on December 3, 1992, authorized UNITAF.

Still riding high from success in the Gulf crisis and moved by the media coverage of thousands of Somalis starving in the midst of a civil war (what many observers label the **CNN effect**), the United Nations began diplomatic and peacekeeping efforts to produce a cease-fire, which it achieved between the two main factions in March 1992. However, there were no peacekeepers in place to monitor the cease-fire. Although in late April 1992 UNOSOM I (the first U.N. Operation in Somalia) authorized the presence of fifty U.N. observers to monitor the cease-fire, the observers did not arrive until four months after the cease-fire. In late August, Security Council Resolution 775 authorized a security force to protect the delivery of humanitarian aid, but the five hundred peacekeepers did not arrive until mid-September (the SRSG in Mogadishu had requested seven thousand). When the peacekeepers arrived, they were unable to move beyond the port. This was just one of what Mohamed Sahnoun, the special representative on the ground, called "missed opportunities."[31] Three months later, UNITAF was authorized, and U.S. resolve to lead in protecting the delivery of relief aid brought twenty-four thousand U.S. troops onto the beaches of Somalia and twelve thousand from elsewhere to ensure access to civilians in the short term.

By May 1993, responsibility for U.S.-led Operation Restore Hope had been passed on to the United Nations through UNOSOM II—the first armed Chapter VII humanitarian operation under U.N. command and control. Starvation had been brought under control, and thousands of lives had been saved. The theft of relief supplies had declined, and warlords were gathering to talk of national reconciliation. However, the killing of twenty-four Pakistani Blue Helmets by faction members on June 5, 1993, led to Security Council Resolution 837, allowing force to be used in order to arrest and detain those responsible. Operation Restore Hope was transformed into "The Hunt for Aidid," the faction leader believed responsible for ordering the deaths of the peacekeepers. General Mohamed Farah Aidid eluded capture, and Washington's resolve to remain in Somalia withered because of its inability to capture one man, the downing of two U.S. helicopters in October 1993, and the deaths of eighteen U.S. soldiers (which included the unseemly dragging of a dead marine's body through the streets of Mogadishu). The Clinton administration, prodded by an anxious Congress, called for U.S. troop withdrawal. U.N. Security Council Resolution 954 ordered the complete withdrawal of all peacekeepers by March 1995. Interestingly, in June 1995 Aidid nonviolently stepped down as the leader of his faction, and the new leader asked for the return of U.N. assistance in the reconstruction and development of Somalia. Critics of forceful intervention pointed to this as proof of the futility of military involvement against the will of the local parties. Interclan violence has fallen below the pre-UNITAF level. As of January 1996, Aidid has regained his position as warlord and is himself calling for the United Nations to assist in rebuilding Somalia.

In addition to criticism of the Security Council's delay in authorizing an effective multilateral response to the Somali crisis—Secretary-General Boutros-Ghali had come under criticism after calling attention to Yugoslavia's higher visibility as a "rich man's war"—the United Nations is also cited for its basic incompetence. Even more critically from the point of view of humanitarian action, U.N. staff were absent because of security and insurance regulations even though the ICRC and four well-respected NGOs (the International Medical Corps, Save the Children/UK, MSF, and SOS) remained amid personal danger—in fact, they increased their staff as the United Nations withdrew its personnel. NGOs took on roles normally assumed by U.N. agencies, whose security regulations required their evacuation. "Save the Children/UK, a relatively small private relief agency, delivered more food to Somalia in 1992 than did UNICEF," and while the UNDP "left untapped $68 million budgeted for Somalia *for lack of a signature* from the nonexistent Somali government," the ICRC devoted 50 percent of its worldwide emergency relief budget to establish massive feeding programs (much of the funding came directly from USAID).[32] Defenders of the UNDP's nonuse of funds state that the money had been budgeted for development, not relief.

The United Nations, in an effort to bring about a peaceful settlement, went through several special representatives. The U.N. invited the violent warlords, Aidid and Mahdi, to New York for peace talks; other clan leaders and especially elders were excluded. Political legitimacy by default was thrown to those in the urban areas who attempted to rule by force and largely excluded those in the rural areas who led by relative consensus.

The Former Yugoslavia

There is a plethora of scholarly work examining the source of violent ethnic conflict in the former Yugoslavia. Some scholars go back centuries looking for root causes in ethnic differences (among Catholics, Orthodox, and Muslims), others point to the beginning of the twentieth century, and still others claim that the late 1980s collision of strong and manipulated nationalism in Serbia with the independence movements in Croatia and Slovenia had more to do with an economic tailspin than with revenge for past ethnic grievances. For our purposes, we need to review the chronology of more recent political and military events and how they affected the vulnerability of noncombatants and the response of the international humanitarian system in Croatia and especially in Bosnia-Herzegovina, where the most acute humanitarian tragedies took place until a semblance of peace was negotiated in a twenty-one-day marathon at Wright-Patterson Air Force Base in Dayton, Ohio, in November 1995.

MAP 2.4   The former Yugoslavia

In June 1990, the Yugoslav Communist Party collapsed, setting into motion Croatia's and Slovenia's desire for more political autonomy. Serbia
adamantly opposed this development given the presence of Serbian minorities in the area (12 percent of the population in Croatia) as well as the
relative economic prosperity of Croatia and Slovenia. Moreover, Serbia
had benefited most from democratic centralism and thus stood to lose the
most from a change in authority.

On June 25, 1991, Croatia and Slovenia each declared their independence, which Serbia and the international community at large regretted.
Maintaining the integrity of Yugoslavia was the overwhelming security objective of all countries that feared a demonstration effect that could unleash
a similar and violent fragmentation of the Soviet Union. The European
Community quickly became involved in peace negotiations. By January 15,
1992, Croatia and Slovenia had been formerly recognized by the EC, by
which time the Soviet Union itself had ceased to exist. The EC found itself
unable to broker a cease-fire between Croats and Serbs in Croatia, where
war was under way, and asked for the assistance of the United Nations.

In September 1991, the U.N. Security Council had invoked Chapter VII and passed Resolution 713, imposing an arms embargo against all parties to the conflict in the former Yugoslavia. Resolution 724 called for the presence of a peacekeeping force in Croatia once a cease-fire had been negotiated. The U.N. Protection Force for the former Yugoslavia (UNPROFOR) was established in four protected areas of the Krajina region within Croatia. They were to be completely demilitarized and Croatian refugees permitted to return to their homes. Under Resolution 743, although a firm cease-fire had not been reached and there was no peace to keep, troop deployment was authorized and peacekeeping began in Croatia. Although the secretary-general estimated that $600 million were needed for the operation to be effective, the Security Council permanent members authorized only $250 million. UNPROFOR was set into motion half-funded, halfhearted, and with its role and authorized range of behavior unclear. The "model" for future actions in the former Yugoslavia was set in place, which would prove particularly problematic for the international humanitarian system.

While the conflict in Croatia waxed and waned, the February 1992 referendum in favor of independence in Bosnia-Herzegovina pushed another thorny political problem before the European Community. Of the 4.4 million people in Bosnia in 1991, 44 percent were Muslims, 31 percent were Serbs, 17 percent were Croats, and the remaining 8 percent were self-described "Yugoslavs." The Serbs had boycotted the referendum. Without any effective guarantees for minorities in place, the United States and the EC recognized Bosnia in April 1992, following Germany's insistence. U.N. recognition in May 1992 was followed by increased ethnic violence by Bosnian Serbs toward Muslims, including the use of **ethnic cleansing**—violence and incentives to ensure that no non-Serb remained in areas under the control of the Serbs.

The international response included everything except the robust use of military force—or in Lawrence Freedman's terms, the Security Council "experimented with about every available form of coercion short of war."[33] Economic sanctions were imposed on Serbia for assisting the Bosnian Serbs, and humanitarian relief operations ran in tandem with diplomatic attempts at the peaceful settlement of the conflicts. Without a cease-fire signed by all fighting parties, the United Nations initially declined to send peacekeepers into Bosnia. At the outset of the conflict in Bosnia, it was clear that the Bosnian Serbs did not acknowledge any special consideration for U.N. protected areas (UNPAs) or for noncombatants. The war was about territory, and the best way to gain territory was to eliminate the presence of non-Serbs in whatever manner was most effective. The means to that end included blocking relief supplies to Muslim populations, systematizing the rape of Muslim women and young girls, shelling civilian populations, and practicing widespread and indiscriminate torture and murder.

UNPROFOR troops, in accordance with Resolution 770, were eventually deployed specifically to assist in the delivery of humanitarian aid within Bosnia, of which only an estimated 25 percent was getting through. France, Britain, Canada, Spain, Pakistan, and former COMECON countries provided the troops at the outset according to a type of special arrangement with NATO, but under a U.N. umbrella. Although authorized to use force to protect humanitarian personnel, especially their own members, the military commanders on the ground were reluctant to provoke further Serbian aggression—soldiers who were unable to act as soldiers for fear that Serbian soldiers would attack, "eunuchs at the orgy," according to local gallows humor. The United States and its European allies disagreed over the use of force to bring about Serbian compliance with no-fly zones and obstruction of relief delivery. Violations by all warring parties, but particularly by the Serbs, of the 1949 Geneva conventions, additional protocols, and numerous other codified and customary norms were obvious and abundant. In the absence of consensus over the use of force against transgressors, the international system focused on humanitarian relief, diplomatic negotiations, and hope, not a particularly effective strategy but certainly with the fewest risks for external actors. It was particularly distressing for humanitarians that their actions had served as "a palliative, an alibi, an excuse," according to José-Maria Mediluce, the UNHCR's first special envoy who subsequently became a member of the European Parliament.[34]

Security Council Resolution 795, passed in December 1992, placed peacekeepers on the northern border of Macedonia to prevent the conflict from expanding its territory, while the conflict within seemed to feed upon all humanitarian and political efforts to ease it. Article 51 of the U.N. Charter, invoked during the Gulf crisis, legitimates the "inherent right of individual or collective self-defense if an armed attack occurs against a Member of the United Nations." Yet there was no collective agreement from the major powers to formulate collective self-defense of Bosnia. And given the disparity in the original distribution of the resources from the former Yugoslav People's Army (JNA)—about 85 percent went to Serbia—the enforcement of the arms embargo against Bosnia as well as against Serbia and Croatia amounted to a variety of collective intervention on behalf of the Serbs.

A tenuous winter cease-fire negotiated by former President Jimmy Carter unraveled in spring 1995. In the last week of May, the Serbs resumed heavy bombing of Sarajevo, which resulted in NATO's bombing Serbian ammunition dumps near the Serbs' political headquarters in Pale. This was the strongest response by the Western alliance since the war began in April 1992. Both NATO and U.N. commanders approved the bombing. French soldiers were the most vulnerable on the ground, numbering thirty-eight hundred. France declared that if its troops did not receive significant reinforcement from NATO and the United Nations, it would withdraw those troops. Within a few hours of the bombing, the Serbs commenced heavy shelling of five of the six so-called U.N. safe areas. Within three days, 325 peacekeepers had been taken hostage by the Serb forces, and some had been chained to poles and placed in strategic locations as human shields against further U.N./NATO military responses.

As a result, the blurring between peacekeeper and combatant thickened. French soldiers had come under attack immediately after NATO planes bombed the munitions site near the Serb-appointed capital of Pale. Radioing into the commander of the French U.N. peacekeepers, Jean-Paul Michel, French soldiers under attack on the ground reported that they were being ordered to surrender by the Serbs. "One of my lieutenants called me and said they were under fire and requested my instructions. As a peacekeeper, it was not easy to know how to respond. I told them to refrain from firing back but not to surrender." When the Serbs increased their fire and the lieutenant called his commander again for instructions, he responded: "I had never faced this kind of decision. We are deployed here as peacekeepers, not as fighting soldiers. I knew I had no way of getting them out and no way of protecting them. I said to myself, 'My men are going to die if they start shooting back. And for what? For peace?' So I ordered them to surrender."[35] The frustration of the French stems in part from contradictions between their action-oriented military training and the peacekeepers' impossible task in Bosnia.

The response of the United States, Britain, France, Germany, and Russia (the **contact group**, which formed in 1994 to facilitate diplomacy by the major powers) was to agree to what on paper appeared to be a more robust military presence. The 22,000 peacekeepers in Bosnia were to be reinforced with 12,500 soldiers from France, Britain, and the Netherlands as part of a rapid reaction force with heavy artillery, tanks, and helicopter air support. In addition, the peacekeepers would be given more aggressive rules of engagement.

The buzz phrase *Mogadishu line* began to circulate. It alluded to the American-led intervention in Somalia, in which U.N. peacekeepers metamorphosed from protectors of humanitarian relief into partial combatants. Military force was heightened. Following Serb retaliation against NATO, the U.N. operation was flooded with an increased troop presence on the ground—the rapid reaction force represented a 50 percent increase in troop strength in Bosnia.

Decisions about the increased military buildup were made by NATO. The secretary-general of the United Nations was *informed* of the decision to augment troops and equipment and to rearrange troop configuration already in place in Bosnia. The command and control of the U.N. peacekeeping operation strayed farther away from the humanitarian planning of the UNHCR and into the strategic military planning of NATO. And what was the Serb response to this flexing of military might? Within one month, safe areas designed for the protection of Muslim noncombatants began to fall, starting with Srebrenica, the first safe area established in 1993 after the theatrical personal vigil of the colorful French commander in Bosnia, Lieutenant General Philippe Morillon. Some forty thousand Muslims had lived in Srebrenica. Women, children, and the elderly were forced to leave everything behind, including their husbands, brothers, and sons of fighting age, as the Serbs entered the city. One week later, only twenty thousand of Srebrenica's residents could be accounted for. The promise by the international humanitarian system—that if the residents stayed during the war, they would be protected—had obviously been broken. As the residents left the city, they passed bodies hanging from trees and lying in the streets and listened to more stories of rape and torture, tragedies that the United Nations was supposed to have prevented by the establishment of the safe areas and a war crimes tribunal to prosecute war criminals. Ironically, perhaps the most unsafe areas in the Balkans turned out to be the safe areas.

A turning point was reached after the fall of Srebrenica and Zepa when NATO agreed to use airpower to deter further attacks. Croatia then took the opportunity to begin an unprecedented offensive against the Serbs. The Tudjman government immediately mobilized soldiers and prepared to return to full-scale war to recover the Krajina and other areas in western Bosnia under Serbian control. In spite of the arms embargo, Croatia's long coastline meant that it had been in a position to secure heavy weapons for its army of one hundred thousand.

In only a few days, the Croatian Army overran Knin, the capital of the self-styled breakaway republic, and recovered most of the Krajina that had been occupied for almost four years. The West talked, but Croatia acted. NATO's bluster had at least served to tie down the Bosnian Serbs so that they could not come to the aid of their Croatian counterparts. In an ironic twist, the largest refugee flow of the war—indeed the largest in Europe since the Soviet crushing of the Hungarian uprising in 1956—resulted from a successful Croatian military campaign. The estimated 125,000–150,000 refugees and 50,000 soldiers this time were all of Serbian origin. They fled into Serbia itself and toward Serbian-dominated Bosnia. The so-called UNPAs were finally "protected," but by Croatian, rather than U.N., soldiers.

In late August 1995, Serbian shells killed thirty-seven people in the same Sarajevo market where over twice as many deaths had led to the first NATO air strikes in February 1994. The Western response this time was far swifter and firmer. The efforts against Bosnian Serbs involved artillery from both the rapid reaction force and sixty NATO war planes. The explanation for the largest military efforts since the founding of the Western alliance in 1949 was twofold: Serbs were on the defensive after the Croatian trouncing in the Krajina, and their leadership was in disarray;

and U.N. soldiers had abandoned the exposed areas in eastern Bosnia, thereby removing the contradiction that the Blue Helmets were potentially endangered by Western military retaliation.

From the beginning of the war, the West's vacillation over the use of military force had led to comparisons between the United Nations and its toothless predecessor. Jamasheed K.A. Manker, about to retire after two years as Pakistan's chief representative to the United Nations, stated: "This is not the League of Nations. That would be an exaggeration." But he also noted the similarities between the international community's performance in the 1930s and its response to the current clash "between a weak multiethnic democracy and a militarily strong fascist regime prepared to use force ruthlessly."[36] Slobodan Milosevic clearly understood that the West was willing to tolerate the worst atrocities in Europe since the Nazi era and that it was not going to force him or his proxies to retreat from the ethnically pure areas that created a basis for a Greater Serbia. Fred Cuny, a veteran of many humanitarian tragedies who lost his own life while on a humanitarian mission in 1995 in war-torn Chechnya, commented on the international community's impotence and misplaced neutrality from his perspective in Sarajevo: "If the U.N. had been around in 1939, we would all be speaking German."

Much of the media attention and rhetoric within national legislative bodies on the issue of the former Yugoslavia center on the failure of the United Nations. However, as one NGO executive stated, "It's particularly hard to find fault with the U.N.'s humanitarian organizations when their failure is more a function of the lack of political support than of their own decisions."[37] In the absence of political consensus from those member states that hold the largest market share on the use of force and resources, humanitarian assistance during an escalating conflict can at best be a Band-Aid, sporadically applied and easily removed.

The UNHCR was designated the lead agency throughout the former Yugoslavia. The complexity and volatility of the environment were unfamiliar and overwhelming. Moreover, the former Yugoslavia had not been host to development IGOs or NGOs prior to the conflict because the country had been a source of recruitment for international personnel and fund-raising. Thus, there was little institutional understanding of local cultures and problems and few "Yugoslav hands."

By late 1993, an estimated 250,000 persons had been killed or were missing in the former Yugoslavia. Bosnia-Herzegovina yielded the largest number of internally displaced, with approximately 2.7 million persons homeless and dependent for their daily survival on international assistance. There was never a guarantee that those who sat at the negotiating table could "deliver" to the peace process those combatants in the field intent upon the vision of a Greater Serbia or those simply looking for gains in material wealth or a feeling of personal **empowerment** through the subjugation of others. This fact was manifested in the field. Commanders of peacekeeping troops in Bosnia, in their efforts to assist the delivery of humanitarian relief, had to negotiate not only with Serb political and military authority in Belgrade, Pale (the Bosnian Serb headquarters), and Sarajevo, but also with Serb and Bosnian Serb officials in the field and at roadblocks. Locally, military and especially **paramilitary** elements called their own shots, regardless of what had been negotiated with higher authorities.

Military contingents were as unfamiliar with this new type of conflict and their new role in protecting humanitarian relief as were the providers. Military strategy for protection forces changed frequently and without warning. Troops were not equipped to wage war. Front lines were constantly shifting. Oral agreements from belligerents were unreliable. At one point in 1995, U.N. peacekeeping uniforms were stolen and donned by Bosnian Serbs in their efforts to capture a U.N. outpost guarding a safe area. The United Nations in Geneva and New York was humiliated, and so were the troops on the ground, who were impotent to respond in kind to blatant violations of human rights and international law.

What should the international humanitarian system do when political authorities do not respect the norms and rules of behavior to which the majority of others adhere? In the case of the former Yugoslavia, the international resolve weakened, and attention turned more toward protecting the peacekeepers than protecting noncombatants—derisory comments in Bosnia suggested inserting the word *self* before *protection* in UNPROFOR. Since summer 1994, the subject of peacekeeper withdrawal from the former Yugoslavia has been a staple on the agenda of the Security Council. And the secretary-general proposed in September 1995 what had been obvious for some time—namely, that the effort become a "multinational" (that is, "NATO") operation rather than a U.N. one.

Before the peace talks began at Wright-Patterson Air Force Base in November 1995, there were some fifty thousand peacekeeping and policy personnel from thirty-six countries in the former Yugoslavia at a cost of some $2 billion annually. The majority were in Bosnia, protecting themselves and the approximately three thousand humanitarians in the region, who were providing life-sustaining assistance to at least 1 million refugees and 3 million internally displaced persons. The UNHCR alone was spending nearly $500 million annually.

At the time the peace agreement was signed on December 14, 1995, the three-and-a-half-year war had left some 200,000 people dead, 30,000 people missing, and another 2.7 million homeless, of which 60 percent were internally displaced. The country was divided into two regions, one under the control of the Bosnian Serbs (49 percent) and the other under the control of a Muslim-Croat federation (51 percent), with Sarajevo reunited and ruled by the Muslim-led government. The long process of rehabilitation and reconstruction was hampered by the presence of some 6 million land mines, of which only 30 percent had been mapped. UNPRO-FOR was replaced with a peace implementation force (IFOR) under NATO command. Efforts to commence war crimes investigations and judicial hearings were a key item on the postconflict agenda.

Rwanda

Article 8 of the 1951 U.N. Convention on the Prevention and Punishment of the Crime of Genocide mandates that "competent organs of the United Nations . . . take such action under the Charter of the United Nations as they consider appropriate for the prevention and suppression of acts of genocide." Perhaps a key word missing from this article is the word *timely*—action must be taken swiftly when the crime against humanity is a massive, fast-rolling wave of genocide. Rwanda is another example of too little, too late from the international humanitarian system.

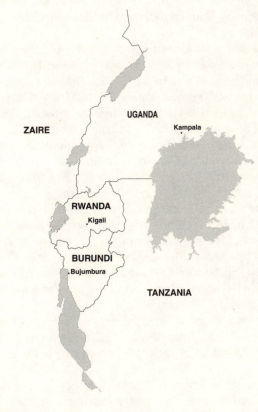

MAP 2.5   Rwanda

In April 1994, the president of Rwanda, Juvenal Habyarimana, was killed when his plane was shot down. The life of the president of Burundi was also taken. Rwanda and Burundi had both been trapped in regular cycles of conflict since the eve of independence from Belgium. Ethnic tension had been exacerbated by the governance structures in Rwanda established by Germany (the colonizer before World War I) and Belgium (U.N. trustee, resulting from the original League of Nations mandate, until 1962), in which the Tutsi minority had always been granted special privileges and authority. The death of Habyarimana in a country with weak political institutions and heightened impoverishment unleashed a level of human massacre whose speed and magnitude had not been witnessed since World War II. The Czech Republic, in its position as a nonpermanent member of the Security Council at the time, pleaded with the permanent members to declare the actions of belligerents in Rwanda as "genocide." To the contrary, the State Department issued instructions to officials to avoid this term. By acknowledging genocide, the international community would have been obliged to respond according to the provisions of the 1951 Genocide Convention. Consequently, the Security Council determined that genocide was not rampant in Rwanda, only "acts of genocide."

Were national interests indeed at work, and could they have been a barrier to an immediate response from the U.N. Security Council during the initial stages of the conflict? In May 1995, the American-based Human Rights Watch accused France, Zaire, South Africa, China, and the Seychelles of violating the 1994 arms embargo by assisting the former Rwandan government in rebuilding its military forces. "The human rights group's report, based on a four-month investigation in Central Africa, said that former Rwandan Government and army officials have rebuilt their military infrastructure and created a force of 50,000 men in about a dozen refugee camps, primarily in eastern Zaire."[38]

In the absence of peace **enforcement** measures, new records for the size and speed of human suffering were set. At least 500,000 persons died (15 percent of the prewar population), and hundreds of thousands of Rwandans poured into neighboring Zaire and Tanzania, where camps were established so that refugees could be adequately fed and medically treated. Almost 50 percent of the prewar population were displaced by the tragedy. The magnitude of human flight across Rwanda's borders was unprecedented. Within forty-eight hours of the death of the Rwandan president, an estimated 250,000 refugees made their way into Tanzania. An additional 500,000 poured out of Rwanda over the next few weeks.

Holly Burkhalter of Human Rights Watch broke the time line of the Rwanda crisis into five distinct phases to demonstrate where the international humanitarian system could have responded in a timely fashion if the commitment to the protection of human life and dignity had been more compelling.[39] During the first phase, between the August 1993 signing of the Arusha Accords formally ending the civil war between the Hutu government and Tutsi opposition and the April 6, 1994, downing of Habyarimana's plane, his party systematically began killing political opponents (Tutsis as well as Hutu moderates). On one occasion, a moderate Hutu cabinet minister and forty Tutsis were murdered by government soldiers. U.N. troops on the ground monitoring the so-called peace process—the U.N. Assistance Mission in Rwanda (UN-AMIR)—did not respond. As Alison Des Forges, a longtime Rwanda watcher, noted, "When they saw they could get away with that kind of violence in Kigali with no reaction from the U.N. troops who were supposed to be responsible for security, it encouraged them to go ahead with the larger operation."[40]

The second phase began on April 6, 1994, immediately after the president's death, which was believed to have been planned by his own army. Prime Minister Agathe Uwilingiyimana, a moderate Hutu, fled to her compound for safety, where she and three of ten Belgian UNAMIR peacekeepers were killed by a mob of militia and presidential guards. The seven remaining Belgian peacekeepers laid down their weapons, as their mandate instructed them not to become involved in combat if unnecessary. The mob mercilessly tortured the soldiers and then murdered and dismembered them. Belgium ordered the return of its 450 soldiers in Rwanda, who had formed the critical nucleus of UNAMIR. Within three and one-half months, between 500,000 and 1 million people had been massacred by the frenzied wave of genocide. The statistics are highly variable and inconsistent.

Those still hiding in schools, churches, and homes of compassionate Hutus became more vulnerable after the April 21 Security Council resolution to reduce the UNAMIR presence to only 250 men, marking the third phase of the crisis. For those doing the killing, the resolution demonstrated the total lack of international resolve and hence a green light for continuation of genocide. Two weeks later, Washington made its intentions clear regarding participation in peacekeeping when President Bill Clinton signed Presidential Decision Directive 25 (PDD 25). The United States would not become involved unless American interests could be advanced at an acceptable risk, and no fewer than seventeen conditions had to be fulfilled to indicate what would constitute an acceptable risk. Somalia-like interventions were to be avoided; the Mogadishu line was not to be approached. As one senior government official quipped in an off-the-record comment: "It is almost as if the Hutus had read it [PDD 25]."

Phase four began with mass refugee outflow and France's deployment of troops on June 23. Although France has been accused of bias toward the Hutus—France had armed and trained the government troops responsible for the genocide—the French did save thousands of lives and did not interfere with the Tutsi-led Rwandan Patriotic Front (RPF) assumption of power. However, Opération Turquoise had protected fleeing militarized and politicized Hutus and allowed them to operate a radio station for a month that continued to broadcast encouragement to slaughter Tutsis.

It was not until the fifth phase, in mid-July, after the genocide was over and the RPF had announced the formation of a national government, that the Clinton administration took any real action. The Rwandan Embassy in Washington was closed, and assets of Rwandans in the United States were frozen. Throughout the prior four phases, Washington had treated the crisis in Rwanda more as an embarrassing irritation than as a pressing humanitarian and human rights disaster.

During the most violent periods of massive slaughter, U.N. agency personnel, who had established offices in Rwanda, were evacuated; but the ICRC and MSF managed to maintain a symbolic presence. As in Somalia, evacuation by the United Nations reduced aid, and withdrawal of its physical presence caused more panic in an already terrorized population. Moving U.N. personnel into the UNAMIR compound until the violence subsided was apparently never an option. A follow-up critique of U.N. performance rang of similar criticism of U.N. operations in other complex emergencies: "Institutional confusion and lack of clarity on the roles of, and relationship between, the humanitarian-development and political-military arms of the U.N. . . . the slow pace of deployment, lack of visible action, and the negative implications of this for . . . overall recovery . . . point to the need for stronger linkages and synergy between the various U.N. components."[41]

At the end of 1995, there were several hundred U.N. humanitarian personnel working in Rwanda and refugee camps and nearly one thousand NGO staff members. The tally for humanitarian assistance has been erroneous—for a country with only 8 million people, estimates vary between $1 and $2 billion of emergency aid in 1994 alone, or between 2 and 4 percent of total overseas development assistance.

The RPF is in control of the government but without the means to pay salaries to government workers and the military. The World Bank has withheld over $240 million of currently frozen project funds from the new government until it pays over $5 million of arrears in loan reimbursements (attributed to the old regime) and presents a balanced budget and a stabilization plan. The European Union is withholding funds until the World Bank is satisfied with the government's actions. Without proper funding during the rehabilitation phase, the government will have to rely on coercion, rather than consensus and incentives, to bring about compliance with government policies.

Refugee camps in Zaire, Tanzania, and Burundi have vacillated in and out of a cholera epidemic and the control of Hutu terrorism and militia building. To intimidate the refugee population, relief workers must be terrorized first, which has been done effectively on numerous occasions. Intervention into the camps by OAU and RPF soldiers has been with the intent to eradicate Hutu terrorism. It is virtually impossible to locate the source of human rights violations at any given time.

The UNHCR, UNICEF, and the WFP have struggled to mobilize and distribute resources in environments that pulsate with violence. The UNHCR took responsibility primarily for the refugee camps, while the DHA took responsibility for the internally displaced within Rwanda. The DHA in its coordinating function worked to bring together the operations of the U.N. and NGO communities by providing information on the evolution of the crisis. Although it lacked resources of its own to make a real difference, a friendly government established under DHA control the Swedish Support Team (SST). The SST made available to the DHA and NGOs its staff; vehicles; state-of-the-art communications; office, food, and medical supplies; and support.[42]

UNAMIR subsequently returned to Rwanda after the French departure. The twenty-five hundred French legionnaires operating under Chapter VII were replaced by over twice as many Chapter VI U.N. soldiers. This revived operation for a time also facilitated U.N. and NGO activities by providing security and logistics support. In August 1994, UNAMIR personnel transported more than fourteen thousand metric tons of relief supplies and produced and distributed more than 7 million gallons of potable water to refugees in and around Goma, Zaire. UNAMIR established humanitarian liaisons within DHA offices. The DHA responded in kind by ensuring the attendance of humanitarian personnel at UNAMIR briefings.

In summer 1995, the new government had come full circle, demanding the reduction of U.N. soldiers. The logic reflected impatience with sizable expenditures on peacekeeping and virtually none on rehabilitation. As UNAMIR had pulled out in 1994 at the outset of violence, the RPF reasoned that UNAMIR would do so again.

As of early 1996, the humanitarian and political crises in Rwanda had not abated. While violence within the country decreased, violence in refugee camps for Rwandese in Burundi, Tanzania, and Zaire rose. Because of fighting among Hutus and Tutsis in Burundi, some fifteen thousand Rwandese refugees fled from their camp in Burundi into Tanzania and were followed a few days later by an additional sixteen thousand

Rwandese and some Burundi asylum-seekers. The U.N. Tribunal for Rwanda has begun the process of handing down indictments, although many suspects are living as refugees. According to a U.N. prosecutor: "Time is of the essence. 1996 must be the year of massive investigations because justice must be done swiftly."[43]

A Contextual Comparison

There are similarities and differences among the contexts of each complex emergency that deserve attention because ultimately they color the effectiveness of action and the quality of dilemmas faced by humanitarians. Such variations are vital to appreciating the complexity of humanitarian action.

Humanitarian assistance during the various wars in Central America was delivered largely by NGOs in the 1980s, most particularly religious organizations, which were in-area addressing development and political issues throughout nearly two decades of conflict between militarized governments and opposition groups. The objective of belligerents was to control civilian populations, not exterminate them. The conflicts varied over time, sometimes slowly escalating and slowly diminishing. The role of the United Nations was largely in managing refugee camps and coordinating repatriation and peace processes. Cold War politics had assisted in strengthening military institutions and power at the expense of civilian institutions and kept international institutions out of the United States' "backyard"—similar to the conflict in Afghanistan until Mikhail Gorbachev's new thinking and the change in superpower relations. This is a characteristic common to the conflicts in Iraq and Somalia as well.

The humanitarian operation in northern Iraq to protect the Kurdish minority was one of three crises within what is referred to as the Gulf crisis. The United Nations initially was conspicuously absent in northern Iraq, was unable to respond to the concerns of countries hosting refugees, and floundered severely in coordinating relief efforts. The succor provided to Kurds in the safe havens in northern Iraq was handled largely by NGOs (some of which had been in-area before the conflict). The protection of the Kurds within encampments was eventually the responsibility of U.N. security guards, not peacekeepers. Elite troops from NATO offered initial protection, and they were followed later by air forces that monitored the no-fly zone over the protected region. The commitment by the U.S.-led coalition in the Gulf crisis has remained strong. The government of Saddam Hussein, whose objective was to beat the Kurds into political submission, was defeated soundly; its supine position did not allow for violations of Kurdish protection.

The crisis in the former Yugoslavia will linger in various degrees for years. The official Balkan peace plan signed in December 1995 cannot erase overnight the personal pain experienced by millions. As of early 1996, thirty thousand were still missing from the war, including seven thousand Muslim men from the fallen safe haven of Srebrenica in mid-1995. The Bosnian Serbs' objective of removing non-Serbs from desired territory set the pattern for Muslim and Croatian forces' behavior once the balance of power shifted in fall 1995 with a Croatian offensive. Refugees were pushed about the Balkans, always one step ahead (if they were fortunate) of military offensives. There were no NGOs in-area prior to the conflict because the former Yugoslavia was more a magnet for tourism than for development aid. Weapons were plentiful to the Serbs in the region because of the Cold War manufacture of weapons in Yugoslavia and the seizure by Serbia and Bosnian Serbs of the vast bulk of hardware from the JNA after the split-up of the formerly unified country. The Bosnian Serbs had shown no respect for international law or the decisions of the Security Council. Until the change in the balance of military forces in mid-1995, there had been no incentives for the Serbs to choose peace over force because of a lack of concerted will among the major powers. Humanitarian action, a massive U.N. peacekeeping effort, and cautious NATO airpower were insufficient to reverse the hunger of the Serbian political elite for new territory or its willingness to resort to war crimes to attain its objectives.

The objective of belligerents in Somalia was to accumulate and consolidate territorial control and power over populations. Somalia is a failed state—there is no functioning national government. Early warning signs of the complex emergency went unheeded. The stronger warring factions showed little respect for either the U.S.-led or U.N. military presence when there appeared to be no incentive for doing so. The humanitarian impulse to assist the vulnerable was helpful in the short term but was severely weakened after U.S. political and military leaders were humiliated following the death of eighteen U.S. soldiers and failed to capture one particular warlord, which was not in the original humanitarian mandate. The availability of weapons contributed to the deterioration of the state and the withdrawal of assistance. Its most important impact, however, was the destruction of civil society. Sean Devereux, an Anglo-Irish UNICEF aid worker gunned down in the streets of Kismayu, noted in a letter home the story of a Somali fight over two camels. "At the end of three days more than thirty people had been killed. If it had not been for the guns, there would have been a few broken bones and some black eyes."[44]

Genocide was the objective of the Hutu-led Rwandan government in 1994. Systematic planning to carry out genocide had actually occurred long before the death of Rwanda's president in April 1994. Early warning signals of the complex emergency were not addressed, as in Somalia. The focus of major donor governments and permanent members of the Security Council was not on humanitarian assistance and the protection of human rights but on peacekeeping, which included a resolution to reduce, not increase, the UNAMIR force in-area before massive genocide began. Humanitarian relief subsequently was an overwhelming task to which the international humanitarian system responded remarkably well but that came after the number of deaths and displaced persons had broken previous records in terms of speed and magnitude.

THREE

□ □ □

Operational Dilemmas
and Challenges

The international community is faced with the paradox of needing ever larger resources to address the immediate survival needs of victims, while simultaneously recognizing that such action may deflect attention and support from initiatives essential to undoing the root causes of vulnerability and strife.

—Boutros Boutros-Ghali, *Report of the Secretary-General on the Work of the Organization, August 1995*

By July 1995, Kenya had become unwilling to continue hosting the more than fifty thousand Somali refugees who had crossed the border three years earlier. The refugees' overextended stay was disrupting tourism, claimed the Kenyan government; the UNHCR was advised to close the camps and begin refugee repatriation. The UNHCR communicated Kenya's concerns to Somali elders, who rejected the repatriation proposal and then arranged a press conference to appeal to the international community. As the Kenyan government, Somali elders, the UNHCR, and the media wrestled with camp closings and repatriation issues, groups such as the International Federation of Red Cross and Red Crescent Societies continued working on major construction projects in and around the camps. Road were being repaired. New police measures were being implemented to reduce theft. Libraries and a football field were being reconstructed. And efforts were being made to increase school enrollment. Along with development projects, relief efforts were also still in effect: Food and charcoal were being distributed, and clinics were treating cholera, malaria, respiratory ailments, and skin infections.[1]

The simultaneous activities of closing camps and reconstructing them seem counterintuitive at best, even to the most amateur analysts; yet the double process is not an uncommon one. The UNHCR was confronting two of its mandates simultaneously: negotiating with a country of asylum so that refugees could remain and convincing refugees to repatriate. The IFRC was involved in providing relief and fostering development to the point of creating incentives for the refugees to stay. After three years of assistance, the refugees were still completely dependent on the international humanitarian system for their basic needs. And the media had to decide between airing a short, attention-getting humanitarian story—suffering Somalis being forced to repatriate by a heartless Kenyan government—or a more lengthy, less sensational story that included a variety of perspectives and issues.

Such challenges are pervasive in humanitarian operations. An external actor can adopt a wait-and-see attitude rather than make a decision, choose to adopt several courses of action even if they are uncomplementary and their resources are limited, or make one choice and accept the negative consequences of the action as necessary evils. This chapter examines choices made by humanitarian actors and the indirect consequences that follow by focusing on four torturous trade-offs encountered repeatedly in recent humanitarian operations. It concludes with a larger, more controversial debate among actors in the humanitarian system: Under what conditions do good deeds do more harm than doing nothing at all? Those who feel a humanitarian imperative would argue that choosing to do nothing is never a consideration; therefore, no dilemma exists. For others, given the strengths and weaknesses of the current international humanitarian system and the nature of particular conflicts, there are times in which humanitarian involvement during active fighting ultimately can hurt more than it helps.

THE CONCEPT OF A DILEMMA

Clashing interests, competition for resources, and the complex organizational structures of external humanitarian actors complicate the traditional definition of a dilemma—that is, two or more alternative courses of action, each with unintended but unavoidable, indirect, and equally undesirable consequences sure to emanate from an actor's chosen course of action after careful deliberation. The simplistic notion of a single actor with the necessary resources to take action is expanded to the three types of institutional actors, each with perceptions conditioned by a multitude of interests and each with various levels of power, influence, and access to information. The alternative courses of action that lie at the crossroads for these actors can bear life-threatening consequences for the civilian populations that these institutions serve and for humanitarian field staff, convoy drivers, and soldiers on the front lines. And the tools required for a comprehensive approach to humanitarian action are seldom held by one institutional actor, thus highlighting the need for cooperation, coordination, and steadfast commitment among institutions that often do not share the same principles, mandates, or procedures.

Moreover, the context in which humanitarian dilemmas in war emerge is always complex and politically charged. Information on which decisions are based is often incomplete or inaccurate, and by the time decisions are implemented, the problems that they were meant to address may have changed. By the time U.N. food and services arrived in Somalia, the peak of the famine had passed. U.S. soldiers who volunteered to assist in the delivery of food were perplexed as to why they did not see any starving people on the streets of Mogadishu. The proverbial bottom line is that choosing a course of action that is guaranteed to be effective throughout the course of a conflict and is free of negative repercussions is an impossible assignment.

In short, the concept of a dilemma is graphically attractive and heuristically useful, but it must be employed with caution. Otherwise, the term can be conceptually misleading as we attempt to describe the uncomfortable and tough choices and trade-offs faced by individual humanitarians and the international humanitarian system as a whole. Fundamentally, a decision to act or to refrain from acting must adequately take into account the adverse and inevitable negative consequences of a particular course of action.

DILEMMAS IN THE FIELD

Refugees, IDPs, or Those in Safe Havens

War scatters people in many directions. Those who can demonstrate a well-founded fear of being persecuted, who manage to avoid the dangers en route to an international border, and who are not turned back by border guards fall into the category of "refugee." (See Figure 3.1.) The rights of refugees are codified in the 1951 Convention Relating to the Status of Refugees and the 1967 protocol. Article 33 of the convention prohibits a contracting or host state from expelling or returning a refugee (*réfoulement*) back to the "frontiers of territories where his life or freedom would be threatened." The U.N. High Commissioner for Refugees has the duty to supervise the application of the provisions of the convention and protocol.

FIGURE 3.1 Global Number of Refugees, 1960–1995 (in millions)

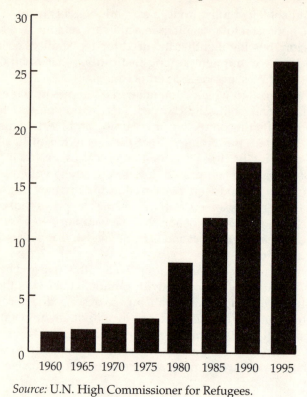

Source: U.N. High Commissioner for Refugees.

Only in environments where human rights and international law are respected are refugees safe from harm. Operational challenges to guaranteeing a secure environment produce a dilemma: There are limited mechanisms for separating those who qualify for refugee protection from armed elements who may enter a camp with relative ease during massive refugee flows. When camps are taken over by militiamen who terrorize refugees and relief workers and establish themselves as the camp's political and military cell, the UNHCR, host governments, and NGOs must decide whether to continue supplying food, water, and medical supplies knowing that they are assisting in strengthening the militia population and their political/military agendas.

Even without the presence of militias, security inside a camp can be precarious. Communities have fragmented during the journey to seek refuge, traditional family and community structures that provided some semblance of law and protection have broken down, the ability to care for one's basic needs is absent, disease can spread easily within a densely populated encampment, and women's ability to get food may require an exchange for sexual favors. Add to the list of security breaches a horde of militias intent on terrorizing and controlling non-combatants through violence, and it becomes debatable whether continued support of the camp has increased, rather than decreased, a refugee's well-founded fear.

The situation in refugee camps in Zaire from April 1994 to early 1996 serves as the epitome of refugee camp disaster. Over 1 million Rwandan refugees and tens of thousands of militias and former Hutu civil servants lived in forty camps, many within a few miles of the border. Hutu militias, rearmed by outside sources, made frequent nightly forays back into Rwanda to challenge the Tutsi-led government and reclaim territory. Within the camps, the militias terrorized or murdered those who did not acquiesce to their demand for new recruits. NGOs such as CARE and MSF, with reputations for staying in the most desperate situations, left in 1995. Alain Destexhe, former secretary-general of the international office of MSF, explained the painful decision to withdraw the French and Belgian branches of his organization: "We can't be a party to slaughter in Rwanda. International aid has allowed the militias to reorganize, stockpile food and recruit and train new members. . . . Agencies like ours are caught in a lose-lose situation; either continue being reluctant accomplices of genocidal warmongers or withdraw from the camps, leaving the refugee population to the mercy of their jailers."[2] Even local humanitarians who volunteered to assist in the collection and burial of refugees struck by cholera were attacked, including thirty Zairean Boy Scouts who collected the dead in the Katale Camp and were tied up and slaughtered.[3] The annual cost to the UNHCR for maintaining the presence of the camps in Zaire and providing food, water, and medical supplies was approximately $300 million (or over one-quarter of its annual budget).

This dilemma continues. The governments of Zaire and Rwanda along with the United Nations began a slow process to close the camps one by one beginning in February 1996. The strategy was to impose an economic embargo—limiting aid and preventing refugees from trading with locals—and hope that life would become uncomfortable enough for the refugees that they would take advantage of the U.N. buses parked outside the camps and return to Rwanda. The Zairean government promised the United Nations that there would be no use of force, although the government had lost control of its soldiers' behavior during previous attempts to dislodge the refugees. Uncertainty concerning the reaction of the Hutu militias inside the camps was also a complicating factor.

Although refugees are protected from *réfoulement*, the 1951 convention does allow for involuntary repatriation of refugees if their presence negatively affects the security of the host country. There are few instances where a refugee presence does not produce negative consequences for the social, political, and economic stability of the hosts. The Rwandan refugee presence in Zaire did more than introduce physical violence to the country. One Zairean official spelled out the nefarious impact: "The refugees are of different cultural ethics and behavior. Carrying weapons and killing are quite common among them; the same goes for stealing and squatting on other people's property. The refugee population has overwhelmed Zairean resources, destroyed our environment, introduced uncontrolled inflation into our market and abused our hospitality. We want them out of here soon."[4] In developed countries of asylum, refugees have been blamed for unemployment increases and a subsequent rise in nationalist sentiments. Guatemalan refugees in southern Mexico have been blamed for inciting revolt among the indigenous population. With few exceptions, refugees become the scapegoats for many ills of the host government. Mozambican refugees in Zimbabwe are one of the exceptions. Zimbabwean tobacco farmers became so dependent upon the abundant and cheap labor of Mozambican refugees that some resorted to locking the refugees up at night to prevent them from participating in the UNHCR's repatriation efforts.

Not all fleeing noncombatants wish to leave their country or, if they do, are successful in their efforts. Turkey rejected fleeing Iraqi Kurds, and the United States returned Haitians. The most populated category of noncombatants is composed of **internally displaced persons,** those who did not or could not cross an international border and who are therefore without internationally recognized rights and an international agency as permanent guardian. In recent years, the UNHCR has assumed responsibility for IDPs on an ad hoc basis, generally following a request by the U.N. secretary-general and with the consent of a particular government, which has sovereign responsibility for IDP emergency assistance and human rights protection. Services provided for IDPs generally include distribution of food, water, medical supplies, and shelter. Education and development programs may be started in nonviolent regions.

The problem of separating the displaced from those not legitimately displaced affects IDP camps and distribution centers as much as it does refugee camps; however, the ramifications are somewhat different. In many developing countries, the provision of emergency relief to IDPs entices local populations experiencing various levels of scarcity to enter the camps as well. The quick emergency relief response, according to some critics, prevents both IDPs and locals from relying on traditional coping mechanisms to pull them out of crisis—that is, relief can breed unwelcomed long-term dependency and yield a victim mentality that prevents noncombatants from being active agents in their own recovery. Afghanistan provides illustrations.

The Afghanistan civil war has vacillated between active and dormant conflict throughout various regions of the country since the end of the 1979–1989 Soviet occupation. Moscow withdrew its troops in 1989, although it continued to support the government. In 1991, Mikhail Gorbachev's leadership brought Moscow into agreement with Washington over their both discontinuing aid to their preferred factions of the fighting mujahideen, or Islamic insurgents. The Soviet Union and the United States would support a U.N. plan for an interim government. The plan was never implemented. The former Soviet-backed government fell shortly after the collapse of the Soviet Union, and the power struggle among the mujahideen intensified. The capital of Kabul became a battlefield. The internally displaced who fled to Pakistan were refused entry at the border, forcing the would-be refugees to the UNHCR relief camps in Jalalabad.

Within one year, the Jalalabad camps housed some 17,000 families (about 130,000 people). A city of tents, each stamped with bold blue UNHCR letters, was organized in blocks of twenty families. A block leader was selected for each. People queued up to receive their share of daily rations: cooking oil, rice, tea, wheat flour, some kerosene, and twelve liters of water per day per person. UNICEF provided vitamin A supplements to children under five. Tools were distributed to families to construct dwellings upon allotted plots. The earth, dry and barren, was the site of daily NGO drilling operations for water. Demining around the camps was also a daily event.

Surrounding the camp were locals who were suffering from lack of water and unpredictable food supplies. It was rational for those locals to give up their own hard efforts to deal with a chronic crisis of scarcity and enter into a dependent relationship with the international humanitarian system. According to some estimates, only one-third to one-half of the Afghan populations in relief camps are bona fide IDPs.[5] Other veterans of humanitarian operations argue that had the IDPs been left to their own coping mechanisms, perhaps as many as 50 percent would have found means of employment or returned to Kabul, where an on-again/off-again pattern of conflict prevailed. Indeed, in 1994 a new flow of IDPs from Kabul to the UNHCR's camps in Jalalabad was turned away and received no outside assistance. Some IDPs camped in town, while others found employment in Jalalabad.

Afghan refugees occupy a Hawai refugee village. UNHCR/19139/09.1989/ H. J. Davies.

An additional operational challenge that refugee camps and IDP camps share is the absence of reliable data. Host countries may inflate or deflate head counts in accordance with their own interests. Refugees may change their status to permanent resident or return to their homeland without notification to authorities. U.N. agencies, governments, NGOs, and journalists arrive at different figures based upon different concept definitions and methods of estimation. Few agencies provide demographic breakdowns of refugee populations, assuming that all members have similar needs. An inaccurate count and ignorance of demographics lead to miscalculation of required relief inputs. Refugee camps and IDPs also face a dilemma in the food distribution process: Should relief agencies respect the norms of the culture in which they operate, or should they bypass the norms and strive for efficiency in input delivery? For instance, many traditional societies subordinate the needs and the leadership of women. In accordance with this traditional gender difference, agencies often call upon the male members of a refugee camp to serve as food distribution coordinators, even though women and children normally make up approximately 80 percent of a refugee population and it has been proved that using women to distribute food results in a more equitable distribution throughout the camp. Male-biased distribution of food has led to unacceptably high rates of severe malnutrition, the swapping of food for sex, and death among female refugees.

IDP distribution centers present another avenue of risk to the internally displaced. IDPs are not physically out of reach of belligerents. The concentration of IDPs at food distribution centers and shelters may lead soldiers and militias to their noncombatant targets. In El Salvador, for example, internally displaced persons congregating to receive assistance from the ICRC were bombed and strafed with bullets by the Salvadoran Air Force. In Guatemala, indigenous peoples preferred to remain hungry in the mountains rather than risk violence at the food relief sites. Although relief organizations provide food and medical attention, they are unable to protect IDPs from physical violence by a warring party.

Safe areas, by their very name, give the impression that noncombatants will be provided the maximum amount of external protection and the least amount of community fragmentation. **Safe havens,** as they were called in northern Iraq, or **safe areas,** as they were incongruously dubbed in Bosnia, are whole communities left intact as protected enclaves surrounded by active fighting. Relief aid is generally transported in by truck, sometimes through **corridors of tranquillity** (access roads agreed to by belligerents for the purpose of delivering humanitarian relief), or airlifted, which is ten to twenty times as expensive as road and rail delivery to refugees. Written agreements or military force establish around the community a cease-fire, which is monitored on the ground by peacekeepers (Bosnia) or U.N. security guards (northern Iraq) and in the air through the use of no-fly zones.

In addition to maintaining the cohesion of a community, U.N.-supported enclaves or safe areas also prevent territorial loss. As in the case of Bosnia, attempting to maintain safe areas within the war zone was a political statement to belligerents that control over the territory occupied by the noncombatants would be decided through diplomatic channels, not through brute force. Among safe areas, refugee camps, or IDP camps, safe areas are the least disruptive of a community's autonomy.

The dilemma associated with the creation of safe havens was painfully demonstrated in Bosnia by the abject failure of the international community to guarantee the safety of those residing in the supposedly safe areas once the Bosnian Serbs decided not to respect international humanitarian law, human rights, and prior agreements. The establishment of safe havens in Bosnia was the decision of the Security Council, as was the decision not to protect them. The resolve of the Security Council and NATO to protect the Muslims was periodically tested by the Bosnian Serbs, who shelled safe areas, stole U.N. equipment and uniforms, and held U.N. soldiers hostage. Safe havens by design have little value if their sanctity is not accepted by belligerents.

Safe areas are supposedly "protected" by peacekeepers. Peacekeepers, however, are permitted to respond with force only when belligerents are threatening their lives.

The mandate of peacekeepers generally does not include the use of force to protect noncombatants. Until August 1995 in Bosnia, NATO limited its retaliatory air strikes against Serbian aggression because of the safety of peacekeepers in the area—that is, the U.N. troops on the ground would pay the price for NATO support because U.N. forces were ill-equipped for the wars in which they were placed. Paris and London adamantly disagreed with Washington's desire to lift the arms embargo and refused to remove their peacekeepers or to arm them for war. Inertia persisted among those governments with the ability to alter the maddening increase in the slaughter of Bosnian Muslims. In the absence of clear leadership or collective consensus, the Bosnian Serbs calculated that there was more to be gained through use of force than through negotiations. The first safe area of Srebrenica, established in April 1993, was also the first to be overrun in July 1995.

In terms of international resolve, it is useful to contrast the safe haven established and still maintained around the Kurds in northern Iraq with the fallen or unsafe areas established in Bosnia to glean those factors that seem to make a difference between success and failure. The primary belligerent in Iraq, the government of Saddam Hussein, had lost the war and was therefore not in a position to contest the will of the allied coalition force by continuing to pursue extermination of the Iraqi Kurds. Elite troops from four NATO countries—marines from the United States, United Kingdom, the Netherlands, and France—arrived in April 1991 to ensure security on the ground. Then, and now, NATO airpower based in Turkey was present *and* used to ensure compliance with Security Council directives. The Bosnian Serbs, in contrast, were in a position of strength for over three years, having already captured 70 percent of Bosnian territory. The war was accelerating during that time, not winding down. U.N. soldiers could not protect themselves, let alone civilians. NATO airpower was part of a cardboard scabbard. Incentives—carrots but no sticks—were presented to the Bosnian Serbs, who decided to continue the slaughter of Muslim noncombatants and to refuse negotiations. Safe areas would have been an expression understood in George Orwell's classic *1984*—it was quintessential doublespeak.

Challenges associated with safe areas, aside from the most important challenge to protect, include calculating how much food is needed and how much food will most probably get through and how to protect the wide variety of assistance personnel (for example, convoy truck drivers, medics, food distributors), media, and peacekeepers from the violence of a war that may intensify, rather than diminish, over time. Humanitarian assistance and protection are both extremely expensive in safe havens. On the debit side of the humanitarian ledger there are life insurance costs for relief workers; transportation costs, including the charter fee for trucks and airplanes and the "taxes," or extortion fees, paid to belligerents in exchange for access routes; costs associated with the theft and replacement of food and medical supplies; and the cost to the legitimacy of and respect for the United Nations and the Security Council.

Safe areas also have a postconflict impact on the noncombatant population. Once a peace settlement has gone into effect, and refugees who fled the violence return to their communities (if they can), resentment toward the returnees by those who remained in the safe areas and suffered greatly for doing so must be addressed. Rehabilitation of an unprotected safe haven community requires a great deal of psychological healing, especially for children. According to 1993 and 1994 psychosocial surveys conducted by UNICEF of children in safe areas, 55 percent of the children in Sarajevo had been shot at; 59 percent had had their homes attacked. In Mostar, 57 percent of the children reported having had at least one parent wounded. One is afraid to ask, What lessons did these children learn?

Refugee camps, IDP camps, or safe areas are the choices when all that is familiar becomes distorted or destroyed by war and noncombatants seek safety for themselves and their families. The context largely determines the best course of action. Refugee camps are preferable if violence encompasses an entire country and a country of asylum can be found. However, the number of displaced people seeking protection across borders is rising at the same time that asylum constraints have increased. With internal ethnic and political disputes and economic hardships, neighboring countries are less and less willing to harbor refugees and import new problems.

IDP camps are preferable if a functioning government is willing to protect its own or if members of the international humanitarian system volunteer in sufficient numbers to assist. But governments involved in civil wars often lack the will and means to assist, and international organizations need their limited resources to deal with those crises that *do* fall under their mandates. Moreover, since one of the fundamental aims of many civil wars is the decimation of civilian populations from the "wrong" groups, many governments cannot be expected to live up to the responsibilities vis-à-vis certain internally displaced persons.

Safe havens are preferable if external governments and their armed forces have a long-term commitment to the protection of the group in need of succor and protection. But donor governments frequently vacillate in their commitments, and IGOs are stymied by the inability of their member states to reach a consensus and back their words with concrete commitments.

Regardless of the site of refuge, internal problems of international humanitarian actors have produced additional challenges to each of the options outlined. To date, the United Nations has not mastered the coordination of relief activities among its own agencies or between them and the NGO community. Governments often expect the United Nations to do the impossible—to use its resources specifically for preferred groups of interest and simultaneously deal with the humanitarian crisis as a whole—governments call for "coordination" while pursuing their own flag-waving agendas. Because of an increase in the number of crises with massive noncombatant casualties, NGOs as well as IGOs in hot spots frequently are handicapped by young and inexperienced staffs. And the burgeoning of NGOs in recent years has encouraged a contract culture based on an economic, rather than an experiential, interpretation of efficiency in the choosing of an NGO to implement a program. Meanwhile, the ICRC is reluctantly expanding its role while holding tightly to its principles, and the military is both confused and frustrated with unfamiliar roles and vague mandates.

Humanitarian Assistance or Human Rights Protection

Governments in war-torn countries have primary responsibility for two critical humanitarian functions: providing emergency relief and protecting basic human rights within their borders. During complex emergencies, a government may be unable or unwilling to fulfill its humanitarian obligations, or it may be selective as to which population subgroups are to be targeted for assistance and which are to be targeted for abuse or neglect. In the absence of a government's fulfillment of obligations to its citizens, actors in the international humanitarian system may respond to one or both humanitarian challenges. The dilemma is that a host government or warring party may withdraw consent for humanitarian actors to access and deliver food and other goods to physically vulnerable populations if it is being criticized openly for gross violations of human rights. However, if the violations are not exposed, there is no incentive for the host government or warring party to discontinue its inhumane practices and violations of international humanitarian law, and there is no future for a durable peace and reconciliation without the exposure and punishment of such human rights abuses.

¿Dónde están? (Where are they?) In parts of Latin America that had strong military regimes, citizens who spoke out for democratic and human rights frequently would "disappear." U.N. Photo Archives/Rob Brouwer.

On the one hand, if attention is devoted solely to providing emergency assistance, lives are sustained during active fighting, and a principle of political neutrality is maintained. Some scholars add that the mere presence of relief personnel in the field reduces human rights violations. On the other hand, if attention is drawn to belligerents' blatant violations of human rights, public opinion may be stirred sufficiently to motivate powerful governments to exert more political, and possibly military, pressure than they would have otherwise on combatants to reach a cease-fire. Inattention to systematized violations of human rights aimed at particular groups increases the personalization of a war and thereby its prolongation. Inattention to the kidnapping, torture, and killing of individuals, such as intellectuals and community organizers, deprives a community of the leadership, charisma, and talent sorely needed during postconflict reconstruction.

Operational challenges arise from the tension between providing emergency assistance and blowing the whistle on massive violations of human rights. Actors operating from a principle of political neutrality and waiting for the consent of warring parties before delivering aid often believe that their diplomatic efforts to secure access are undermined by aggressive human rights NGOs. Actors who speak up about human rights violations can place relief personnel at risk. In the past, relief workers have encountered administrative harassment, such as having difficulty getting their visas or work permits renewed, or physical harassment or even death. Moreover, if relief organizations cannot perform their tasks—that is, prove to their donors that they have successfully supplied food and other goods—they become susceptible to slashes in funding. Therefore, to access physically vulnerable populations *and* to maintain organizational credibility and survival, relief organizations may be willing to look the other way or remain silent when individual human rights are being violated, sometimes even blatantly.

Human rights NGOs do not respect the principle of political neutrality. If human rights abuses are part of a Faustian pact made with a devilish government in order to feed the hungry, then a key resource for short- and long-term empowerment of vulnerable groups has been ignored, while only the physical symptoms of war have been addressed. In fact, the practice of certain NGOs' ignoring the principles of sovereignty and noninterference in domestic matters came about in part as a backlash against egregious human rights violations and the ICRC's unwillingness to intervene without consent or even to make public declarations.

The organization MSF, as mentioned earlier, was founded in 1968 by former ICRC staff who were unable to contenance waiting for government consent to help the Ibo population in the Nigerian civil war while simultaneously withholding knowledge regarding extensive violations of human rights. The breakaway staff compared these actions to silence before Nazi atrocities, which in fact had also been a criticism of ICRC policies during World War II. Particularly since the mid-1980s, more and more NGOs have been crossing borders without the consent of governments to secure access to vulnerable populations and indirectly undermine the legitimacy of abusive governments. The logic is that human beings are more important than state sovereignty. As a result, host governments are often more willing to work with the ICRC than with organizations such as Amnesty International or Human Rights Watch. It is debatable which group is more humanitarian.

NGOs do not necessarily coordinate their actions, particularly if their philosophies are not in agreement. The ICRC, an example of an NGO that performs both relief and advocacy functions, does not as a matter of institutional policy make public statements regarding human rights abuses by governments toward civilian populations, even though the ICRC has privileged access to such violations because of its mandate to protect political prisoners. The ICRC, like the U.N. Commission on Human Rights during the Cold War, protests privately. Visceral adherence to an NGO's principles without reflection or links to the efforts undertaken by others can lead to a level of inefficiency that does not serve either the organization or the victims of war. Increased communication could, at a minimum, affect the timing of an NGO speaking out in a way that would be least disruptive of the objectives of relief groups.

The tension between relief and human rights in the NGO community also exists within the U.N. system, although the human rights arm of the United Nations has only recently begun to express views openly and consistently. Prior to 1992, the U.N. Commission on Human Rights kept private all investigations of states' human rights violations. The commission met only six weeks a year and never convened for an emergency session to address urgent situations of massive human rights violations. August 1992 was the first time that an emergency session was convened, at the request of the United States, to address documented atrocities in the Balkans. In Somalia, even before large-scale humanitarian operations began, NGOs and individuals repeatedly communicated human rights abuses to the Commission on Human Rights. The commission, however, never issued a public resolution or published a report. In Iraq, the commission was aware of the government's gassing of the Kurdish population between 1988 and 1989 but did nothing. Following the 1993 World Conference on Human Rights in Vienna, a U.N. High Commissioner on Human Rights was appointed, and special investigators have been assigned for particular crises. To date, however, the publicizing of human rights violations has taken a back seat to peace processes, a situation that has frustrated U.N. personnel with a professional duty to ensure that ongoing violations of human rights are addressed. H. E. Tadeush Mazowiecki, a U.N. special rapporteur on the situation of human rights in Bosnia, resigned from his position because the international community did not respond to his seventeen reports of massive violations. Those involved in peace negotiations fear that the exposure of human rights violations might interfere with the political process of reaching settlement among warring parties.

Operationally, humanitarian assistance is more straightforward than investigating and prosecuting human rights violations; it is concrete and visible. For example, U.N. budgetary constraints and priorities restricted the number of staff available and experienced to handle the Bosnian Serbs' government-condoned military policies of mass rapes of women and girls. At the outset, virtually all of the UNHCR's $500 million annual budget for the former Yugoslavia was allocated to emergency succor. Instead, incidents of mass rapes and executions were placed on the agenda of the International War Crimes Tribunal for the former Yugoslavia and would be dealt with at the close of the war and from a specific tribunal budget. To date, the tribunal has had difficulty gathering sufficient voluntary contributions from governments to meet the investigative tasks at hand. Human rights NGOs are assisting the tribunal as best they can. Some use their field sources to gather information, and a few regularly update an Internet site on the tribunal's efforts and the political barriers to its success. The relationship between human rights NGOs and the U.N. tribunal is a remarkable example of institutional solidarity.

The logic in waiting until after a peace agreement has been reached to address massive violations of human rights is weak. Rape, torture, and murder of noncombatants increase the personalization of a conflict and feed into a cycle of violence and retaliation that escalates until exhaustion sets in. Unaddressed human rights violations also make a country's rehabilitation process more difficult. Although physical needs are easier to satisfy, psychological damage to individuals and their kinship take longer to heal and may in fact serve as an impetus for future retaliations, renewed war, and further humanitarian assistance. Revenge for past atrocities, as we know, is often cited as one of the root causes of repeated cycles of violence.

The need to reinforce neutrality provides the most sanguine explanation for preferring humanitarian assistance over human rights protection; it amounts to "looking the other way" until it is politically more convenient to look in the direction of obvious abuse. The better explanation is that the Security Council as well as the heads of governmental, intergovernmental, and nongovernmental organizations wish to sidestep human rights confrontation with states, move ahead whenever possible with negotiations, and be seen as impartial partners once cease-fires are in effect. The protection of human rights is a victim of such misplaced evenhandedness. By acting as if the most, and sometimes only, essential undertaking is the delivery of assistance, members of the international humanitarian system, and particularly the U.N. system, in many instances ignore opportunities for documenting and denouncing abuses. The treatment of human rights protection as a nonessential luxury has led Human Rights Watch to lament the "lost agenda" of the United Nations by overlooking the U.N.'s ability to make a difference in operations in the former Yugoslavia, Cambodia, Somalia, and the Persian Gulf.[6]

That said, events after the December 1995 signing of the Balkans peace agreement may hint at an advance in the evolution of the humanitarian idea and a step forward in the development of human rights as a universal norm. The Dayton Peace Agreement requires Serbia, Croatia, and Bosnia to cooperate with the war crimes investigation, to give unrestricted access to human rights monitors, to cooperate with ICRC efforts to account for missing persons, and to release all who were detained during the war. IFOR, the peace implementation force spearheaded by NATO, was given the authority to arrest indicted war criminals should they be recognized at IFOR checkpoints. Although all seemed straightforward, NATO troops were hesitant at first to assist the tribunal in extraditing indicted war criminals to The Hague—Bosnian Serbs might view IFOR's assistance as a violation of political neutrality and would retaliate, drawing IFOR into unwanted conflict. IFOR's hesitancy was short-lived. Rumors that IFOR soldiers had allowed Bosnian Serb political leader Radovan Karazdic, an indicted war criminal, to pass through checkpoints were followed by public condemnation of NATO. In the wake of institutional shaming, an American C-130 flew two war criminals detained by the Muslim government to The Hague, and the tribunal was offered additional intelligence information. Less than a week after pleading that IFOR's involvement in detaining alleged war criminals was undesirable, updated photos of seventeen and microbiographies of fifty-two indicted war criminals (forty-five Bosnian Serbs and seven Croats) were posted at IFOR checkpoints. Then "Wanted Posters" were widely distributed for the "War Criminals Indicted by the International Criminal Tribunal for the Former Yugoslavia." In spite of an initial reluctance, public pressure forced NATO to respond to the requirement for human rights accountability.

Public demand for human rights accounting also was present in El Salvador, where the Truth Commission was incorporated into the peace negotiations. Peasants experienced in organizing their collective voice of dissent and desire for political participation through the humanitarian efforts of church groups demanded a role in the peace process. Although these organizations were denied a seat at the negotiating table, their determination to contribute to their own healing led ultimately to the establishment of the Truth Commission. The commission was designed to investigate the atrocities committed against opposition politicians, whole communities of peasants, and church leaders, such as Archbishop Oscar Romero, who had been murdered.

Public opinion often plays a role in forcing different actors to uphold human rights responsibilities and international humanitarian law; the shaming of IFOR and the pressures on El Salvador's peace process are indicative. Concerned global citizens and war victims do not see a dilemma between humanitarian assistance and human rights protection. Both are possible; both should be done. The tension between willing citizens and unwilling states trickles down to the United Nations and emerges in the form of unclear, yet all-encompassing mandates, insufficient funding, and tentative responses. As the U.N. secretary-general has noted, the United Nations' reach is beyond its grasp. The United Nations has stumbled into broad humanitarian and human rights action or, perhaps more correctly, been pushed by states that are themselves pushed by democratic societies imbued with the humanitarian impulse. The human rights rhetoric that permeates international rhetoric has yet to be matched by political will and institutional mechanisms capable of altering belligerents' behavior toward noncombatants. The human rights mechanisms in the United Nations are still weak in authority and finances—only about 1 percent of the regular budget is devoted to human rights. Rhetoric without funding and authority prevents the international humanitarian system from responding to gross human rights violations while they are in progress.

Emergency Aid or Reconstruction and Development

Victims of war need both emergency aid during acute stages of fighting and assistance in reconstructing their lives and communities after violence has abated. The dilemma is that funds are increasingly in short supply for all forms of humanitarian action and available funds generally are not fungible—that is, emergency funds, because of agency mandates or donor preferences, cannot be used for anything but emergency aid. Funds for reconstruction and development, in turn, cannot be used for emergency situations. The UNDP had millions of dollars available for development work in Somalia that could not be used for emergency aid during the height of the famine. Since the end of the Cold War, a trend has emerged: Emergency aid is on the rise, and postconflict reconstruction and development assistance is dwindling, although victims' needs for both remain the same. "Emblematic of this trend is Somalia: the U.S. contribution to the relief effort under Operation Restore Hope—some $1.6 billion—was five times greater than total U.S. development assistance to Somalia over the last three decades; U.S. government figures also show that this same amount is equivalent to two years of U.S. development assistance *for all of sub-Saharan Africa*."[7] Some U.N. agencies have altered their funding activities. As mentioned before, the majority of past World Food Programme resources were directed to development and food-for-work programs; now 80 percent of its food resources are devoted to emergency assistance.

Once a conflict has been politically and militarily resolved and a "loud" emergency becomes quieter in terms of the attention of external governments and the media, emergency funding often dries up. Victory is declared, somewhat prematurely, as donors and journalists move on to the next crisis.[8] Except for such geostrategic allies as Egypt and Israel, where cease-fires were followed by American aid, which now accounts for almost half of total American overseas development assistance, most refugees and displaced persons return to their homes with few or no prospects for remaking their lives. They are welcomed by a host of basic survival problems caused by the destruction of homes, factories, schools, hospitals, roads, and crops; the theft of personal property and cash savings; and a physically and psychologically damaged community. A list of reconstruction efforts would include transforming the security environment, strengthening local administrative capacities, reconstructing political processes, reconstructing the economy, and rebuilding the local social fabric, including troop demobilization and war crimes trials. Demobilizing soldiers frequently need an incentive, either cash, in-kind items, or workable land, to disarm and agree to pursue lawful means to economic gain. Disarmament and demobilization measures failed in Somalia because U.N. appeals for contributions to "reward" belligerents for turning in their weapons failed. Disarmament was successful in Central America because incentives were available. In Nicaragua, for instance, some $44 million was provided for demobilization efforts.

Ethical dilemmas and operational challenges emerge from the dearth of funding and from the preferences of donors for emergency relief rather than reconstruction and development. Logically, if the humanitarian system knows that reconstruction and development funds will not be available during the postconflict period, efforts to relieve acute suffering should try to incorporate actions to empower locals and to use relief inputs in a manner complementary to longer-term objectives. Operationally, this is difficult because the entities that deliver emergency relief and those that assist in reconstruction and development frequently are different and do not communicate with each other.

Professionally, relief and development agencies—or the emergency personnel from UNICEF as distinct from its development staff—are asking different types of questions, leading them to believe there cannot be one common strategy. Institutions or individuals who address complex emergencies with the provision of emergency relief in mind are asking, "How do I relieve these manifestations of human suffering? What are the most urgent requirements for food, medicine, sanitation, and protection?" For those involved in development, the questions asked may include "What are the root causes of this crisis? How do we address the social, political, and economic factors that have contributed to the destabilization of this society?"

Operational considerations of rehabilitative and development work are distinct from those of relief operations. There are, for instance, increased costs associated with providing the additional calories needed by workers rebuilding infrastructure; the cost of tools and seeds for a subsequent harvest; salaries to local personnel; and the cost of housing and feeding expatriates (although development programs are generally much less expatriate-staff intensive than relief operations). Costs calculations are justified on a number of other grounds. How vulnerable was the civilian population prior to the outset of the conflict? How resilient was that population—was it in a state of permanent emergency, and had it developed substantial coping mechanisms? Was it empowered one day and disempowered the next? What societal behavior results from overwhelming attention from the international humanitarian system one day and its virtual complete withdrawal the next?

The conceptual divide between emergency relief and rehabilitation or development work manifests itself in the field in the isolated behavior of relief versus development humanitarians to the detriment of both. Humanitarian action in Iraq following the Gulf War provides an example. Nonemergency U.N. agencies worked on reconstruction and development programs without interfacing sufficiently with agencies providing emergency relief or other development groups. The International Labour Organisation was conducting studies and launching appeals for employment counseling and job retraining programs as early as November 1990. The U.N. Environment Programme was analyzing future environmental impacts of the war, while the International Maritime Organization was concentrating entirely upon coordinating international aid for oil-slick cleanup.[9] No effort was made to tie the projects together, to look at the possible negative impacts that one project might have on another, or to aggregate resources and approach the humanitarian and development projects in a comprehensive fashion so that gaps in short- and long-term need were diminished.

Given the constraints and unpredictability of funding, the international humanitarian system is faced with an ethical question as well: Is it more prudent to deliver emergency relief not to the extremely vulnerable populations that have only a minimal chance of remaining "stable," but to candidates that have a reasonable chance for reconstruction and development and for breaking the cycle of active and dormant conflict? Distinctions among victims on the basis of who can survive past the acute emergency situation and handle recovery themselves may seem inhumane; indeed that is why the choice between emergency aid and development is an ethical as well as an operational dilemma.

Those most in need of emergency relief when a crisis hits are generally those who were marginally surviving at the outset; armed conflict exposes and depletes coping mechanisms traditionally employed to sustain what in many cases have already been impoverished lives. Given the constraints of limited resources, we can either save more lives now and not address the probability of future symptoms of distress based upon the same underlying problems, or we can save fewer lives now with the hope that the local population will be empowered enough through reconstruction and development efforts to ward off any future need for external humanitarian assistance or be trained sufficiently to handle future crises itself.

The tension between offering relief to the most destitute and ignoring those who need more development assistance is not missed by potential beneficiaries of assistance. The Ethiopian Red Cross Society established food distribution centers for those who qualified as completely destitute, approximately 24 percent of the population. Those who owned one donkey, ox, or camel, when told they were not poor enough to receive assistance, said that they would sell what little they had in order to slip into destitution and receive aid. There are no easy answers for a country in which millions are at risk of starvation and resources are limited.[10]

Conceptual constraints also pose challenges to war victims' receiving the type of aid most appropriate for their condition. The United Nations' state-centered mandate has led to missed opportunities in interstate regions that require reconstruction and development assistance while other areas are more in need of emergency aid. Somalia is a good example. Unlike Germany's immediate recognition of Bosnia as an independent state, no major power stepped forward in 1991 to recognize officially the new Republic of Somaliland and its administrative structures. Somaliland continued to be grouped with the overall emergency situation that encompassed primarily southern Somalia and urban areas. The longer-term reconstruction and development assistance required by Somaliland did not appear on U.N. and NGO budgets, and the emergency aid being offered did not wholly suit the stated needs of Somaliland. Moreover, Somaliland's administrative structures were bypassed because of a lack of international recognition by the international community. With a definition of sovereignty that includes only those in the capital, all of Somalia was defined as without any administrative structures with sufficient authority to permit development work.

In cases where there is a clear state authority and conflict is localized rather than widespread, simultaneous relief and development activities have produced rather ironic consequences. Angola provides one such example. The two-decades-long war between the Movimento Popular de Libertação de Angola (Popular Movement for the Liberation of Angola) government and Jonas Savimbi's União Nacional para a Independência Total de Angola (National Union for the Total Independence of Angola) led to large-scale starvation in some areas, while other areas were left relatively untouched by food insecurity. After the peace process seemed finally on track in 1994, in areas originally affected by starvation there was little malnutrition to be found.

However, in the urban slums and coastal cities where starvation had not formerly been an issue, the population was subjected to IMF conditionality and World Bank structural adjustment, which involved the removal of several social safety nets that had formerly helped protect these populations. As a result, while malnutrition decreased in the area provided with emergency relief, severe malnutrition increased substantially in the area unaffected by war but subjected to a stringent new "development" policy.[11] This juxtaposition of simultaneous and largely autonomous outside aid efforts highlights the reality that the government of Angola had as little control over the actions of the Washington-based financial institutions (whose approval was necessary to secure loans) as over international NGOs (whose help was essential to provide for the welfare of the population). Again, the multifaceted potency of the dilemma of the continuum from relief to rehabilitation to development is striking.

Another unusual operational challenge results from a negative consequence of emergency assistance. Dependency theorists have documented the destruction of local markets by relief agencies' delivering of free food over an extended period. Local farmers cannot compete with free or generously subsidized food. The disincentive to grow crops is often followed by a migration into the cities or ports where the free food is distributed, thus directly contributing to a swelling urban population and indirectly contributing to future susceptibility to food crises, disease, and potential political instability. In addition to food distribution, cash salaries to locals and expatriates distort the local economy. The surge in income into an impoverished country alters many social and political relations. The surge is then followed by a dramatic drop once relief providers depart, sometimes leaving local institutions and groups in disarray and in competition for whatever outside sources still remain. The activities and resources of international NGOs in Central America during the 1980s led to a substantial growth in local NGOs. The end of Cold War rivalry, and thereby government funding of international NGO work in Central America, led to competition for resources, rather than cooperation in development work, among many local NGOs.

Some policymakers may determine that there is no dilemma between relief and development assistance. Relief is clearly a more immediate need; the inability of the noncombatants to care for themselves is more obvious. The quick offering of reconstruction and development assistance ignores some evidence that those populations that live in a constant state of structural poverty are more adept, through long experience, at employing coping mechanisms that allow them to weather *expected* episodic crises, such as famine. But even they are ill-equipped in the face of war-related deprivation from long-term political instability. Policymakers may look at these self-help coping strategies and determine that external assistance is not a priority as it would interfere with the empowerment process by which the already marginalized actually can handle crises. This analysis may neglect the fact that each successive crisis weakens the local capacity to cope. Individuals sell off accrued personal assets, such as land or farming equipment, that are required as insurance against the next crisis; families separate to find employment, thereby leading to another thread pulled from an already threadbare social fabric. Without the space to stabilize economically and socially after a disaster, future instability becomes more likely. Evidence exists to support both arguments.

Even if a conflict has wound down, refugees rationally choose not to leave relief camps if the infrastructure in or near their home villages is not equally life sustaining. Demining operations are essential to the return of refugees; so, too, is the repair of water resources. In Afghanistan, water is carried from areas beneath the mountains to various villages via *karezes*, or underground canals. *Karezes* have vertical shafts spaced at equal distances. They must be kept free of debris so that the underground water system does not become clogged or tainted. Traditionally, every spring each village—sometimes composed of different tribes—would work together to clean the *karezes*.

Because fighting in Afghanistan had prevented the annual cleaning of the *karezes*, the United Nations began to finance projects to do the job and thereby induce refugees to return. The UNDP channeled the material resources, and the WFP dispatched food resources through its food-for-work activities, along with the necessary tools. NGOs made the local contacts and supervised the work. The project seemed to be running smoothly until one day a group of villagers stopped a U.N. team and held it captive. They argued that their *karezes* had not been cleaned, whereas all the *karezes* of villages governed by one particular tribe had been. The U.N. team explained to the villagers that an organized gathering of elders from all the villages had determined the priority of *kareze* cleaning. Further research, however, proved that indeed all the *karezes* that had been cleaned had belonged to one particular tribe and that all of the elders present at the meeting belonged to that tribe. Now, instead of working together, the tribes have isolated themselves from future contact. Now, instead of coping with the problem themselves, the villages wait for external assistance to come. The result of the project is disempowered communities and additional and unwanted dependency. The history of post–Cold War relief, if written, would contain many comparable events when relief and development organizations were not knowledgeable enough regarding local culture and social relationships to prevent well-intentioned efforts from backfiring. These events also fuel the debate that gives more funds for relief work and less for development projects.

An additional concern about who is empowered through relief and developmental activities is that the U.N. system usually works through central governments rather than local political authorities. By routing development projects through government institutions, the United Nations is participating in the political process of the host country. Giving governments necessary development resources assists in buttressing the legitimacy of a regime. Ironically, the good news is that funds channeled through government institutions can empower those institutions and the people within them. Funds channeled through NGOs, however, can weaken the political and social institutions of the state unless the NGO projects are programmed with care and the state apparatus itself is legitimate.

Although this section has highlighted relief and development actors' disagreement over humanitarian strategies, these actors share a common barrier to both relief and development efforts. The estimated 110 million land mines planted in the earth today impede the safe delivery of humanitarian assistance and the development and rehabilitation of postconflict regions. All of the country studies mentioned in Chapter 2 suffer from various degrees of land mine problems, with Iraq being the most pronounced. Warring parties can purchase one land mine from a global stockpile of some 100 million land mines for as little as $3.00. The cost to the international humanitarian system for removing one land mine is between $300 and $1,000. Relief and development organizations have consolidated their lobbying efforts to eliminate antipersonnel land mines from the militaries' pallet of weaponry and have recently been rewarded for their collaboration. In May 1996, President Clinton called for a global ban on antipersonnel land mines.

Coercion or Consent

There are three simultaneous objectives to be met by external actors involved in complex emergencies: the provision of assistance (humanity), the protection of human rights (justice), and the stabilization of overall security (order). The first objective, as we have seen, is the most straightforward: to mobilize resources from various public and private sources. The second frequently, although not necessarily, follows. However, the third, the decision to utilize economic or military coercion, is often pursued reluctantly or not at all. The dilemma is that forms of coercion, such as sanctions and military force, cannot be applied without having an effect on humanitarian efforts. The term *surgical strike*—illustrated by televised videos of U.S. missiles going through front doors of Iraqi military command posts—may cause some television viewers to cheer for their "team." However, the visual misleads the public into believing that massive high-tech weaponry is infallible and can discriminate between combatants and noncombatants. Indeed, little was reported of the bombed

An Iraqi boy stands in front of destroyed building in Baghdad following U.S. surgical strikes. UNICEF/ 4566C/91/John Isaac.

Baghdad air raid shelter and the subsequent deaths of hundreds of Iraqi women and children who had sought safety there. But coercion may also be the only way to stop or retard massive waves of violence. There was a role for coercion in Rwanda immediately following the death of the president; its absence is history.

Decisions between force and patience require accurate information and timeliness; operational challenges affect both. NGOs can provide the most accurate information about problems in the field, but routine communication channels are nonexistent between NGOs and the U.N. Security Council, which determines when to invoke Chapter VII.

NGOs are also in the best position to determine whether economic sanctions are having an unbearable effect on the noncombatant population. However, the Security Council may be more interested in the political sphere than in the humanitarian one, and sanctions may be left in place regardless of human consequences. The humanitarian and development organs of the United Nations also do not have a clear line of communication with the Security Council, although they are required to respond to the humanitarian consequences that flow from policies of coercion.

The application of military force to achieve humanitarian ends can also suffer operational weakness such as unclear mandates, poor coordination among all actors, and miscommunications. The resort to arm-twisting and arm-breaking is perhaps the most acute dilemma to emerge for humanitarians in the post–Cold War era. Operationally, the professional culture and agendas of armed forces and humanitarians have had great difficulty in finding a common ground and a common language.

It is worth examining a typical scenario in which the movement is from consent to coercion. Many NGOs and U.N. agencies, particularly with development agendas, are already in the field prior to the eruption of widespread war. This was the case in Somalia long before December 1992 and is the case today in Sierra Leone as this country descends into civil war. Once violence escalates, other NGOs and U.N. agencies are called upon by their constituents and governing bodies to deploy relief personnel to the area. Attempts at the pacific settlement of disputes, as outlined in **Chapter VI** of the U.N. Charter, run in tandem with humanitarian action. Consent by the government to the presence of humanitarian personnel generally has been negotiated, although often heavily conditioned. If a cease-fire or other agreement has been negotiated, U.N. peacekeepers may also be deployed to the area to monitor compliance.

However, if consent to assist the most vulnerable is not forthcoming or is so heavily conditioned that humanitarian assistance cannot be administered without tilting the political balance in favor of one of the belligerents, humanitarians then consider whether to withdraw or limit operations or to ask the Security Council to contemplate more forceful measures. If the lives of humanitarian personnel and peacekeepers are targeted, the Security Council may move from Chapter VI to Chapter VII responses. There is a stream of decisionmaking at various levels and within various institutions as violence escalates and **populations** become more **at risk** or begin migrating to equally unstable neighboring countries. Development NGOs must decide when to ask for relief assistance, relief personnel must decide when to ask for diplomatic and peacekeeping assistance, and the Security Council must determine how and at what point it becomes necessary to move toward force and away from traditional diplomacy, impartiality, and political neutrality. Additional questions follow: What tools of Chapter VII should be employed—economic, communications, and diplomatic sanctions and the use of force by land, sea, and air—and how will they affect relief efforts and personnel? Should the level of force be proportional to the force exerted by the warring parties upon noncombatants, or is it better to dismiss caution and overwhelm belligerents?

Previous case studies may have already raised such questions for the reader. Economic sanctions—in Iraq, Serbia, Haiti—hurt most those whom the international community is supposedly trying to help (women, children, the sick, and the elderly) while leaving targeted regimes and elites ensconced in power. From the beginning of Chapter VII action in the former Yugoslavia, proportionality of force was the strategy. Its ineffectiveness was obvious and left uncorrected until the Croatian offensive and NATO attacks in August 1995. Within four months of overwhelming force by a Croatian-Bosnian alliance and NATO air strikes, a peace agreement was signed. Many argue that the years of diplomatic negotiations produced nothing but borrowed time for war criminals and unnecessary loss of life; war-making and peacemaking are not compatible. Shashi Tharoor, special assistant to the Under Secretary-General of the Department of Peace-keeping Operations, agreed: "It is extremely difficult to make war and peace with the same people on the same territory at the same time."[12] A distinction must be made, however, between the use of force and a display of force, Somalia being a striking example. The display of force was overwhelming, particularly initially, but the use of force was constrained and later underwhelming (total withdrawal) when it became clear that twenty-five thousand soldiers could not capture one warlord and that outside soldiers would have to be casualties in order to bring about stability in the failed state. *Mission creep* is a new catchphrase used by the military to describe unwanted variations away from an operation's original mandate. Critics of military performance and fecklessness argue that the armed forces do not understand the difference between mission creep and flexibility.

The great controversy within the international humanitarian system about the use of coercion to achieve humanitarian objectives and the compatibility of institutions of force and compassion in the same operation has yielded operational as well as ethical questions: What would be an effective sequencing of humanitarian and military action to replace contemporary ad hoc and ineffective responses? What are the institutional constraints that prevent either humanitarian efforts or military objectives from being relatively successful when both are operative?

Does humanitarian assistance in an unstable political environment obstruct the long-term viability of a community and fuel the prolongation of human suffering? If there is no functioning government, how can the international humanitarian system assist in constructing an environment stable enough to facilitate the treatment of food insecurity and disease? Imagination and institutional reform within NGOs, IGOs, and governments and their militaries are key, as is listening to advice from the beneficiaries of international assistance. At the close of 1995, nonstate actors from Nigeria begged the international community to impose sanctions on the military regime even though sanctions would have caused hardship for the poor; nonstate actors in Iraq begged the international community to lift the sanctions—the Security Council ignored both pleas.

At present, movement from Chapter VI to Chapter VII—and frequently back again—often introduces contradictory actions that can cancel each other out or even inflate the degree of suffering by noncombatants. Mandates and strategies are further complicated when Chapter VI and Chapter VII actions are used simultaneously (as in the former Yugoslavia) or switch back and forth (as in Rwanda). Chapter VI is theoretically impartial and neutral; Chapter VII makes a highly political statement regarding which belligerent is at fault and needs to be brought back into line by concentrated and coercive actions of the international community—first by sanctions and then by military force if the nonforcible sanctions are ineffective. Too many humanitarian practitioners have failed to integrate into their operational philosophies the basic incompatibility between their traditional operational principles (based on impartiality and neutrality) and the requirements of working in a war zone where Chapter VII actions are in effect. Chapter VII is anything but impartial and neutral. It is the only instance in the world organization's constitution in which finger-pointing is condoned and blame is attached to decisions. To try pursuing a traditional humanitarian style within a Chapter VII operation is to try forcing what is definitely a square peg into a round hole.

Chapter VII allows for economic sanctions against the accused; its objective is to bring about a change in behavior by the governing authority. The logic of economic sanctions is that they create pain and suffering at the lowest strata of society, which within time will trickle up to the governing authority and bring about policy changes or perhaps a change in regimes. Economic sanctions are applied, often as a knee-jerk reaction, regardless of the fact that authoritarian regimes are not accountable to civil society and are not affected by the pain and suffering of noncombatants. In the words of Boutros Boutros-Ghali: "Sanctions, as is generally recognized, are a blunt instrument. They raise the ethical question of whether suffering inflicted on vulnerable groups in the target country is a legitimate means of exerting pressure on political leaders whose behaviour is unlikely to be affected by the plight of their subjects."[13] Moreover, repressive governments may even be strengthened because they can mobilize local support to counteract the targeting of outsiders—a kind of "martyr" effect that plays upon the most shrill nationalist chords. To counter the effects of economic sanctions on the most vulnerable parts of populations, humanitarian agencies are then called upon to increase assistance. The effects of sanctions and humanitarian assistance in many ways cancel each other out and at a high price.

Coercion to encourage belligerents' compliance with Security Council resolutions can have extremely negative consequences on vulnerable populations—not only IDPs and refugees who must wait for humanitarian supplies to pass the scrutiny of the Sanctions Committee on admissible imports into conflict areas, but also, and perhaps as importantly, those populations that are not uprooted but whose livelihood is hindered or completely eliminated by the hardships produced by sanctions. For example, sanctions against Serbia affected the ability of host families caring for roughly 95 percent of incoming refugees from Bosnia and Croatia to care for themselves. One study concluded that "90 percent of the *resident* Serbian population . . . was unable to meet basic food needs."[14]

"Diplomacy without force means nothing," stated the vice president of Bosnia in June 1995—a saying that he garnered from Republican senator Bob Dole's earlier article in *Foreign Affairs*. While futile efforts to negotiate a settlement continued between the warring parties with the assistance of the five-nation contact group (the United States, France, Britain, Germany, and Russia), Serbs stepped up their aggression against safe areas, with sporadic and ineffective NATO response. Economic sanctions previously had been eased against Serbia in exchange for that government's agreement to desist from supplying the Bosnian Serb forces with armaments and other support, an agreement that was respected in the breach as Bosnian Serbs continued to be in a position to overrun U.N. safe areas. International law was continually violated, and civilians continued to be the primary targets of snipers and other efforts at ethnic cleansing. Although the vice president of Bosnia was requesting that Chapter VII be employed to its fullest alongside Chapter VI, would it not have been preferable to pull back from Chapter VI action and the involvement of the U.N. Secretariat and relief agencies, increase Chapter VII military action to stabilize the region, and then revert back to Chapter VI humanitarian action? Until Chapter VII has been effective, it may be desirable for Chapter VI to wait in the wings.

UNPROFOR peacekeepers monitor a checkpoint patrolled by Bosnian and Croatian police. U.N. Photo/186715/J. Isaac.

In the cases involving military operations, the protection of Kurds in northern Iraq led by the United States in Operation Provide Comfort, and the stabilization of the crisis in Rwanda, led by France in Opération Turquoise, are two examples of clear intent, coordinated implementation, and commitment of adequate military means. In northern Iraq in particular, the willingness to maintain a secure environment for the Kurds was present in April 1991 and remains today with NATO airpower poised to respond, as it has in the past. The actions in northern Iraq and Rwanda were led by a coalition and a major power unilaterally; there was a U.N. blessing but no U.N. commander. In both cases, force was utilized first to establish a protected area and later to maintain it.

Other cases are not so clear, partially because there is a tendency to group different operations with different mandates together under an all-encompassing label of "humanitarian intervention." For example, military actions taken in Somalia by the international community were driven by different mandates; thus, the three phases of UNOSOM I, UNITAF, and UNOSOM II should not be confused with one another. In the same manner, we should be clear about the effects of the action in northern Iraq on humanitarian efforts in the rest of the country.

The diplomacy and subsequent military action approved by the Security Council were decisive in reversing Iraqi aggression against Kuwait and its own Kurdish population. But the combination of previous and continuing economic sanctions with military force in the Gulf also produced negative humanitarian consequences. U.N. Security Council Resolution 661 had called for economic sanctions against Iraq. Exempt from the sanctioned items were food and medicine earmarked for humanitarian efforts, but the review process by which shipments were inspected before entry into Iraq created a critical lag in the delivery of relief supplies and an aggravation of human suffering. In the immediate aftermath of the war, UNICEF and the World Health Organization managed to push a convoy of trucks carrying medical supplies into Baghdad, where civilians were being hit by U.S.-led air attacks on the city. The attacks also destroyed the water and sanitation infrastructure. Ironically, intergovernmental and nongovernmental organizations were called upon to deal with the humanitarian debris caused by the actions of the international community.

Although a continuum from consensus to coercion appears to exist, the system for managing activities by the international humanitarian system along that continuum is rudimentary at best. The diplomatic and bureaucratic structures of the United Nations are hostile to initiating and overseeing military efforts when serious fighting rages—where coercion, rather than consent, is the norm. There are two reasons that stand out for this aversion to managing enforcement. As noted earlier, political and military enforcement under Chapter VII is not only inconsistent with and compromises fundamental humanitarian principles, but also goes against the grain of a world organization whose operating procedures are overwhelmingly based on consensus—some would say obsequiousness to the lowest common denominator of state sovereignty. And the use of force sometimes places in peril the lives of peacekeepers and relief workers and jeopardizes the international legitimacy of the United Nations and the Office of the Secretary-General, which is based on neutrality and impartiality. Former Assistant Secretary-General Giandomenico Picco, for one, has warned against "transforming the institution of the Secretary-General into a pale imitation of a state" because this office "is inherently inappropriate to manage the use of force."[15]

Others disagree and contend that military intervention in support of humanitarian objectives represents a necessary, although insufficient, last-ditch effort to create enough breathing room for the reemergence of local stability and order. This has been the case in Haiti, northern Iraq, and Rwanda. This line of argument formed part of the logic for the use of force in Somalia, which ultimately and unsuccessfully led to the "manhunt" (complete with reward) for General Aidid. Interestingly, Aidid did not fall until after humanitarian intervention had ceased and all foreign troops had departed from the country. Although Aidid's capture was never a specific part of the original mandate, failure to capture him was seen as a failure of the entire U.N. operation and has cast a long shadow on forceful humanitarian efforts—the powerlessness of the "Somalia syndrome," which is the post–Cold War equivalent of the Vietnam syndrome. Aidid was *peacefully* ousted by a former ally, Osman Hassan Ali Atto, a businessman who turned on the general for having impeded efforts to rebuild Somalia; he urged the United Nations and investors to return. (Subsequently, it became unclear which warlord controlled this violent faction.) The militarization of a humanitarian operation and the use of coercive measures to capture a faction leader appear to have heightened the power of the leader, or at a minimum were factors in the equation, and to have inhibited opportunities for peaceful nation-building.

Positive and negative experiences of military and humanitarian collaboration in Rwanda have been reported by various NGOs and U.N. agencies. There were three joint military/humanitarian phases: the multilateral peacekeeping forces of UNAMIR during the worst wave of genocide, the French unilateral security action and the U.S. Support Hope humanitarian action, and the national military contingents involved in humanitarian activities under UNHCR invitation and direction. The designated functions of military units during the Rwandan crisis were to provide a secure environment for humanitarian activities, to assist humanitarians, and to carry out various relief activities on their own.

Because UNAMIR troops did not have the mandate to use force except in self-defense, they were unable to provide a secure environment for victims and humanitarian personnel, a task in which military contingents supposedly have a comparative advantage. Only French troops in Opération Turquoise were capable of fostering a secure environment, but not without heavy criticism from the French NGOs that viewed the military's show of force as undermining the ability to deal with all victims impartially. Even after the humanitarian emergency had stabilized, more humanitarian organizations had arrived on the scene, and troop operations had wound down, some NGOs maintained their distance from military units performing strictly humanitarian activities. Dutch NGOs, such as MSF-Holland, which were thankful for Dutch military transport to Goma, nevertheless maintained the view that the presence of the military compromised their organizations' humanitarian mandate. Many others, however, were pleased with the professional working relationship between the military and humanitarians. Irish soldiers made the task easier by assisting NGOs while wearing T-shirts and leaving their weapons at home; the Irish government, unlike wealthier countries, also provided its military personnel at no cost to the relief organizations. The cost of UNAMIR was $162 million. The official figure for Opération Turquoise is about $200 million; and Operation Support Hope, about $135 million, although unofficial tallies are much higher, some four or five times greater.[16]

The positive aspects of military/humanitarian collaboration in Rwanda include the military's financial, technical, and logistical capacity; its can-do approach; its ability to attract media and public attention to human tragedy; and its focus on evaluation of performance once tasks were completed. On the negative side, military units were less willing than humanitarians to take risks (the Japanese troops, for example, refused to work inside refugee camps for security reasons, and some U.S. troops were not allowed to leave the Kigali airport); contingency planning did not occur until the last moment; and the timetable of military involvement was problematic (humanitarian personnel were reluctant to form working relationships with military units not scheduled to remain in the area for long). Perhaps the clearest lesson concerned physical protection—unilateral action was more effective than action under U.N. command and control.

Once coercion is viewed as the best plan of action, individual countries begin internal legislative processes to determine whether to contribute troops. Considerations for international military involvement by the United States include the requirement that the president consult with and report to Congress (the War Powers Resolution); cost, readiness, and budgeting mechanisms; command and control issues; and force structure.[17]

Danziger, © *Christian Science Monitor.*

A LARGER, MORE CONTROVERSIAL DILEMMA

Historians are not the only persons fond of counterfactual analyses—
"What if?" Would the hundreds of thousands of Bosnian Muslims have
been better off if there had been no humanitarian action, if no safe areas
had been established, if no future war crimes tribunals had been touted?
Perhaps fewer Bosnians would have died or been psychologically destroyed. Perhaps more robust diplomacy and military might could have
been deployed by NATO earlier than September 1995, instead of prolonged reliance on humanitarian action to salve Western consciences into
believing their governments were "doing something." Before NATO
ratcheted up its actions in September 1995 side by side with the Croatian-
Bosnian offensive, the deputy commander in chief of the U.S. European
Command, General Charles G. Boyd, remarked, "It pushed for more humanitarian aid even as it became clear that this was subsidizing conflict
and protecting the warring factions from the natural consequences of
continuing the fighting."[18]

Yet upon closer scrutiny, it would be too simplistic to write off humanitarian action. The norm created by the evolution of the humanitarian idea
has not been totally lost; the bottom line is to act effectively, not to aban-
don, even if one could, those who suffer. Those who believe that an imperative exists that requires a global response to all suffering caused by
war would argue that this book's overall approach to problems it articu-
lates reflects an inadequate understanding of the complex emergencies of
the 1990s. However, other bona fide humanitarians are more reflective before jumping or stumbling into a crisis. It is essential to ask in each crisis,
"Would humanitarian action in this particular crisis do more harm than
good?" Stumbling into a crisis without experience or sufficient resources,
except for a plethora of goodwill, is not responsible humanitarianism.
Given the current institutional structures and arrangements for conducting humanitarian efforts, the lack of accountability to war victims, and
the seemingly irreconcilable perspectives of the means to protect human
welfare, counterproductive humanitarianism can occur. Although those
who believe in the humanitarian imperative would argue vehemently,
depending on the circumstances and context, a legitimate and ethical decision can be made by humanitarians not to get involved in a particular
crisis or to withdraw (either temporarily or permanently). In short, it may
not be unthinkable "to just say no" to humanitarian action in a particular
context.

The larger dilemma posed to humanitarians—whether doing something may be worse than doing nothing at all—is in fact becoming more
acute as resources become in shorter and shorter supply, as parliaments
slash foreign assistance allocations, and as donors at all levels become

"fatigued" by the seemingly endless stream of human tragedies that are the media's daily bill of fare. As U.N. High Commissioner Sadako Ogata already noted in 1993, "The time has come for a major dialogue on the hard choices that will have to be made in the face of finite humanitarian resources and almost infinite humanitarian demands."[19]

As we have seen earlier, delivering humanitarian assistance in an active war zone can be extremely expensive (airlifts, life insurance, percentage of aid that actually gets through). If the international humanitarian system mobilizes resources and treats as many victims as it can, it is no doubt reducing the quality (and possibly the long-term effectiveness) of assistance to other suffering populations. If triage is employed, addressing first the requirements of the most needy who are also able to survive, then how many more lives are sacrificed? Part of the larger dilemma about when and where to conduct humanitarian action thus concerns the fundamental issue of quantity versus quality of life.

There is a bias in the international humanitarian system toward responding vigorously to **loud emergencies**, meaning wars, which are generally recognizable by the abundant media attention they receive. These loud emergencies by their nature and media coverage drown out the more feeble and less dramatic calls to address the **silent emergencies** of malnutrition and preventable diseases, which could be treated by a well-planned mobilization of far fewer resources. For example, the international humanitarian system and the media reacted vigorously to the half a million deaths of Somali children under the age of five in 1992, but the deaths due to poverty of 13–14 million children around the world (that is, thirty-five to forty thousand per day, according to UNICEF estimates) during that same period went relatively unnoticed. In the age of channel surfing, the drama of loud emergencies holds the attention of the world far better than a lengthy documentary of preventable human suffering caused by underdevelopment.

We are then left to wonder whether the trend in the international humanitarian system of responding energetically to emergencies with high decibel levels may in some ways contribute to the creation of future loud emergencies. This line of questioning builds upon the justifications for preventive medicine: What is left untreated in its early stages becomes more difficult and more expensive, in both financial and human terms, when the crisis stage is reached. If we carry the medical analogy one step further, when an emergency room receives multiple patients at one time because of a large, unforeseen accident, the overburdened health care staff treats first those seriously hurt but most likely to survive. Those barely clinging to life must wait. By the time attention can be paid to the latter, they may have expired. Would one say that the medical team was "successful" because it managed the crisis thoughtfully, taking into consideration the long-term viability of its patients and efficient use of financial, medical, and human resources because providing triage to those most vulnerable would certainly have cost more? Or would one say that the medical staff was callous?

This ethical subtheme to our larger dilemma is uncomfortably painful, some would say morally repugnant. Judgments ultimately, although not overtly, are made regarding the value and viability of particular populations. The fact that we seldom pose such awkward questions openly does not mean that decisions are not being made about the use of limited resources. In December 1992 when the international humanitarian system responded massively to Somalia's suffering, those victims in neighboring Sudan, or across the continent in Liberia or Angola, received virtually no international attention. Those children in Niger dying from vitamin A deficiency were even less visible.

Moreover, humanitarian efforts to sustain noncombatants in complex emergencies, where any semblance of law and order is absent and civil society is fragmented, are more costly as well as dangerous to relief workers and peacekeepers. In the words of retired General of the U.S. Marine Corps Bernard Trainor: "One would like to use the doctrine of limited tears. We can't cry for everyone, so we should have some sort of measure that helps us decide when and where to get involved."[20] In those cases where there is little hope for long-term political and social stability, extensive humanitarian assistance and peacekeeping efforts appear futile, which creates an acute problem in Africa. Ethiopian president Meles Zenawi, whose government is trying to strike a delicate balance between democratic change and long-suppressed ethnic aspirations, believes that "every country in Africa is a potential failed state."[21]

The politicization of humanitarian action—or the perception of its politicization, which has the same impact—in Bosnia, Somalia, and Rwanda has altered civilian humanitarian orthodoxy. London's International Institute for Strategic Studies put forward possible new guidelines that were based on an internal U.N. memorandum about humanitarian action when outside military forces are involved. The new bottom line was the recommendation that civilian humanitarians "should not embark on humanitarian operations where, over time, impartiality and neutrality are certain to be compromised." "If impartiality and neutrality are compromised," the document went on to say, "an ongoing humanitarian operation should be reconsidered, scaled down or terminated."[22]

This argument would have been anathema to humanitarian practitioners only a few years ago, when there was an unquestioned imperative to respond to every human-made tragedy. But the conclusion of a comprehensive evaluation of humanitarian conflict management in Somalia prescribes "tough love"—the heretical notion that the international community should have left when it became obvious that looting, corruption, and extortion of assistance were fueling the war. Although it may seem callous to walk away from suffering, this may prove to be the most humane option: "It would likely have led either to improved protection allowing the continuation of aid or to an opportunity, with departure from Somalia, to channel scarce aid resources to other countries' emergencies."[23]

What kinds of policy responses from the international humanitarian system will such a statement generate? The logic is compelling and rational—use funds to assist vulnerable populations with strong institutions rather than apply emergency triage to extremely vulnerable groups that do not even have a political and societal infrastructure to survive on their own. Use limited resources to help development in stable societies not at war rather than to intervene in hot armed conflicts. Such decisions are of course void of the basic compassion that drives humanitarians. They also overlook any responsibility by major powers for destructive national policies during the colonial period or the Cold War that have contributed to the inability of some populations to empower civil institutions and dismantle their own war machines.

Yet the dilemmas and challenges encountered by humanitarians are not insuperable. The response should not be to throw the baby out with the bathwater. There have been successes—lives saved, rights protected, societies back on their own feet. The idea of humanitarian action has become more firmly rooted. Institutions are grappling with reform at all levels. While critics of the institutions call for the creation of new institutions and the death of the old, training manuals to improve professionalism are circulating among true professionals in many agencies. The latter option, to do nothing at all, is a difficult one to contemplate, particularly for humanitarians working directly on children's issues.

One tactic that has been tried since the mid-1980s is the creation of protected space around vulnerable groups, especially children. In 1983, Nils Thedin of Sweden proposed to UNICEF that children be treated as a "conflict-free zone."[24] The logic was that the next generation was innocent and should be protected from harm and provided with essential services. As unrealistic as this suggestion initially appeared on paper, the first experiment occurred in El Salvador in 1985 when three days in three consecutive months were devoted to vaccinating small children in the midst of warfare. The notion of temporal and spatial temporary safe havens was applied in other disputes—in 1986 in Uganda the warring parties permitted a "corridor of peace" for supplies; in Lebanon in 1987 hostilities were suspended for vaccinations; in 1988–1989 in Afghanistan vaccination teams operated in both government-controlled and mujahideen-controlled areas.

Probably the most sustained experiment was negotiated by UNICEF's late executive director, Jim Grant, for the Sudan. The country had been torn by an on-again-off-again civil war for three decades when drought and renewed fighting in 1988 killed 250,000 people and displaced 3 million. Fearing a similar disaster in 1989, Grant managed to launch Operation Lifeline Sudan as both the government in Khartoum and the rebel Sudan People's Liberation Army (SPLA) agreed to eight "corridors of tranquillity" along which fighting would stop and relief proceed.[25] At least along the corridors, there was hope. Significantly, the SPLA agreed in 1995 to abide by the provisions of the Convention on the Rights of the Child, the first nonstate (or insurgent group) to do so.

The debates, as they unfold in the next chapter, are constantly on the agendas of actors in the international humanitarian system. The bottom line is that more thoughtful humanitarian efforts are required. It is to this challenge that we now turn.

FOUR

□   □   □

International Policy Choices

Glendower: I can call spirits from the vasty deep.
Hotspur: Why, so can I, or so can any man;
But will they come when you do call for them?
      —William Shakespeare, *King Henry IV, First Part*

Senator Strom Thurmond, chairman of the Senate Armed Services Committee, opened a June 1995 hearing on U.S. involvement in Bosnia with the observation that the "Bosnian crisis confronts us with critical choices, and perhaps none of them are good."[1] In informal and formal policy discussions, personal and professional opinions about humanitarian action in war zones are often polarized. On the one hand, there are those who recommend on idealistic moral grounds that the international humanitarian system react to every conflict. On the other hand, there are those grounded in realpolitik who prefer to look the other way or wait for others to do the job, conserving their state's resources until suffering within another country has a more direct impact on their state's own internal and external security. Many observers, and perhaps many readers of these pages, have been frustrated by institutional inertia and the entangled web of power politics that thwart better responses to life-threatening suffering.

Amid counterproductive, black-or-white debates, a truism is often overlooked in the gray area in between so-called idealists and realists. The international humanitarian system is in a state of transition where it cannot remain. Inertia will further cripple credibility and states' ability to act rationally in the collective interest of international peace and security, as outlined in the U.N. Charter, and in the interests of the people caught in the throes of armed conflict, as called for in such documents as the Universal Declaration of Human Rights and the Geneva conventions and additional protocols.

135

A revolution of the imagination is required to carry the international humanitarian system out of its turbulence and into the twenty-first century. A first step involves efforts to get the mix of responses right, given political constraints and available resources. A second and simultaneous step concerns institutional rejuvenation or new forms of cooperation. It is to these two tasks that the present chapter is devoted.

GETTING THE MIX RIGHT

Evolution of the humanitarian idea is inevitable; but pro-active steps to move it constructively through the next stage are also essential. What kinds of policy choices do international actors make daily that affect the lives not only of refugees, internally displaced persons, and besieged populations but also of humanitarians themselves? Governments can choose to accept or reject asylum-seekers on an ad hoc basis or to work with other governments and international institutions to make a standardized, collective response. Governments along with intergovernmental and nongovernmental organizations can choose to design and implement preventive measures for potential crises before they explode, or they can adopt a wait-and-see strategy, which ultimately is more expensive. Governments and humanitarian agencies can design new strategies for improving security in safe havens for future crises, including a rapid reaction humanitarian unit constituting a trained nucleus to implement quick responses, or they can continue to proceed randomly.

The turbulence and frustration generated by the current transition period in world politics and state-to-society relations can lead policymakers to oversimplify the problems of the international humanitarian system under broadly constructed concepts that hinder, more than help, rational thought and effective action. For example, **compassion fatigue** is blamed for dwindling resources. In an environment with ever-expanding needs, donors of humanitarian aid are reducing their contributions or becoming more selective in where and how they want their money spent. Donors are becoming exhausted financially and compassionately by the daily bill of fare of human tragedy—tired of throwing their money at both recurring problems and less-than-optimal programs. This view, however, assumes that humanitarian actors have been utilizing funds in a cost-effective, result-oriented fashion and that resource problems lie solely or even primarily in war zones themselves. One can argue that the problem has been not that resources have been drained, as enough of them and goodwill exist to address adequately a multitude of human tragedies, but that resources have been applied without a comprehensive strategy. As such, the whole of the international humanitarian system adds up to less than the sum of the parts.

Do the physical tools already exist for responding to the food, shelter, medicine, and protection needs of suffering noncombatants? Yes. Do various international agreements, the U.N. Charter, and international law adequately set out the ethical and legal guidelines for the treatment of noncombatants and the rules of war? Yes. Is the humanitarian impulse sufficiently rooted in international society to motivate responses when people are in need? Yes.

Then what prevents the design and implementation of cost-efficient, thoughtful, and cooperative humanitarian action? One answer is that institutional structures of states and intergovernmental organizations prevent many policymakers from imagining a productive and effective "right mix" of responses beyond what are believed to be given and insurmountable constraints. Yet all social constructs are malleable and dynamic. The altered power relations within and among states following the Cold War's demise have weakened some international and governmental institutions while strengthening others. In the realm of humanitarian action, these changes are reflected in the increased presence, funding, and authority of nongovernmental organizations, which may be in a position to better represent various peoples of the world in state or interstate forums where concerns of state-to-state relations are expressed and state-to-society relations ignored. If social constructs are flexible and we expect them to change over time, the question with regard to humanitarian action is, What can be done now to facilitate changes in social constructs favorable to a positive evolution in humanitarian norms and collective humanitarian action?

If states can be convinced that it is in their security and material interests, in addition to salving their consciences, to consider the full range of humanitarian and military responses to human tragedy (and some countries in some instances have), policy choices could become more pro-active, rather than reactive, when crises surface or, preferably, before they disrupt the social, political, and economic cohesion of communities, regions, and an interdependent world. If the United States, which is in the most influential position to take a new tack toward consistent and accountable involvement in humanitarian crises, continues to demonstrate ambivalence, another country or group of countries will rise to assume the mantle of leadership. The ideology of that new world leadership or hegemony will be synthesized into the current humanitarian idea and its codification and institutionalization. With or without the United States or the United Nations at the helm, the evolution of the humanitarian idea will proceed. The menu of policy choices is sufficiently stocked; imagination and will are required to discontinue the adoption of a wait-and-see strategy—processes of choice that have proved to be frequently distasteful and often counterproductive for those in need of assistance and those rendering it.

Without understanding sufficiently or choosing to ignore the actual political nature of humanitarian concerns in war, states and institutions are often making ill-suited choices. The nature of the humanitarian emergency and the responses presented by actors in the international humanitarian system must be logically compatible, not simply logistically achievable at minimum cost. For instance, if the problem is rampant genocide, is the appropriate response to begin long-term peace negotiations while doing nothing militarily to stop the slaughter, as was the case in Rwanda? If the problem is famine exacerbated by warlords fighting for political power while clan elders and women's groups attempt to construct a peaceful society through cooperation and consensus, is the appropriate response to negotiate and offer incentives only to the warlords, as occurred in Somalia? Although hindsight is always more accurate than foresight, nonetheless better contextualizations and analyses of the situations underlying acute dilemmas are the sine qua non for humanitarians at the dawn of the twenty-first century.

Particular policy choices are required to dismantle barriers to getting the mix of responses right. Asylum and preventive deployment must be supported, and the establishment of safe havens must be coupled with genuine military commitment to long-term protection. The actors in the international humanitarian system must determine how best to divide the labor and resources required in all phases of a humanitarian crisis, based on various institutions' strengths and weaknesses—in short, a better international division of labor, with minimal overlap and gaps. Those who commit crimes against humanity must harbor no doubt that once the conflict has ended, they will be prosecuted and punished. Local populations and institutions must be given a decision-making role in their own immediate and long-term needs through projects designed to relieve suffering and to foster development. Societies and donors within the great and medium powers must have their preferences altered through education and the media's coverage of silent and loud emergencies with equal vigor. And those conflicts that defy the concerted efforts of the international humanitarian system must be allowed to run their course once noncombatants have had the opportunity to leave the area and are guaranteed temporary security and sustenance in a country of asylum.

It would be misleading to suggest that the global safety net does not support a considerable number of war victims. The holes in the net and its constant shifting are a reality, however; and the fabric can be mended only by more thoughtful policymaking. Getting the mix right requires clarification of policy choices followed by expedient international implementation.

CLARIFYING POLICY CHOICES

Ironically, the word *policy* means a definite course of action adopted for the sake of prudence, in its first dictionary definition, and a method of gambling, in its second. The true meaning as it relates to humanitarian policymaking by the various actors in the system often vacillates somewhere between the two definitions. With sagacity and chance at opposite ends of the spectrum, the policy choices of the ICRC, with its strict principles and mandates, most probably lie closer to the former; the policy choices of governments, with unpredictable pressures from domestic politics, often lean toward the latter. When the major actors' own political considerations are calculated into humanitarian policy choices, the survival of war victims is sometimes gambled away on a strategy of hope. For example, after the bombing of Baghdad's water and sanitation infrastructure during the Gulf War and the imposition of economic sanctions, the governments of the coalition were hopeful that the United Nations and NGOs would ameliorate the humanitarian crisis that inevitably followed. In Bosnia, after three years of successive cycles of Bosnian Serb aggression against Muslim civilians, toothless NATO and U.N. retaliatory threats, followed by more brazen Serb aggression, hope appeared to be the only consistent strategy employed by the United Nations, NATO, and the contact group. In short, one policy choice of state actors has been to support relief work as an alternative to taking stronger political and military action. When diplomats and soldiers are reigned in, humanitarian efforts equate to doing something.

Apart from political and organizational considerations that may blur assessments of particular crises, what do the actors know to be broad truths about complex emergencies and humanitarian crises—truths that should guide future policy formation for the inevitable humanitarian crises to come? The truths of the post–Cold War era include an increase in the number and duration of complex emergencies. And inherent in complex emergencies are massive dislocations of peoples; death and human suffering; the destruction of economic, transportation, and communication infrastructure; and the collapse of a myriad of social and political institutions that bind communities together and buttress law and order locally, regionally, and internationally.

In part, these complex emergencies will continue because no viable and politically acceptable solutions have been found to deal with resource scarcity, political manipulations, and adaptive measures (of which conflict is one) of economically marginalized societies incapable of competing in the world market. Moreover, decreases in private investment and development assistance leave international crisis management as the sole predictable source for external material inputs and worldwide attention; as such, an incentive to engage in internal conflict often may be present and pertinent. Conflicts may also continue because they are profitable for certain merchants and justify the maintenance of troop levels and military budgets. There have been, for example, dramatic increases in sales of weapons from developed to developing or politically unstable countries since 1989 (41 percent of 1993 U.S. arms exports went to nondemocratic regimes), while some militaries develop and train for peacekeeping responses to justify their budgets. In addition, economic immigrants refused visas today, so they can find work and send remittances home, may very well be tomorrow's refugees refused asylum.

In some developing countries, remittances sent home by relatives working abroad are as important a source of foreign exchange as foreign aid. As immigration laws tighten in response to domestic factors such as limited resources, social unrest, and nationalist sentiments, remittances drop and survival mechanisms kick in, including violence and crime. Demands for international humanitarian assistance are therefore expected to rise. The breakdown of states and increase in humanitarian need are also rooted in privatization trends. Weak states can no longer depend upon state-to-state cooperation as a source of legitimacy, which frequently rests in a state's ability to provide social services. Without social services, local military forces become the preferred vehicle to distribute resources, and they do so by taking from other groups within the same society.

In sum, actors following and affecting world politics know that crises will appear, whether they are prepared to address them or not. What policy choices are available? Long-term development assistance, although it may appear to be *the* answer to all ills, is not a panacea for humanitarian problems, although more often than not economically satisfied countries have buffers to prevent them from imploding. Not all geographical areas are good candidates for sustainable development because in some locales the environment is not sufficiently life sustaining. Many people are affected by chronic famine resulting from the infertility of the soil and abusive climate conditions. Throwing development funds at unsustainable land is not appropriate.

The point being made in this wide-ranging introductory comment is that policies must reflect an accurate assessment of underlying reality. This has not always been the case. The following five policy choices facing the international community as a result of the mini- and larger dilemmas discussed in the previous chapter illustrate how and why. Suggestions about improvements follow in the final chapter.

A woman hangs her laundry at a camp for some of the estimated twenty-five thousand displaced from the fallen safe haven of Srebrenica. The barbed wire is to keep people from straying into mined areas. UNICEF/95-0538/Roger Lemoyne.

The Need to Choose Among Asylum, Preventive Deployment, and Safe Havens

Conflict strikes. People suffer and are uprooted. Asylum, preventive deployment, and safe havens are three policy choices that, if adopted and implemented, could save lives and reduce suffering and destruction at less expense to the international humanitarian system. The experience of the past few years, however, has been for state actors to adopt them arbitrarily and halfheartedly or in some cases to retreat from traditional behavior.

In the latter category, governments tend to view policy choices about **asylum** as an either/or, ad hoc decision and have in recent years tightened up both procedures and quotas. Either they broadly accept asylum-seekers, such as the U.S. policy of blanket acceptance toward Cubans (or to anyone escaping a communist country during the Cold War), or broadly reject them, such as the U.S. policy toward Haitians. There is, however, room to expand asylum options. Choices include the negotiation of agreements among several countries to share the burden of massive population movements of people in crisis so that one country does not bear the economic, social, and political brunt of accepting nonnationals. Additional alternatives to accepting asylum-seekers are to fully guarantee safety within designated safe areas or to financially compensate, in advance, third countries willing to host "guests" for a determined amount of time.

In the absence of thoughtful policy, we witness many countries with the means and political stability to host asylum-seekers hiding behind the narrowest possible interpretation of the conventional definition of refugee. Rising in tandem with the number of refugees seeking asylum are rising barriers and more stringently applied conditions for meeting asylum status—well publicized, for example, in Western Europe, but in fact increasingly prevalent as well in many developing countries. However, restrictions on accepting refugees does little to deter effectively those fleeing from persecution, as the rising tide of refugees demonstrates. States do not want refugees, and the number of refugees is expanding. This puts into question the long-term ability of international organizations to carry the burden for states, but without the means or autonomous authority.

Asylum-seekers themselves are responsible for the burden of proof upon which their application for admission to a conflict-free country is based—according to the language of the 1951 convention, upon the "credible" fear of persecution if returned to their native country. The precise meaning of credible is largely determined by the prospective host country and therefore allows for the political concerns, domestic and foreign, of the host country to bear upon acceptance of refugees. Thus, subjective judgments determine how many refugees are able to meet the criteria detailed in the 1967 protocol to the 1951 Convention Relating to the Status of Refugees.

Some policy choices rely upon outdated bureaucratic processes. The asylum process, unlike immigration laws, was designed to meet individual, not group, requests for protection. Because cases are reviewed on an individual basis in most developed and developing countries, backlogs of asylum applications are mounting. By the time Haitian refugees began to arrive on U.S. shores after the military overthrow of the democratically elected Aristide government, the Justice Department's Immigration and Naturalization Service already had a backlog of almost four hundred thousand applications.[2] Their treatment was quite unlike that of asylum-seekers from El Salvador and Guatemala in the mid- to late 1980s, who were permitted immediate entry and granted work permits while awaiting final determination of their asylum status. Haitian refugees were sent to safe haven third countries, such as Grenada and Antigua, or they were quickly sent back to Haiti.

Asylum is linked at least as much to foreign policy objectives and to domestic considerations (including xenophobia and a concern for cohesion and identity) as to humanitarian objectives and international conventions. Without a clear threat to state sovereignty or an overriding commitment to the notions of asylum and human solidarity, there does not appear to be any obvious national interest or economic advantage advanced by the acceptance of civilians fleeing war. Appeals to a history of accepting immigrants increasingly have a hollow ring in comparison with the more strident populist appeals of halting the flow of poor refugees thought to exacerbate inner-city ills and deprive native-born or already nationalized citizens of employment.

States are not obligated to grant refugees sanctuary if the state can identify a willing third country that will accept them. States that have signed the 1967 protocol to the 1951 convention are only informally required to provide a camp environment until the fear of persecution has subsided. Unfortunately for asylum-seekers, the increase in terrorism and the rise in right-wing groups have lumped together refugees, terrorists, immigrants, and all nonnationals in the minds of many citizens in potential host countries. Fearful people seeking refuge in fearful societies do not an optimistic scenario make. UNHCR data show a continual rise in asylum-seekers in Western Europe as a result of the collapse of the Soviet Union and the crisis in the Balkans and elsewhere in Eastern Europe: 420,000 refugees applied for asylum in 1991; 560,000 in 1992; and more than 400,000 in the first half of 1993 alone. Roughly 9 percent of asylum-seekers had their applications accepted. Even with a UNHCR budget increased to $1.5 billion for 1995, the UNHCR was ill-equipped to adequately safeguard those rejected for asylum.

The asylum debate has produced vastly different solutions to the same problem. Is asylum really needed if in-country protection can occur, including the construction of safe havens within the conflict areas? Can conditions be created to hasten the return back to the countries of origin for most refugees? Formal expansion of the UNHCR's mandate to include internally displaced persons and other casualties of wars would reduce the burden of responsibility and guilt upon the conscience of well-off developed countries. In addition to the UNHCR—whose staff has serious reservations about "diluting" the coverage of refugees by broadening it to include all victims of armed conflict—safe havens can be constructed and maintained multilaterally, as in northern Iraq, or even unilaterally by governments with an interest in the area, such as the French did for fleeing Hutus once the Rwandan Patriotic Front was strong enough to pursue those deemed responsible for the slaughter of thousands of Tutsis. Although the French have been criticized for their obvious bias toward the

Hutus, Opération Turquoise did act as an effective fire barrier to further human tragedy in the short run and to further refugee movements.

Another possible solution to refugee problems is to distribute refugees fairly among a number of countries so that one country alone does not have to bear the political, social, and economic burden of nonnationals. For such an option to be taken seriously, however, there also need to be more formal guidelines regarding the conditions upon which host countries accept refugees, as different states appear arbitrarily to place various conditions and time limits on the presence of nonnationals.

Although countries may be amenable to accepting refugees or willing to do so under duress, host country behavior should be carefully monitored to prevent abuse and manipulation of relief agencies. The presence of UNHCR operations caring for refugees as well as other war casualties may lead political authorities to manipulate the civil or military components of a humanitarian operation to further unacceptable political, economic, military, or criminal interests of their own, thereby narrowing the opportunities to provide relief to the suffering or even adding to such pain. It is obvious that negotiations continue in the country in conflict to bring about political and military stability. What may be less obvious is that diplomacy is also ongoing in refugee host countries to maintain an environment conducive to meeting the needs of the refugees.

Some argue that better early warning mechanisms would help mitigate humanitarian crises before they grow exponentially and require either asylum for refugees or safe havens for the internally displaced. Others counter that catastrophes in Rwanda, Somalia, and the former Yugoslavia did not take the intelligence or humanitarian communities by surprise. Rather than focus more time and resources on increased early warning mechanisms, rapid deployment capabilities and better coordination are more effective antidotes than better information.

Preventive deployment as a policy choice is seen as a potential stopgap between early warning and massive human tragedy. According to paragraph 28 of the secretary-general's oft-cited *An Agenda for Peace*, preventive deployment includes, but is not limited to, early posting of civilian, police, and/or military personnel to help stabilize political and social unrest within a country, along both sides of the border between disputing states, or on only one side of the border if only one government requests the presence of security personnel. A weakness in the secretary-general's interpretation of preventive deployment is caused by the United Nations' state-centric approach to crises—preventive deployment would require the consent of governments so as not to undermine state sovereignty. U.N. bias toward the consent of governments in effect legitimates them without considering that such an interlocutor does not necessarily reflect the will of society or that a functioning central government is a fiction.

The secretary-general steers clear of this particular issue by focusing his discussion of preventive deployment on interstate conflicts rather than the far more prevalent intrastate variety.

The early presence of military personnel in strategically important locations can assist in alleviating further disintegration of the political, social, economic, and cultural infrastructure necessary to sustain populations in the short and long term. They can encircle and protect hospitals; schools; energy, water, and sanitation sources; food and commercial production; and cultural properties that give meaning to the lives of noncombatants. Preventive military deployments serve a symbolic as well as deterring function by demonstrating the resolve and attentiveness of the international community. According to a recent internal guidebook, the UNHCR, for one, is optimistic that preventive deployment and early assistance to civil authorities after a cease-fire will accelerate the transition from crisis through stabilization and into reconstruction, rehabilitation, and development.[3]

However, in the absence of a cease-fire or of a central authority, what is to be done? Preventive deployment could be utilized without the consent of the warring parties if consensus is reached by regional powers choosing to deploy early for the sake of regional security. The Liberian civil war merits examination along these lines. The contested military presence by the troops of several members of ECOWAS, and particularly of Nigeria, provides interesting grist for preventive analytical mills. Scholars and practitioners are currently debating whether the military presence helped negotiations or prolonged the war.

If policymakers take a detour around preventive deployment, they eventually will be confronted with choosing between refugees camps crowded with asylum-seekers or havens within a war zone. If nothing is done to lower the rising barriers confronting asylum-seekers, the establishment of havens is, by default, the main policy alternative to building a wall around a country torn by war. Experience has shown a correlation between the deterioration of the concept and the loss of U.N. credibility. During the crises in the former Yugoslavia, the term *safe areas* was a travesty as Serb transgressions against them went largely unchecked for three and a half years before two of them (Srebrenica and Zepa) were overrun in 1995. Ironically, there was probably no place in the Balkans less safe than the safe areas. The so-called safe areas became "formerly known as safe areas." Unless safe areas are actually guaranteed security from outside aggression, refugees and internally displaced persons—the raw material for asylum-seekers—will continue to trouble the conscience and territorial boundaries of less troubled countries.

Efforts to strategize about the security of havens are becoming more visible. There have been signs that military units are trying to fashion an identity and a reliable response that were absent in the former Yugoslavia. In August 1995, military units from the United States, Great Britain, and Canada met at Fort Polk, Louisiana, to construct a possible NATO-peacekeeping scenario linked to the relief of large-scale human suffering. Such events are important to humanitarian intervention for two reasons. First, they demonstrate a commitment from militarily strong governments to the idea of developing contingencies for humanitarian intervention, even after the military debacle and governmental disagreements over the use of force evidenced in Bosnia and Somalia. Second, they represent another stage in the evolution of NATO as a security institution. Left without an agenda following the collapse of the Soviet Union, NATO countries are entertaining the thought of continued participation, as a collective security institution, in humanitarian action—a path begun by the late NATO secretary-general Manfred Wörner and continued by his successors Willy Claes and Javier Solana. In a February 1996 speech given in Munich, Solana identified IFOR, NATO's international coalition for peace in the former Yugoslavia, as the "first concrete expression of an integrated and cooperative approach to security in the new Europe."[4] With NATO's own reputation on the line, one can be assured that strategies to improve the security of safe areas are being brainstormed in military circles.

Danziger, © *Christian Science Monitor*.

It is difficult to imagine how the international humanitarian system would respond should another complex emergency arise that is as similar in context and geographical proximity to Western Europe as the one in the former Yugoslavia, particularly if tough policy choices are not made soon to address straightforwardly the problems associated with asylum, preventive deployment, and the security of safe areas. Interested eyes should look to Burundi, a troubled country currently sending out early warning signals to the international humanitarian system. In October 1995, after two and a half years of internal unrest, two hundred thousand Burundis became refugees, many of whom were women, young children, and the elderly fleeing attacks by security forces and armed opposition groups. An additional four hundred thousand Burundis were internally displaced. An estimated hundred thousand have died. To many, Burundi is perched on the brink of a tragedy to rival the horror of neighboring Rwanda, while the international humanitarian system watches.

Improvement in the Division of Labor

Even thoughtful policy decisions can be rendered ineffective if the institutional constructs that implement them are inept or inefficient. Most international humanitarian actors are aware of the tasks that they perform best and those in which they are weak. Some agencies focus entirely upon distributing food, while others concentrate on conflict prevention and still others on conflict resolution. Some are well respected for their work in highly volatile environments, such as the ICRC, while others are better known for their development work once cease-fires have been reached, such as Oxfam. Strengths and weaknesses also may vary during different phases of a crisis. These factors should be considered in the formulation of a comprehensive strategy for noncombatants and the division of the labor and resources of various actors accordingly. Even staff culture and internal regulations are important. For example, because of insurance coverage, U.N. relief personnel can be forced to evacuate an area, while other agencies' personnel are able to stay with victims throughout a crisis.

Included in a comprehensive strategy should also be mechanisms for monitoring the effectiveness of actors' contributions. Transparency is important for determining whether a perceived strength of an actor actually exists in practice as much as it does in theory. For instance, development organizations, which normally are present in a country, enjoy long-standing relationships with governments and local groups, and have an informed view about local culture and social relations, would seem to possess a comparative advantage as the "eyes and ears" of the international humanitarian system for collecting and reporting human rights abuses before they burst into full-blown crises. Yet prior to the massive wave of genocide that swept over Rwanda, development documentation in the form of mission reports, country development strategies, sector analyses, and plans of action from donor agencies (such as USAID and the Belgian and Swiss development cooperation agencies), from U.N. agencies (such as the UNDP and FAO), and from the World Bank made virtually no reference to ethnic tensions. Instead, development specialists gave glowing reports of Rwanda's improved infrastructure and economic growth per capita. The early violence and ethnic tension leading up to the slaughter were glossed over, perhaps so as not to undermine the working assumption among professionals that development is social progress and will eventually calm whatever social tension exists.[5]

An appropriate division of labor of humanitarian activities that begins with early warning activities must take into consideration the organizational agendas of each actor and how they constrain field personnel. Although development personnel may have the greatest opportunity and apparent capacity to report human rights abuses and political instability, their doing so could result in decreased funding to their agencies or their eviction from an area and cessation of their development programs. Hence, they are unlikely to be in the forefront of such denunciations.

A possible solution to this challenge may lie in expanding the role of those actors whose primary purpose is simply to supply food and medical equipment to civilians caught in a conflict. Those who deliver emergency aid could also serve as the eyes and ears of the international humanitarian system regarding human rights violations. It may be possible for those in the field to pass on information regarding human rights abuses to an actor designated as the one to expose belligerents guilty of abusing individual human rights without jeopardizing the physical welfare of the civilian population at large. ICRC personnel were forced out of Iran in 1992 for allegedly sharing with human rights groups information gathered during their relief activities. The release of a joint communiqué outlining human rights violations is a possible tactic to protect the eyes and ears in the field under the cover of a consortium of agencies while continuing to serve suffering populations, unimpeded by political backlashes.

The challenge is expanded once again if there is no follow-up action to exposed violations; if war criminals are not held accountable after their deeds are exposed, the credibility of humanitarian action is further weakened. The argument for allowing the politics of making peace to take priority over the pursuit of justice is clear, yet not readily defensible: If there are a number of factions fighting, it is strategically important to strengthen the legitimacy of certain faction leaders so that those leaders are able to "deliver" armed followers at the negotiating table. Given this scenario, no matter how atrocious the actions by belligerents toward civilians, realistic politics dictates that war crime charges be dropped even in the face of international law and moral reasoning. As mentioned earlier, the cases of Bosnian Serbs and Rwandan Hutus accused of war crimes will be critical for an understanding of the international priorities among the trade-offs of providing emergency relief, protecting human rights, and pursuing a politics of peace.

When preventive deployment has not been entirely successful in halting increased escalation of human suffering, the second best alternative is a quick and thorough response to the crisis. Here a different division of labor is required, one that includes institutions with similar skills and profiles, perhaps with responsibilities assigned by sector or by geographical area. Alleged bureaucratic incompetence and infighting within the U.N. system, multiple NGOs on the ground performing overlapping functions, and the military tendency to engulf an operation without consideration of formerly established networks of cooperation have contributed to the paradoxical combination of turf-battling, on the one hand, and gaps in the negotiation and delivery of humanitarian assistance, on the other.

In fact, how much of the rapid increase in relief expenditure is due to inefficiencies and rising administrative costs is not clear. Having literally hundreds of subcontractors delivering similar goods and services in a disjointed and competitive fashion during the chaotic conditions of civil war necessarily means that part of the dramatic growth in resources devoted to complex emergencies is driven by humanitarian agencies themselves. The result is the inability of the international humanitarian system to respond as quickly and effectively as it could and should to some complex emergencies. Potential solutions to this problem include the adaptation of the economic concepts of a **division of labor** and **comparative advantage** to the realm of humanitarian assistance.

The term *division of labor* was coined by Adam Smith, founder of classical political economy, in his 1776 *An Inquiry into the Nature and Causes of the Wealth of Nations.* Applied to humanitarian action, the term implies that each actor should assume a specialized functional role toward a common objective. Through specialization, actors should become more experienced in their roles and therefore better able to respond quickly, almost automatically, to crises as they erupt. The international humanitarian system would thereby become more efficient.

There are two problems with transferring the idea of a division of labor from the economic to the humanitarian realm. The first is associated with identifying a common objective. Actors must be convinced that what they believe to be their primary objective—peace settlement and cease-fires, relief distribution, reconstruction, and development—are part of a higher common objective, that being the long-term viability and prosperity of a community of people. In business, the common objective as well as decisions regarding the distribution of functions is determined largely by the factory owner or shareholders. There is little room for those performing the functions to debate the leadership. In the international humanitarian system, in contrast, there is no agreement among the various actors as to who the legitimate leader is or should be and who decides what function each actor will perform.

The second problem is one that continually plagues the humanitarian system. For a division of labor to be effective, resources have to be allocated efficiently among actors so that they can perform their functional role while other actors are simultaneously fulfilling theirs. In a better world, the UNHCR would expand its formal mandate to include the protection of all casualties of war, while government mediators or contact groups focused on negotiating a cease-fire, the UNDP began a development project in an unaffected area, and U.N. military forces ensured secure access. However, if the necessary resources are not made available to the UNHCR or donors insist on tying contributions to assistance rather than to protection, then the actor cannot be efficient in its assigned task and the collective humanitarian peace operation suffers. If governments are unable to negotiate, or have hidden agendas that prevent them from doing so, the collective effort fails. If the UNDP has unqualified staff or is poorly placed because there is an alternate source of bureaucratic power, the collective effort falters. If U.N. soldiers are equipped for peacekeeping when peace enforcement is required, the collective effort stalls.

Moreover, organizational imperatives for fund-raising and turf-building place barriers in the way of a comprehensive division of labor. Because private donors as well as governments often transmit their own agendas by tying their contributions to NGOs, the functions that particular NGOs perform may overlap with those of other NGOs. Governments are particularly prone to want their contributions clearly recognized, and the penchant for flag-waving works against a more rational coverage of sectors and areas of a country in distress. A population in need may find itself with dozens of NGOs distributing food and clothing but not one with funds earmarked for what are deemed less immediate requirements, such as rebuilding a sewage system. Efficiency is lost, along with the integrity and credibility of the international humanitarian system or, at a minimum, of the particular agency that does not seem able to achieve its mandate.

Classical comparative advantage theory applies to the division of labor. It incorporates notions of specialization and efficiency maximization with considerations of each actor's comparatively better resources and inherent qualities that make it more suited for particular tasks. For mutually advantageous cooperation to occur, arrangements among actors must provide incentives for actors to achieve efficiency. The United States is thought to wield a comparative advantage in leadership, which stems in part from its military and economic strength. The ICRC is believed to have a comparative advantage in accessing political prisoners and negotiating with belligerents. NGOs are supposed to possess a comparative advantage in reaching and networking with local grassroots groups. The military is reputed to have a comparative advantage not only with its means of coercion but also with certain kinds of technical and logistic expertise in insecure situations. The United Nations is supposed to be neutral and well placed to orchestrate efforts without hidden agendas.

If each actor can do what it does best given its resources and learned skills, then a rapid and efficient response is more likely to occur. The efficiency of a true "system" of international humanitarian action would reduce each actor's present costs by diminishing overlapping functions, filling in logistical gaps, and reducing the cost of information gathering and resource mobilization. Communication among actors could be established through liaison offices. For example, some military units have already demonstrated the strength of the notion of comparative advantage with respect to liaison communications. The desire to increase transparency and coordination of action among civilian and military actors has led to the creation of Civil-Military Operations Centres (CMOCS) within military headquarters. At CMOCS, civilian agencies can gather information, become more familiar and comfortable with military structures of command, and request military assistance for various phases of a relief operation.

As the previous cases have undoubtedly made clear, the so-called advantages of the actors listed earlier have not always been present in post–Cold War crises. One problem in putting the theory of comparative advantage into practice in the realm of humanitarian action is the lack of concrete incentives to cooperate in joint endeavors. In spite of recent efforts to alter the pattern of sticks and carrots for cooperation through the establishment of the Inter-Agency Standing Committee and the new Central Emergency Revolving Fund, existing organizational structures provide more of an incentive to continue with business as usual than to submit to a bottom-line litmus test for their successes or failures. In economics, if an actor is not efficient in producing results, it is replaced by another actor that can. Some critics might argue that the historical division of labor within the United Nations, for example, has not been economically or functionally efficient and that it should therefore be disbanded. Although the fifty-year history of the United Nations is filled with countless proposals and recommendations to reform aspects of its security, humanitarian, and development divisions, there has been little evidence of actual implementation of reform suggestions.

As discussed, in 1992 the Department of Humanitarian Affairs was created as a coordinating mechanism for U.N. humanitarian activities, specifically to overcome the problems encountered in the Gulf War. It was supposed to garner support for humanitarian action from the Security Council, the secretary-general, and people in positions of power and authority. The United Nations has often assigned a lead agency to act as a coordinating body in the field (UNICEF in the Sudan, the UNHCR in the former Yugoslavia) or relied on ad hoc coordinating mechanisms. These fuzzy concepts gloss over the fact that each U.N. body is autonomous and independent from the other agencies in the system, although in a particular crisis one of them is supposed to function less as a feudal baron than as a leader of a confederation.

Although the DHA, a lead agency, or the secretary-general may make recommendations for the involvement of other U.N. organizations in a particular fashion, the latter cannot be cajoled into participating in a humanitarian action in a particular manner if they choose not to, regardless of their strengths and weaknesses. A lead agency, in theory, acts as a focal point for information and coordination for all actors in an area. Sometimes the lead agency is chosen because of its comparative advantage in a particular substantive area, at other times because of field personnel already in-area at the time the crisis exploded or of the reputation of the executive head. There are no rules, regulations, or standard operating procedures for a lead agency. Moreover, past experience has shown that the ability of a lead agency to acquire a "following" varies substantially; much has depended upon individual personalities.

For a true division of labor to occur in a humanitarian crisis, actors must agree upon appropriate actions, assignment of tasks to reach objectives, and leadership. A more hierarchical arrangement of authority— over funds, functions, personnel—must exist. In particular, the international humanitarian system must manage cooperation, or at least ensure orchestration, among the various actors to achieve seven common challenges resulting from human need during complex emergencies: assessing the severity of a particular crisis, negotiating access to affected populations, mobilizing human and financial resources, delivering services, ensuring coordination, pursuing education and advocacy activities, and looking beyond the emergency. Cynicism abounds when the United Nations cannot achieve cooperation and efficiency within its own system. In such light, the chances that the international humanitarian system as a whole will improve significantly under U.N. leadership are considered nominal.

What has been labeled **donor fatigue**—a stagnation or reduction in resources and interests believed to be due to weary, overwhelmed donors—in truth may stem from a "lack-of-efficiency fatigue." Analogous to the weariness about substantial domestic welfare spending without commensurate results, donor governments have started bypassing public intergovernmental bureaucracies and are working more directly with NGOs on a contract basis to get a better buy for their dollar or yen. NGOs have picked up on the value that governments assign to efficiency and have become more market oriented and bottom-line directed to win government as well as U.N. bids. If an NGO does not "deliver" what it outlined in its proposal, its contract will not be renewed and a presumably more efficient NGO will assume control of the project.

Interestingly, we now return to an earlier debate concerning victim-oriented versus market-oriented humanitarian action. By focusing on the bottom line, NGOs must spend considerable and increasing time quantifying results to prove success—the number of tons of grain delivered, the number of tents erected—rather than on the extent to which inputs have had any significant impact on victims, a far more difficult analytical task. Policy decisions that focus on cost efficiency and comparative advantage may save money without saving lives.

Those organizations whose objectives are more single-minded have a comparative advantage in situations that demand impartiality and neutrality. The ICRC and NGOs with strict humanitarian agendas are less constrained in their actions and negotiations with local authorities than are organizations with multiple agendas, such as the United Nations, external governments, security coalitions, and regional organizations. In the case of Iraq, for instance, U.N. agencies such as UNICEF had to wait for permission from the Security Council's sanction committee before releasing needed humanitarian aid. Conversely, the ICRC notified the committee of items being transferred to Iraq but did not wait for the committee's permission before sending them on to those in desperate need of relief. Ironically, the actors most often excluded from discussions of divisions of labor are the ones that have the strongest comparative advantage when it comes to understanding the needs of the suffering population and the strongest incentive to cooperate—local populations themselves.

A local woman feeds women and children at a refugee feeding center run by French NGO Action Internationale Contre la Faim, which is partially financed by UNICEF. UNICEF/94-1004/Betty Press.

Empowerment of Local Populations and Building of Institutions

As argued earlier, development assistance is dwindling, and more and more of it is devoted to emergencies rather than to investments in a self-sustaining future. Interestingly, some development NGOs are countering the drop in government and U.N. funding with appeals to businesses interested in promoting a benevolent company image. For example, *Food and Wine Magazine* contains a glossy spread that advertises, "In partnership with CARE, the international relief organization, Starbucks® coffee is helping bring clean water to Guatemala through funding of the Rural Water and Health Project." Other development NGOs are less fortunate in their search for funding at the same time that demand for assistance is increasing as a result of human-made catastrophes. The challenge of rebuilding war-torn societies is immense—transforming the security environment, strengthening local administrative capacities, reconstructing political processes, reconstructing the economy, and building local social fabric.

Given limited resources and virtually unlimited demands for multilateral help, the most pressing and doable assignment in front of policymakers would appear to be the transformation of the security environment.

This is also the arena where previous peacekeeping principles and some recent experience (especially in Rhodesia and El Salvador and perhaps also in Namibia and Cambodia) are pertinent. Disarmament, demobilization, and reintegration of regular and irregular troops, although costly, are urgent assignments at the end or near-end of every armed conflict. The demobilization in Nicaragua cost some $2,000 per soldier, or $44 million total; Zimbabwean demobilization cost $3,000 per soldier, or approximately $230 million. Yet however costly, these tasks constitute a prerequisite for any meaningful rehabilitation and development efforts. And they should be the priority of multilateral efforts, building upon the new generation of multifunctional operations involving unprecedented intrusion into domestic affairs.

In a related and potentially crucial step, it should also be possible to associate more closely the Washington-based financial institutions with demobilization schemes. The disconnect between U.N. efforts and those of the World Bank and the International Monetary Fund have been striking in Rwanda and El Salvador, for instance. The World Bank was unwilling to release development funds to the new Tutsi-led Rwandan government until the emergency situation subsided. However, the government needed those funds to bring about political and social stability as well as to bring refugees back from Zaire, Burundi, and Tanzania and to begin war crimes trials. In both El Salvador and Nicaragua, a similar situation occurred when the parties to conflicts had agreed to a particular peace package under U.N. auspices, while the IMF and the World Bank pursued separately a reconstruction and development program. Unfortunately, the U.N. peace process that ended the emergency crisis was then, in the view of the principal negotiator, Alvaro de Soto, on a "collision course" with reconstruction and development.[6] A possible solution for bridging similar gaps between emergency aid and development and reconstruction efforts might be to include the IMF and World Bank in settlement negotiations among belligerents. The Washington-based institutions are autonomous and, in spite of organigrams in textbooks, not really part of the so-called U.N. system. But they are clearly a critical component, probably the most essential one at the multilateral level, of the international community's arsenal to move beyond humanitarian relief in war zones.

The World Bank, the IMF, and other lending or assistance institutions should consider involvement even while armed conflicts are raging. Political instability often has roots in resource scarcity. An infusion of confidence into local efforts by international financial institutions, particularly in stable regions of a country in conflict, may assist in reducing violence there and elsewhere. Wars require soldiers and militia. Empowering local communities during a conflict may provide incentives for soldiers to considering dropping their swords and returning to their plowshares.

Whatever else the secretary-general implied in 1992 when he wrote of an "integrated approach to human security" in *An Agenda for Peace*, intergovernmental organizations' decisionmakers working on demobilization as a prelude to sustainable development and those working on longer-run development should work in tandem rather than at cross-purposes. Institutional changes—for instance, involving the IMF and the World Bank in peace negotiations from the outset rather than after the fact and creating a unified U.N. presence, rather than multiple sources of authority, in postconflict countries—are required to make the most of multilateral action.

In addition to this type of closer association, there is a need for more conceptual work. How can emergency inputs be conceptualized so that they include a greater consideration of capacity-building for societies in crisis? Pioneers in this area have been Mary Anderson and Peter Woodrow, whose efforts have become a cornerstone in an alternative analytical edifice to reconceptualize humanitarian help.[7] Humanitarian delivery and protection should obviously strive to be as cost-effective as possible in the mitigation of suffering. However, as war and conflict are rooted in underlying problems of poverty and powerlessness, humanitarian action—even in the eye of the storm, literally for natural disasters and figuratively for human-made ones when the bullets are flying—should also improve the medium- and longer-term prospects for sustainable development and peace. At a minimum, humanitarian action should do no harm—that is, not undermine or needlessly delay those prospects. In short, the challenge is to conceive emergency inputs so that they maximize the programmatic ways that will help a society care for itself once the natural or human-made catastrophe has passed.

This approach has begun to permeate the rhetoric and sometimes the reality of emergency relief policies. The conventional trade-off between immediate and effective relief and slower and more problematic development and peace is unclear and probably artificial. The more valid and sensible approach is to visualize a continuum of actions from relief through to development and peace. However attractive in theory, case studies of successful experiments are scarce and, in any case, do not yet provide an adequate basis for general theory-building or operational guidelines. Moreover, there is also considerable debate among experts about whether the linear depiction in the alternative model (that is, in the notion of a continuum) of relief from reconstruction to rehabilitation to development is "conceptually wrong and operationally misleading."[8]

The concept of a continuum from relief to development is straightforward. Its underlying premise is the concomitant necessity for emergency inputs to serve longer-term objectives or, at a minimum, to do no harm to local coping capacities. The problems that constrain choices along the relief-to-development continuum are that resources are limited, donors prefer loud emergencies, relief agencies emphasize delivery of assistance rather than locals' empowerment, and the media focus on outsiders helping "victims" rather than insiders taking charge of their own future. The concept of a continuum is misleading in that there are no distinct points in time when emergency relief has stopped and rehabilitation, reconstruction, and development have begun. Getting beyond a philosophical commitment to do no harm and to maximize local participation requires conceiving a more organic framework of such external assistance and how it fits with a local system with complex feedback loops. Again, the need for conceptualization and applied research is obvious.

What this all comes down to is asking the following question: What policies would support communities under stress so that the period of their dependency on external assistance is short and the social, economic, and political recoveries are longer lasting? Is it enough to save lives if nothing is done to save livelihoods and lessen vulnerability through rehabilitation and development efforts? How can an interactive dialogue begin between the international humanitarian system and its "clients"? Given that certain funds are fungible and can be distributed as seen fit by policymakers and donors, are there institutional or political barriers to incorporating the brain and brawn of local populations in the relief-to-development continuum?

If we glance back at the five humanitarian crises outlined in Chapter 2, the case of Central America stands out because local populations and institutions played an active role in their own recovery, along the entire continuum from relief to development and in the democratization and nation-healing processes. In short, and to use the latest conceptual jargon, these persons were "empowered"; as the UNDP's *Human Development Report* contended: "Development must be *by* people, not only *for* them. People must participate fully in the decisions and processes that shape their lives."[9] In Guatemala, El Salvador, and Nicaragua, the myth of apolitical humanitarian assistance did not prevail, and the concept of noncombatant remained a difficult one to pin down. Religious groups and many NGOs with strong biases toward a particular population took great pains to organize and educate noncombatants. Their humanitarian efforts were undeniably political. In Nicaragua after the Sandinista government lost the elections, for example, a considerable number of pro-Sandinista NGOs left the area, just as they had come when the Sandinistas had triumphed over the Somoza regime. In a related fashion, during the conflict between the Sandinista government and the contras, the U.S. government based its humanitarian assistance on its own political agenda. There was very limited space for U.N. agencies and their nonpolitical or neutral application of humanitarian assistance until after peace had found its way to the region.

Empowerment of local populations requires that policymakers choose the side of the victims. Regardless of political or apolitical principles, empowerment of populations is a highly political process. When empowerment is the objective, traditional intrasocietal relations may experience the repercussions and be subject to debate among cultural relativists. For instance, if the culture being assisted ignores the human rights of women, can the international humanitarian system be true to international humanitarian law if it does not ignore local mores and empower women?

Women in camps for refugees and the internally displaced are frequently ignored if there are cultural constructions of gender roles and concepts of authority that subordinate women, even though women and their children represent the majority in encampments. An efficiency argument can be made in support of organizations that override these cultural norms. Studies have found that when women are given a role in food distribution, there is a more equitable distribution throughout the community than if males are given the responsibility. The UNHCR's own Guidelines on the Protection of Refugee Women, adopted in 1991, specify that women should be considered the first point of control for distribution of food and other goods. Ignoring in practice what is known in theory has contributed to the high death rates and levels of malnutrition among refugee and internally displaced populations and the leakage of aid to black markets.[10] Empowering populations may mean ignoring tradition or being intolerant of local culture for the sake of effectiveness and justice.

Empowerment can take a number of forms. In northern Iraq, the protective shield placed around the Iraqi Kurds enabled them to begin the process of nation-building, which they have begun intermittently since earlier in the century, but now with less fear of persecution. Protecting a persecuted minority is certainly one way to empower them. Rwanda presented little opportunity to empower local populations during the rage that swept the country in spring 1994. However, once the Rwandan Patriotic Front assumed control of the government, the World Bank and other financial institutions had an opportunity to contribute to the empowerment of state institutions in Kigali by disbursing reconstruction funds, but these institutions did not.

The majority of humanitarian emergencies discussed in this book occurred among largely agrarian populations with distinctly different social structures for cooperation and vastly different forms of individual and collective identity. Attempts to empower local institutions and people must be tailored to the social, economic, and political constructs of a society rather than applied in one-size-fits-all relief and development packages. Traditional hierarchies of power cannot be dismissed as channels for relief distribution simply because they do not conform to "modern" constructs. The viewpoint that tribal relations are primitive and must be eradicated through the adoption of a democratic political system is inappropriate in many instances. Moreover, it stands in the way of designing a relief-to-development strategy for vulnerable groups that can be incorporated easily into existing institutions that provide meaning, in addition to physical sustenance, to their lives.

It can be argued that channels for empowering local institutions are bypassed largely because they are least understood, not because they would be ineffective. A failed state presents grounds for highly intrusive outside intervention and may present an exceptional challenge. But a state that does not have a Western-looking institution for societal leadership is not necessarily lacking consensus on leadership in some other form, such as in Somalia. As pointed out on several occasions, those who hold a monopoly of force and are in a position to exercise unabashed violence on their own people are too readily acknowledged by Western institutions to be the rightful heirs to state leadership.

Regional institutions are another important and underexploited factor for maintaining peace and security within states and for responding to humanitarian crises. Whereas other international actors tend to apply to a variety of cases a model of procedures that have been used elsewhere with relative success, regional institutions are more familiar with local culture and traditions that may require a custom-designed approach to assistance and diplomacy. For example, African traditions of conflict management include the use of elders to mediate and reconcile differences.

Chapter VIII of the U.N. Charter allows for regional arrangements deemed necessary to restore stability. Incentives for regional involvement are strong. The flow of refugees into neighboring countries is usually economically unsettling and can bring about or exacerbate preexisting social unrest. Wars disrupt normal patterns of trade, which can be distorted further once economic sanctions are imposed. Personal contacts among regional leaders are usually intense, if not always warm. Shortcomings of regional collective action include the fact that regional blocs of power and influence routinely require a regional hegemonic power to lead a collective response to political and social instability and to respond to humanitarian needs. However, a regional "anchor" with the backing and monitoring of the international community may be well placed to spearhead regional military, diplomatic, or even humanitarian efforts.

It is and will continue to be difficult to buttress the local welfare system of a state and society during and after a crisis without creating dependency, a theme that has repeatedly entered this analysis. One way for the international humanitarian system to disengage from assistance along the relief-to-development continuum with minimal dislocations for those who have leaned on the humanitarian system during a crisis is to engage as far as possible local populations and institutions from the outset of a crisis. One could argue that a humanitarian system is functioning best when its presence is least obvious; when the population and its familiar institutions are clearly engaged in working toward a stable future without an overwhelming presence of expatriate personnel.

Empowering local individuals and groups represents a danger in that humanitarians work toward making political decisions that will affect the long-term viability and cohesiveness of a society. There are inherently political ramifications in this because some groups will receive assistance, while others will not. Local conflicts can be exacerbated through the injection of external personnel and funding into resource-scarce environments. Competition for outside resources arises, internal resources can be directed more toward war than toward the welfare of noncombatants, local economic activities can be distorted, and warring regimes can be legitimized by association with the international humanitarian system.

However, finding appropriate policy to empower local groups may be the only way to ensure that material inputs of humanitarian assistance reach their targets. In an effort to get the mix of strategies right, there has been an increased focus on integrating development strategies with humanitarian mandates. But some scholars argue that the process by which the relief-to-development continuum is structured carries with it another set of problems. So long as relief agencies, contracted to distribute certain inputs—such as water, doctors, and instructional kits—succeed in that distribution process, and so long as the target number of health care providers and teachers has been deployed, there is a tendency to consider an operation successful. Whether or not the mandates of various organizations have been achieved or victims helped in their struggle to gain control over their future lives may be inconsequential.

All too often, in implementing such a process, however, the humanitarian system considers victims objects of assistance. The process of delivering humanitarian assistance has in some instances taken priority over the objective of making civilians self-sustaining as soon as possible. Providers can ignore whether the application of material inputs is making any substantial difference in alleviating human suffering or empowering parties to assume full responsibility for the welfare of society and peace in the region. Working with, rather than for, victims of war automatically injects an element of accountability into relief programs. It also forces victims to eventually take full responsibility for their own recovery and coexistence with former enemies. U.N. peacekeepers have kept watch over Cyprus since 1964. Governments such as Canada, which has provided troops since the outset, are increasingly asking, How much responsibility for peaceful existence have the parties to the conflict been forced to assume?

Not all humanitarian actors agree that consideration must be given to empowering local groups at the outset of a relief operation when the sense of urgency is most pronounced. As one U.S. aid official remarked about the exigencies of mass starvation in Somalia, "We're rightly indifferent to people's cultural needs and to appropriateness issues."[11] Others would argue vehemently with the official that vulnerable populations require a sense of empowerment and participation in decisionmaking about their situation at the beginning of a crisis, before dependency, complacency, and hopelessness set in. Research suggests that the most successful operations are those that attempt to incorporate local populations and institutions early on, which is why the merits of the Central American case are so salient.

Before we leave this discussion, it's important to take a critical look at why relief agencies sometimes choose policies that do not empower local populations to deal with future crises. Would the recruitment and training of local authorities have caused an unreasonable delay in the delivery of humanitarian aid, or did the expatriate relief staff avoid a cooperative expatriate-local relief effort owing to expatriate cultural biases against locals? How real is the problem of "can-do" expatriates from a developed country treating locals as if they were incapable of contributing anything of value to expatriates' projects? If this bias truly exists, the problem can only get worse because the majority of staff members of the international humanitarian system are Western, while those they are assisting are not. Increasingly, those populations requiring considerable humanitarian relief are Muslim.

Conversely, a more active disempowering policy occurs when outside institutions contribute to the "brain drain" of a country by hiring local professionals and encouraging their departure from government and the private sector, where their wages and benefits can be far less than in relatively well-heeled Western-financed aid projects; nowhere is this risk greater than in war-torn countries. Again, there are few easy answers. When emergency relief is urgently required, providers often claim that there is no time to establish working relations with locals or that they are not qualified, which is sometimes true, particularly in failed states where many professionals have been executed or have gone into exile. At the same time, when local staff are hired away from local institutions, they may never return, or, alternatively, the local economy may become overly dependent upon infusions of assistance and foreign exchange.

Empowerment policies themselves, therefore, clearly are not dilemma-free. There are ethical and operational problems associated with every choice. The care of children presents the humanitarian system with a painful dilemma: choosing between taking full responsibility for providing food and shelter for the young and giving the resources to the community with the expectation that the interests of this most vulnerable group will be met. Relief agencies are quick to respond to the needs of children and adolescents in crisis—a stratum of society that usually accounts for 50 to 65 percent of displaced populations. Orphanages and temporary care facilities are erected immediately following, if not before, a crisis explodes into physical violence. For those populations that have spent their lifetime in absolute poverty, the advent of a heightened state of emergency can lead some households to turn over the care of the young right away and for prolonged periods. The dilemma is either to establish orphanages and camps that address the needs of children separate from their families or to empower families and communities with the hope that the children will benefit. If the international humanitarian system takes full responsibility for the care of children, it can disconnect the community from its own obligations, thereby contributing to increased fragmentation of community and family life. Moreover, some countries in crisis have cultures whose values subordinate the nourishment of children and women to the needs of males, even though the children and pregnant or lactating women have greater nutritional needs. If the humanitarian system does not continue to support the needs of children directly, their suffering may remain acute.

Another important issue confronting efforts to empower local capacities to assist in their own relief efforts, but one that is frequently ignored, is first to guarantee the personal security of females within refugee camps and encampments for the internally displaced. Women cannot be empowered if they are not freed from fear of the sexual violence that occurs too frequently when they are dislocated from their homes and families and forced to exist in relatively lawless environments. The substantial number of rapes by other refugees and security personnel in Somali refugee camps in Kenya in 1993 brought this issue to light. A refugee camp can be a dangerous place for women and girls, who become victims of sexual exploitation by camp members, border guards, camp officials, police officers, and military personnel. Women cannot be empowered during the day by relief and development programs and then disempowered at night by sexual violence.

Conflict Management

There are at least two rational reasons for decisionmakers not to choose coercive military intervention for a humanitarian crisis. One is that a mil-

Somali citizens welcome the arrival of U.S. soldiers at Mogadishu. U.N. Photo/159819.

itary presence can heighten the violence toward relief personnel or obstruct, rather than assist, the delivery of emergency relief. The other is that there is often only halfhearted support for a military presence in the post–Cold War era of no-casualty foreign policy when substantial geopolitical interests are absent or perceived to be by the electorate.

It is undeniable that the presence of coercive external military force can stoke the fire of an already violent conflict. Because military force and other coercive instruments of Chapter VII, such as economic sanctions, point an accusatory finger at one of the warring parties, defensive nationalist sentiments may be aroused. Negotiations among belligerents may stall or be postponed.

One of the most articulate critics of the "new interventionists" is Stephen Stedman from Johns Hopkins University. Because the potential number of possible cases for intervention far outstrip available resources, "only a combination of coherent strategy, sufficient leverage and a keen sense of timing will allow a third party to bring peace." He saw very few such cases arising; and without sufficient national interests involved in a crisis, it is foolish to intervene since the credibility of both the United Nations and the United States will suffer along with the victims. In short, "humanitarian concerns are not enough."[12]

Stedman was skeptical enough about intervention but even more negative about the prospects for acting earlier through preventive deployment to impede violence from erupting in the first place. He compared some naive foreign policy analysts to "alchemists" who are searching for miraculous solutions to civil wars whose risks and costs as well as feasibility are vastly understated. Calling into question the "idea that early intervention can prevent civil war, state collapse, and attendant humanitarian tragedies," Stedman saw "little basis for optimism in the ability of social science to precisely forecast the outbreak of violent domestic conflicts" or in the political ability to mobilize "appropriate responses to incipient violence."[13]

This part of the policy debate turns on the costs and benefits of a particular use of military force. This means that, in principle, intervention would still be possible and desirable should the threats to international peace and security (and U.S. interests, if Washington is to participate) be great enough or the potential risks low enough. Presumably, northern Iraq qualified under the first category and Haiti under the second. Public debate about sending twenty thousand U.S. troops to enforce the peace in Bosnia demonstrated a mixture of the two.

But an even more fundamental criticism is that humanitarian military intervention is undesirable because it simply puts off until later the local reckoning that must occur. If there had been a United Nations in the nineteenth century, according to this reasoning, it would have been inadvisable to prevent the slaughter at Gettysburg and elsewhere because it would only have postponed the inevitable bloody clash between North and South. Similarly, it would have been better and ultimately less lethal to have permitted Charles Taylor to have assumed power quickly in Liberia in 1991 rather than for ECOWAS to have intervened, or for the RPF to have quickly overrun all of Rwanda rather than for the French to have shielded Hutu war criminals.

From the point of view of this book, there is clearly a growing requirement to employ military might to help quell ethnic violence, create humanitarian space, and protect fundamental human rights. Yet it is undeniable that political pressures at present point toward skimping on humanitarian intervention. The critics are correct that international intervention in such civil wars as Somalia and Bosnia is messy and should be timely and robust or shunned altogether. If there is inadequate commitment to stay the course, it is better not to begin.

But it is important not to ignore the fact that military force made, and continues to make, a difference in northern Iraq, as it did in Rwanda by the French and in Haiti by the Americans. After almost four agonizing years in Bosnia, the combination of Croatian and NATO efforts shed light on the value of a paper humanitarian tiger. The old adage about

Rwandan boys perform a "psychodrama" to act out the killings they witnessed, part of a trauma treatment. Some 90 percent of surveyed Rwandan children witnessed the murder of a parent or an acquaintance. This type of treatment is often underfunded as it may fall under the category of a silent emergency. UNICEF/ 94-0588/Betty Press.

diplomacy without force being meaningless has been learned anew. With or without military protection, some international organizations and the ICRC will no doubt continue to send relief personnel into harm's way to offer assistance while waiting for the parties to exhaust themselves or for one side to predominate (including the possible annihilation of the opposition).

Loud over Silent Emergencies

In this "crisis of crises," all institutions and analysts are playing catch-up, trying to understand and redefine their roles in the post–Cold War era. More specifically in relationship to this book, there is a sense that the communications revolution and the nature of modern civil wars have together conspired to produce what is loosely termed the **CNN effect**—a shorthand used to convey the impression that Ted Turner and Rupert Murdoch are more in charge of policymaking than is, for example, the U.N. secretary-general or the president of the United States. Whatever one's opinion, it has become clear since the Gulf War that the media (particularly U.S. television) draw the attention of government, business leaders, and societies at large toward loud emergencies associated with active warfare and unintentionally mute the sound of the silent emergencies of grinding poverty.

From a historical perspective, media influence on foreign policy is not really new. Before the Spanish-American War, for example, William Randolph Hearst is widely reported to have commented to Frederick Remington, "You furnish the pictures; I'll furnish the war." More recently, the media have played a role in galvanizing international action for civil wars: in Biafra in the late 1960s, in Bangladesh in the early 1970s, and in Ethiopia in 1973 and again in 1984. Their motives for doing so are at times morally void. In the novel *Scoop*,[14] based on a true experience but disguised as fiction to avoid Britain's libel laws, a local news reporter is told to pack his bags and head for Ishmaelia. "What's the story?" he asks. "Well," the editor remarks, "a lot of niggers are having a war. I don't see anything in it myself, but the other agencies are sending feature men, so we've got to do something."[15]

Technological communications developments have implications for information about humanitarian crises, for access by people around the world to such information, for the roles of editors and producers, and for the wherewithal of the international community to respond to breaking events. Thanks to new satellite technologies, the media are indisputably a more major factor in the humanitarian arena now than in earlier periods. Both the immediacy and the intensity of its involvement have been affected. Yet the graphic images from Srebrenica and Zepa were no more sufficient to move Western governments to intervene soon enough to halt more ethnic cleansing. Although scholars are fond of counterfactual history, CNN's cameras in the Germany of the 1930s would probably not have changed the course of events more than those in Bosnia. As a leading commentator on these issues wrote: "Real time TV coverage of armed conflicts like Bosnia and Rwanda helps those people (the attentive public and policymakers) know a little more, but not enough to persuade governments to show greater political will."[16] Or as another prominent observer of Bosnia more wryly noted, "Had there been cameras in Auschwitz, the world might very well have done as little as it did in that pretelevision age, unless, of course, it had suited the people who have power in the world to act."[17]

It thus appears safer to argue that media influence in post–Cold War crises has taken a quantitative, if not qualitative, jump. This explains the coining of the term *CNN effect*, but this term hardly explains adequately the causal links between information and opinion, on the one hand, and decisions and actions, on the other. Despite greater access to information and images—the former head of MSF noted that "the victim and his rescuer have become one of the totems of our age"[18]—neither the public nor policymakers necessarily have a better command of the state of affairs in war zones now than they did a decade ago. Even though the connections between the media and political and humanitarian action in civil wars are thus recurrent, the chemistry of interactions between public exposure and international engagement requires more serious analytical review than it has received to date.

There is consensus that technological changes in communications have quickened and sharpened interactions between and among the three key sets of outside actors responding to civil wars: the media, civilian (both from NGOs and the United Nations) as well as military humanitarians, and government policymakers. None of the three sets of institutions is a monolith, however, and any discussion that fails to take into account their variegated nature risks obfuscating, rather than facilitating, our understanding. Although often referred to in the aggregate, "the media" in reality consist of print and electronic entities, journalists and editors, owners and publishers, traditional and alternative news organs. "Humanitarians" are made up of nongovernmental, governmental, and intergovernmental groups, presidents and CEOs, headquarters and field staffs, program managers and specialized personnel, civilian and, increasingly, military versions. "Policymakers" include elites as well as midlevel staff in the State Department, executive branch agencies, and Congress.

We frequently overlook that all institutions have gatekeepers, those who control information and determine the priority of problems to be solved. Bureaucratic politics impedes the tackling of humanitarian agendas more effectively until they are absolutely embarrassing and unavoidable, which automatically puts hot wars on the front burner and silent poverty sometimes completely off the stove. Each media, humanitarian, and governmental organization has limited financial and human resources, which force selectivity among crises. Each includes committed people with humane values. In short, a discerning analysis of the media in its humanitarian interactions needs to involve precision in identifying which media influence which policymakers and which humanitarian groups in which directions on which issues.

Even though everyone seems to have a view—our consumer roles as viewers, listeners, and readers seem to qualify each of us—there are really more anecdotes than data. There is widespread agreement that the media exercised decisive influence on political decisionmakers and on military and humanitarian organizations alike in Somalia and Bosnia. If the wrong conclusions are drawn from failed initiatives, these actions may come to represent the high-water mark of assertive post–Cold War action by the international community in civil wars.

Within this context, it is worthy inquiring how one could determine a "successful" humanitarian operation. According to the UNHCR, it "is one which delivers the greatest good to the greatest possible number of people in need."[19] The greatest number of people in need—the more than 1 billion persons in the world living in absolute poverty—far exceeds the 50 million or so refugees and internally displaced persons directly of concern to humanitarian actors. Equity and need do not seem to determine which crises receive attention. The difference between loud and silent emergencies appears to be public and donor perceptions about the level of urgency. It is easier to visualize children being struck by bullets than by the hidden hand of structural violence through abject poverty. Treating loud emergencies seems more doable and requires a shorter commitment than eliminating silent emergencies.

Altering preferences for loud emergencies is a key policy strategy for alleviating chronic conditions that lead to conflict and human suffering. The public must be better educated, and the international humanitarian system must change the ways that it measures success: How would one determine if a loud emergency had been prevented by treating a silent one? How does one move away from measuring success by inputs rather than results? And perhaps most important, how does the international community come to terms with global economic interdependence that frequently hinders the development of less developed economies? Treating silent emergencies means that the international humanitarian system must address the root causes of loud emergencies, two of which are economic marginalization and the perception that the use of force is the only remaining route to economic survival.

Not all poor countries erupt into civil conflict. Attention should thus be paid to the adaptive measures of economically marginalized societies that have led to civil conflicts and violent ethnic rivalries. Civilian populations have been targeted in recent years because belligerents have been led to believe by their political and economic elites that their survival is challenged by the continued existence of another group. This type of manipulation is not new. Adolf Hitler used fear for economic survival to incite the people of Weimar Germany into supporting his policy of cleansing the region of Jews.

The new humanitarian agenda includes preventive conflict management. But when a source of loud emergencies is the international economic system, there appears little hope that developed countries will join in the humanitarian effort when battles elsewhere over resources have yet to escalate into war. Once silent emergencies have burst into loud ones, it becomes more difficult to find the root cause or perhaps far easier to conceal it. Many developed countries are not interested in discussing the negative externalities of the international economic system and may prefer to deal with negotiating peace, distributing food, and providing protection rather than tweaking laissez-faire.

The challenge is thus what has commonly been referred to as "development education." This is a task of NGOs that is distinct from their assistance and protection efforts in war zones but that may in fact be more critical in the longer run to help alter preferences in order to attack silent emergencies. We have been focusing in this book almost exclusively on the targets (victims of war) for operational NGOs, whereas those for educational and advocacy NGOs are their own contributors, the public, and decisionmakers. Educational NGOs seek primarily to influence citizens, whose voices are then registered through public opinion and bear fruit in the form of additional resources for NGOs' activities as well as new policies, better decisions, and, on occasion, enhanced international regimes. Educational NGOs often play a leading role in promoting the various "days," "years," and "decades" that the U.N. system regularly proclaims. Nongovernmental organizations can reinforce the norms promoted by intergovernmental organizations through public education campaigns, which in turn can help hold states accountable to their international commitments.

Western operational NGOs are under growing pressure from their Third World partners to educate contributors and Western publics about the origins of poverty and violence. Without such efforts, one commentator remarked that "conventional NGO project activities are manifestly 'finger-in-the-dike' responses to problems that require nothing short of worldwide and whole-hearted government commitment to combat."[20] Going hand in hand with operational activities is the need to educate populations and mobilize public opinion about the requirements for fundamental alterations in the structure of global distribution of power and resources.

Nongovernmental organizations focusing exclusively on education in their own countries without overseas activities within at least some internal conflicts are not numerous, but they exist. The most effective educators are those with credibility, knowledge, and convictions gained from substantial operational experience or from firsthand experience with war-torn societies. Examples are Oxfam and Save the Children efforts in development education that are linked to the origins of poverty and injustice and are part of their overall campaigns to deal with the victims from wars in Bosnia and Somalia. Many NGOs have moved away from an exclusive concern with projects and toward a focus on preventing the need for relief projects in the first place through the promotion of structural change and prevention of violent conflicts. The shift is toward educating the public about its attitudes and the necessity for systemic change, while moving away from a preoccupation with relief. Two observers summarize this logic in the context of their negative views about the World Bank and the IMF: "Many of the causes of under-development lie in the political and economic structures of an unequal world . . . and in the misguided policies of governments and the multilateral institutions (such as the World Bank and IMF) which they control. It is extremely difficult, if not impossible, to address these issues in the context of the traditional NGO project."[21]

Linked to education are the related concerns of those NGOs working primarily in the corridors of governments and intergovernmental organizations, where international responses to internal conflicts are shaped. These advocates pursue discussions with national delegates and staff members of international secretariats in order to influence international public policy. "Lobbying" is perhaps an accurate image but an inaccurate description because the definition of lobbying applies only to legislators. In seeking to inform or alter the policies of governments as well as of governmental, intergovernmental, and nongovernmental agencies, advocacy NGOs seek to influence a wide variety of policymakers and not simply parliamentarians. Prominent examples in the humanitarian arena in the United States include the Lawyers' Committee for Human Rights, the Refugee Policy Group, Refugees International, and the U.S. Committee for Refugees. In spite of the pertinence of advocacy NGOs, they are not numerous and have the most difficulty in raising funds.

A great deal of NGO advocacy in the past has been directed against the official policies of governments and U.N. organizations. Recently, however, many nongovernmental organizations have moved toward institutionalizing a "full-fledged partnership with the governmental members of the United Nations."[22] Historically, NGOs have had some responsibility for the implementation of treaties drafted mainly by representatives of states. But now these NGOs aspire to more direct involvement in the drafting of language and in the political processes resulting in treaties. When governments or international institutions are trying to decide upon the shape of actions in the face of humanitarian emergencies in war zones, NGO views can be influential, as responses in northern Iraq, Somalia, Rwanda, Haiti, and even Bosnia suggest. Both through formal statements in U.N. forums and information negotiations with international civil servants and members of national delegations, advocacy NGOs seek to ensure that their views, and those of their constituencies, are reflected in international texts and decisions. They sometimes offer research and drafting skills and provide scientific or polling data to support their positions. Also, firsthand reports and testimony from field staff can be powerful tools before parliamentary committees.

FIVE

□　□　□

Immediate Improvements for the Post–Cold War Humanitarian System

It is common sense to take a method and try it.
If it fails, admit it frankly and try another.
But above all, try something.

—Franklin Delano Roosevelt

The international humanitarian system is in need of improvement. A robust humanitarian impulse has stirred global citizens and forced reticent state actors into humanitarian action when they may be institutionally ill-equipped to be effective or be complementary to a multi-institutional, multinational effort. A market for cost-efficient implementers of humanitarian policies has spawned an industry of new NGOs that at times are more concerned with proving or improving their market value than with determining if their operations are effective. And the United Nations operationally cannot live up to the Charter's idealism—the organization's humanitarian, development, and security organs suffer from internal mismanagement, insufficient resources, and competing interests. The abundance of thorny policy choices outlined in Chapter 4 reflects the magnitude of improvement needed in how and when the international humanitarian system addresses complex emergencies.

Perhaps the first improvement needed is increased public awareness of the successes of the current system so that the shortcomings can be situated. Although the media shower sufficient attention on where the system has flopped, such as in Bosnia, "nonevents" or avoided catastrophes are largely ignored. The public has lost sight of the fact that the conflict in

171

the former Yugoslavia has not spread to the people of Kosovo, Macedonia, or Albania. And despite barriers of political will, national interests, and bureaucratic mazes, hundreds of thousands of lives have been saved in Somalia, northern Iraq, and elsewhere around the globe; hundreds of thousands more are finding their way back home in Central America. The rebuilding and healing of communities continue as the international community turns its attention to mayhem elsewhere. The corps of humanitarians and accompanying norms are growing, not diminishing, with successive generations. A more knowledgeable public is the first imperative for improving the international humanitarian system—a public less willing to accept from their governments, IGOs, and NGOs anything less than the achievable.

Informed and dedicated people do not readily accept conventional wisdom or political rhetoric that limits the possibilities of humanitarian responses. For example, a major NGO published a large advertisement in the *New York Times* listing its achievements in assisting noncombatants in Bosnia. It accompanied its call for donations with side-by-side photos: one of a young Jewish boy with his hands held high as Nazi soldiers stood by, the other of a clearly frightened Bosnian woman clutching an equally frightened little girl. The caption under each photo was "Ethnic cleansing." The text stated, "You can't stop the ethnic cleansing in Bosnia, but you can save a life [through your generous donations]."[1] Of course you can stop it. More people believing that they can leads to more pressure on legislatures that say they cannot.

A thoughtful international citizen must recognize how misleading the previous comparison is between Nazi Germany and Bosnia. Although helpless victims and abhorrent perpetrators of violence were present in the 1940s and 1990s, ethnic cleansing *was* stopped in 1945, and the perpetrators *were* killed or prosecuted. Ethnic cleansing *could have been* stopped much earlier in Bosnia, and war criminals could have and still could be held accountable for their actions. To dismiss the latter is to limit severely the range of responses to humanitarian crises and to extinguish the hope that noncombatants have in the humanity of those with the ability to stop genocide who instead send food and blankets. It took forty-three months before a peace agreement was signed among the warring parties in the former Yugoslavia. The political negotiations mediated by the international community did not win the peace; it was won by force through a successful combination of a Croatian-Bosnian offensive and NATO-backed artillery and air strikes against Bosnian Serbs. The members of the Security Council were unwilling to surrender the rhetorical shield of political neutrality, even after Bosnian Serbs made it clear they had no intention of respecting international law, because the council members had no vision of how they wanted the war to end. "The old United Nations' policy was impartiality to the point of appeasement," one senior U.N. official lamented in anonymity. "That has not changed."[2] The Security Council's subjectively selective policy of political neutrality to the point of inertia has also not changed.

The World War II imagery—in the NGO's reference to the Holocaust and in the U.N. spokesman's to appeasement in Munich and elsewhere—is an apt way to recall that human beings are not captives of their fate. The late visionary economist Kenneth Boulding has been quoted often as saying "we are what we are because we got that way." Ideas and theories, like their concrete manifestations in institutions and material resources, can be changed and in fact are changing all the time. The host of choices in the post–Cold War era illustrate that structures can be modified or transformed. President Franklin Roosevelt would give a nod of agreement: The humanitarian regime can and must be improved.

Everywhere and every day, scholars and practitioners muse over how the tensile strength of the military and civilian safety net under war victims can be improved. That in itself seems to signal a general consensus that internal conflicts and international humanitarian responses may not be part of a transitional period in world politics but a more permanent characteristic of global affairs and conflict management for the foreseeable future. Ignoring the complexities and the dilemmas previously outlined is not an option or a strategy. The demons of war must be staved, the rights of the innocent must be protected, and postconflict societies must be rebuilt. There is much work to be done; let us begin.

BUILDING UPON LOCAL RESOURCES

There is a paradox between wanting to help non-Western victims of war and at the same time appearing not to trust them to administer to their own needs with donated resources. Buried beneath the humanitarian impulse of some external actors may lurk what has been identified in domestic welfare circles as "blaming the victim" for his or her current vulnerability and dependency on outside aid. To build the capacity of local resources requires that we first begin with abandoning notions of a "right" way to assist vulnerable groups. Second, external humanitarian actors must examine their own institutional and personal barriers to allowing victims, often from dissimilar cultures, to manage their own recoveries. Probably no other task for humanitarians is more urgent or more feasible. Such an approach requires fewer resources but greater imagination.

A local teacher works with students using a "school-in-a-box" provided by UNESCO and UNICEF as part of a Teacher's Emergency Package. UNICEF/94-1018/Betty Press.

Reluctance to transfer responsibilities to local NGOs and individuals may stem from a common complaint. U.N. agencies and NGOs have been criticized for sending inexperienced personnel or for placing unqualified personnel in positions of authority. If staff in the field are inexperienced, they may be in some ways motivated to demonstrate their previously untried skills to their home offices and therefore bypass local experts. Or they may be professionally immature, which renders them unable to judge when it is most appropriate to draw upon local resources to implement programs.

Strengthening the capacity of local people to assist in their own relief, rehabilitation, and reconstruction empowers them to ward off future crises as well as lays the groundwork for self-sustaining development. In a highly volatile arena, local populations and institutions understand subtle, yet powerful social and political relations as well as networks for community action. Many external humanitarians regularly hire locals as part of their field staff. In Somalia in 1992, for example, the ICRC organized Somali women's committees to operate open air soup kitchens that fed hundreds of thousands of people. The women's committees, once formally organized, took it upon themselves to reestablish the Mogadishu school system, paying some five hundred teachers with ICRC food aid to continue the education of approximately twenty thousand students.

Project budgets should specifically earmark for each phase of a response a certain percentage of funding for local institutions, including funds to train local personnel. Allocating such a desirable percentage of funding would establish in advance a sensible benchmark. It would also help emphasize the disparity between the salaries and benefits paid to locals and those to expatriates, which is as glaring a comparison as one of their living conditions. Based on a percentage of funding, a considerable number of locals could be hired for the same cost as one expatriate. In this manner, governmental donors and their executing agencies in the U.N. system or NGO world would facilitate the use of local resources by insisting upon maximum participation in project execution.

In view of expertise available locally, it would be better for cost savings *and* future viability to maximize local participation. There are plenty of glaring examples of missed opportunities to think creatively and maximize the use of local populations during emergency operations. Aid agencies attending to the medical needs of refugees who poured into Jordan during the Gulf crises flew European and North American doctors into the country even though Jordan had plenty of doctors unemployed because of an economic recession—the cost was about ten times higher than the estimated cost of local doctors. Aid agencies providing relief to refugees who moved into Iraq during the same period flew in young and inexperienced expatriates while hiring highly qualified, English-speaking Iraqi professionals only as drivers and messengers. The bypassing of local resources to administer humanitarian relief causes the low-level animosity, which is not far from the surface, toward the largely Western world of relief providers to harden and become a potential impediment should another crisis occur. External humanitarian actors are not the only groups that mentally file lessons learned from past experiences.

ENHANCING PROFESSIONALISM AND ACCOUNTABILITY

Humanitarian decisionmaking and action in a war zone are not for amateurs, although the number of inexperienced field personnel is increasing as seasoned veterans become less willing to work in increasingly high-risk environments.

The international humanitarian assistance business is flourishing. As new NGOs crop up to meet the market's demand for cost-efficient suppliers and implementers of humanitarian assistance, the business of relief continues to represent one of the most unregulated markets in the world today. As one scholar wrote: "One of the greatest practical problems facing NGOs today is the fragmentation of effort, the hundreds of look-alike organizations spawned more by ego than goodwill, and maintained more by charity than by clarity of purpose. Fragmentation is the amateur's friend."[3] The lack of professionalism, accountability, codes of conduct, field experience, and personal maturity affects the reputations of many less established NGOs operating in complex emergencies and indirectly of the system as a whole. The paradox here, however, is that older NGOs adhering rigidly to principles and codes of conduct may be handicapped or even paralyzed in extremely politicized and volatile conflicts. Unrelenting adherence to principles, regardless of varied contexts, may lead to a general inability to learn from past errors and produce a more effective and flexible international humanitarian system.

More experienced IGOs, NGOs, scholars, and practitioners of humanitarian action are rising to the challenge of educating new arrivals as well as informing seasoned professionals about lessons learned from past actions and ideas for cooperation yet to be tested. One of the objectives is to present a more united front on behalf of war victims by collective acceptance of humanitarian principles and standard operating procedures in the field. The hypothesis is that those who are clear and consistent in their articulation of principles will be more successful in their efforts than those who are not. An opportunity for solidarity, mutual trust, and cooperation among the community of humanitarians is missed without a clearly articulated and agreed-on code of conduct to guide relief workers from various organizations through highly charged emergencies. The agenda for creating a united front involves institutional reflection and reform.

With each new crisis, institutions—from governmental aid agencies to the military to religious-based private organizations—are reconfiguring traditional strategies to meet the changing character of wars. U.N. agencies, such as the UNHCR, are reviewing their mandates and response procedures, and the DHA continues to take organizational form while trying to wrestle hold of responsibility for coordination during complex emergencies from other powerful U.N. players. Analyses about improving response and effectiveness of humanitarian action are ongoing, with feedback from practitioners on the front lines an increasingly essential component. Disaster management training programs have been designed by the UNDP and the DHA, and NGOs are also working hard to enhance management. The DHA has embarked on joint ventures with non-U.N. organizations, such as the International Federation of Red Cross and Red Crescent Societies, to educate diverse humanitarian actors about operational relationships, such as those between NGOs and the military.

Manuals have been published for IGOs and NGOs concerning military strategies and standard operating procedures. Others have been published as guidelines for proceeding with humanitarian aid in insecure environments. *Catholic Relief Services Guidelines for Humanitarian Assistance in Conflict Situations*, the ICRC's *Implementation of International Humanitarian Law Protection of the Civilian Population and Persons Hors de Combat*, and *UNHCR, Coping with Stress in Crisis Situations* are examples of publications written specifically for humanitarians trying to be effective in environments that often are not readily amenable to their efforts.[4]

For the ICRC and the IFRC, an effective code of conduct for behavior by relief workers revolves around the principles of neutrality and impartiality and the strategy of continual communication among governments, victims, and relief staff. Although neutrality is not accepted by all NGOs, for those interested in following standards of professionalism adhered to by the ICRC and IFRC, the annual publication of *World Disasters Report* provides a template for humanitarian behavior as well as published results from the IFRC's research, training, and evaluation of field operations. To date, over fifty NGOs have adopted the IFRC code of conduct as their own, including International Save the Children Alliance, the Lutheran World Federation, Oxfam, and Caritas Internacionalis. An independent effort to synthesize current thinking by Brown University's Humanitarianism and War Project resulted in the 1993 *Humanitarian Action in Times of War: A Handbook for Practitioners*, which offers eight principles for humanitarian action.[5] Excerpts from these two sets of guidelines are found in Boxes 5.1 and 5.2. It should be noted that these principles govern the political behavior of agencies working in conflict situations. Similar principles have yet to be extended to professional actors, for which there are as yet no agreed-on standards or recognized criteria.

Along with establishing guiding principles for behavior prior to entry into a conflict area, some humanitarian organizations are increasingly confronting tough decisions about whether to arrive on the scene at all. Still others are actively preparing themselves to participate fully in the thick of violence by ordering military gear such as flak jackets and armored vehicles, studying military training manuals and strategies for engagement, and hiring former military personnel as consultants. Getting into the tactical mind of belligerents may better position humanitarian actors for negotiating access to war victims, protecting personnel from harm, and avoiding extortion by warring parties. It also may cause significant discomfort among groups of practitioners that traditionally have attracted pacifists and antimilitarists to their ranks.

As noted earlier, nongovernmental organizations are becoming the emergency agencies of choice for many donors, public and private. Although there is a tendency to applaud blindly any move toward privatization, donors should insist on greater NGO self-regulation and enhanced professionalism as a quid pro quo for more resources channeled through NGOs. Encouraging efforts have begun in a variety of settings. For example, major players such as Catholic Relief Services (CRS) have drafted a code of con-

---

BOX 5.1   Principles of Conduct for the International Red Cross and
Red Crescent Movement and NGOs in Disaster Response Programs

- The humanitarian imperative comes first.
- Aid is given regardless of race, creed or nationality of the recipients and
  without adverse distinction of any kind. Aid priorities are calculated on
  the basis of need alone.
- Aid will not be used to further a particular political or religious stand-
  point.
- We shall endeavor not to act as instruments of government foreign policy.
- We shall respect culture and custom.
- We will attempt to build disaster response on local capacities.
- Ways shall be found to involve program beneficiaries in the management
  of relief aid.
- Relief aid must strive to reduce future vulnerabilities to disaster as well as
  meeting basic needs.
- We hold ourselves accountable to both those we seek to assist and those
  from whom we accept resources.
- In our information, publicity and advertising activities, we shall recognize
  disaster victims as dignified humans, not hopeless objects.

Source: International Federation of Red Cross and Red Crescent Societies, *World Disasters Report 1995,* ed. Nick Cater (The Netherlands: Martinus Nijhoff, 1995), p. 146.

---

duct, and consortia such as the Washington-based InterAction and the
Geneva-based International Council for Voluntary Agencies (ICVA) have
also been urging their members to improve performance through training
and the adoption of codes of conduct.[6] At the Citizens Conference on NGO-
U.N. Relations in San Francisco in June 1995, a self-righteous early draft
about U.N. accountability became a more accurate "Declaration of Accountability for Global Governance" whose set of principles began, "All partners
in global governance have responsibility to each other and are accountable
to the global community as a whole for their actions."[7]

Even more salient are nascent efforts among major operational agencies
to regulate themselves. International "antitrust legislation" is far-fetched,[8]
but greater self-regulation and, more important, self-questioning are certainly in order for the largest nongovernmental organizations. In September 1995, two NGO consortia (InterAction and ICVA) began an open discussion of a certification process for NGOs that would signify their
professional wherewithal to be active in war zones. The notion of certifying
only those NGOs that satisfied prescribed standards met with a surprising
assent from participants.[9] The moral high ground, which they often claim
to occupy, would be firmer and their own place in the pluralized system of

BOX 5.2   Providence Principles of
Humanitarian Action in Armed Conflicts

- *Relieving life-threatening suffering:* Humanitarian action should be directed toward the relief of immediate, life-threatening suffering.
- *Proportionality to need:* Humanitarian action should correspond to the degree of suffering, wherever it occurs. It should affirm the view that life is as precious in one part of the globe as another.
- *Nonpartisanship:* Humanitarian action responds to human suffering because people are in need, not to advance political, sectarian, or other extraneous agendas. It should not take sides in conflicts.
- *Independence:* In order to fulfill their mission, humanitarian organizations should be free of interference from home or host political authorities. Humanitarian space is essential for effective action.
- *Accountability:* Humanitarian organizations should report fully on their activities to sponsors and beneficiaries. Humanitarianism should be transparent.
- *Appropriateness:* Humanitarian action should be tailored to local circumstances and aim to enhance, not supplant, locally available resources.
- *Contextualization:* Effective humanitarian action should encompass a comprehensive view of overall needs and of the impact of interventions. Encouraging respect for human rights and addressing the underlying causes of conflicts are essential elements.
- *Subsidiarity of sovereignty:* Where humanitarianism and sovereignty clash, sovereignty should defer to the relief of life-threatening suffering.

Source: Larry Minear and Thomas G. Weiss, *Humanitarian Action in Times of War: A Handbook for Practitioners* (Boulder: Lynne Rienner, 1993), p. 19.

global governance more authoritative if NGOs were to pursue the highest professional standards for recruitment, posting, and promotions. The incentives—essentially more united resources and greater access to decision-making—should be sufficient to elicit more cooperation than in the past.

Although military codes of conduct exist at national levels, for the multinational military contingents involved in humanitarian intervention, a standardized code of conduct and a comparable system to monitor, evaluate, and punish offenders are also required. Military abuse toward civilians, such as the killing of Somali noncombatants by Canadian soldiers involved in UNOSOM, severely weakens the legitimacy of the "protectors" and compromises the humanitarian agenda as a whole. Other recent incidents involving soldiers under U.N. auspices have involved illegal commerce in contravention of sanctions and prostitution rings. At a minimum, education of military troops and other security personnel in "right" behavior toward civilians must begin with an international standardized code of conduct with standardized punishment for violators. It was the Canadian government, not an international criminal court, that rendered judgment and punishment against those soldiers. From a more critical perspective, achieving "right" behavior for humanitarian military personnel would require a complete transformation in consciousness from a warrior identity to a protector identity that would not weaken under stress and would ameliorate the differences in military cultures that cause friction in the field.

Professionalism goes hand in hand with accountability. Because of the nature of humanitarianism, high standards of performance and ethics have been assumed that do not match reality in the field or at the negotiating table. The international humanitarian system must aspire to a higher level of professionalism and accountability, one that parallels the lofty ideals and inherent importance of humanitarian tasks.

ESTABLISHING A NEW HUMANITARIAN UNIT FOR WAR ZONES

There are some situations in which only forceful persuasion can stop starvation, genocide, and massive violations of human rights, which is one of the many possible contributions of the military to humanitarian missions in the accompanying table. The beckoning question is how to effectively operationalize "military humanitarianism." "HUMPROFOR"—our own unofficial acronym for a humanitarian protection force—is one idea for humanitarian intervention that takes into consideration the strengths, weaknesses, and organizational constraints of the present array of actors in the international humanitarian system. In a sense, HUMPROFOR is an effort to add a central brain to the international humanitarian system during peak moments of violence. Until the brain is operative, existing humanitarian actions and their functions appear to flop about, relying more upon the hope that they will meet their objectives than on the institutional capacity that would guarantee them. (See Table 5.1.)

HUMPROFOR would be activated as Chapter VI consensual action moved into a Chapter VII coercion. Once Chapter VII had been invoked by the Security Council, all U.N. agencies would be evacuated from the war zone and replaced with a different type of humanitarian—a volunteer, preferably with a military background, appropriately insured and compensated for the risks he or she would face in delivering humanitarian assistance in a more militarized environment. By having the new cadre of humanitarians report directly to the Security Council, rather than the U.N. secretary-general, the decentralized approach to humanitarian action—which has resulted in infighting among U.N. agencies and barriers to coordination efforts—would be replaced by centralized command and control of a joint humanitarian and protection operation.

TABLE 5.1   Possible Uses of Military Force for Humanitarian Missions in
Complex Emergencies

Armed Activity	Humanitarian Objectives
Military forces deliver relief supplies but do not carry weapons.	Provide food and relief to suffering civilian populations while minimizing potential for entanglement in local conflict.
Armed forces deliver relief aid, using forces only in self-defense and to protect relief supplies.	Provide relief aid, with somewhat greater security for personnel, while deterring interference by hostile groups.
Armed monitoring or enforcement of sanctions; blockade.	Pressure the offending government to modify its behavior to better protect civilians; deprive it of arms that might be used against civilians.
Armed suppression of air traffic in the offending country.	Prevent or reduce air attacks on civilians; protect delivery of relief supplies; pressure the government to modify its behavior.
Air strikes against selected military targets, such as artillery or airfields.	Prevent use of particular weapons against civilians; punish the offending combatant; demonstrate resolve to protect civilians.
Air, ground, and/or naval actions against the armed forces of one or more combatants.	Deter or reduce attacks on civilians or relief shipments; pressure the offending government or other combatants to modify behavior.
Armed forces create safe havens or "zones of peace" and defend them against local combatants.	Shelter displaced civilians until the conflict subsides.
Peacekeeping: armed forces monitor a cease-fire or peace agreement with the consent of combatants.	Protect civilians and encourage a resumption of normal life through efforts to prevent a resumption of hostilities.
Peace enforcement: military action to enforce terms not accepted by the government and/or other combatants.	Restore peaceful conditions and allow resumption of normal life; arrange a transition to a new regime more likely to respect civilian lives.

Source: U.S. Mission to the United Nations, *Global Humanitarian Emergencies, 1995*
(January 1995), p. 19.

The organizational structure and culture of such a unit would be more homogeneous and less sensitive to miscommunication than the present decentralized model. Belligerents may find more resistance to their pilferage of humanitarian supplies or extortion strategies for obtaining cash to purchase more weapons and thereby prolong a conflict. In addition, humanitarian assistance would be under the same command and control center as military protection forces, thereby adding to the diplomat's bag of carrots and sticks during peace negotiations.

Throughout the activation of HUMPROFOR, humanitarians and soldiers would adhere to the principles of the Geneva conventions and additional protocols and would be held accountable for violations. Humanitarian efforts would revert back to U.N. agencies once HUMPROFOR had accomplished its objective. Left untainted by involvement during the Chapter VII operations, the U.N. secretary-general would be in a better (apolitical) position to work with the host government on purely humanitarian concerns after the halt in the armed conflict, when consensus, rather than coercion, is the standard operating procedure. During a HUMPROFOR operation, the ICRC would continue its work with prisoners of war and its own humanitarian efforts. It would be expected to distance itself, as it always has, from warring parties that do not wish to cooperate. It would be unlikely for the work of the ICRC and HUMPROFOR to clash, compete, or contradict each other.

NGOs cannot be stopped from operating in a war zone, unless, of course, they have no funds or are bound by conditions in contracts with donors. If HUMPROFOR was adopted, there would be fewer government and U.N. agency funds available for NGOs. Donor governments would channel more funds into HUMPROFOR, rather than NGOs, or place conditionality clauses in NGO contracts that would remove them from the field once Chapter VII operations went into effect. Thus, the NGO population in active war zones would decline until the bullets stopped flying and Chapter VII was successful.

Pieces of a HUMPROFOR puzzle are yet to be put in place. The resources for this effort would be taken from the emergency operations of the central U.N. agencies—UNICEF, the WFP, and the UNHCR—and government allocations that are often channeled directly to NGOs. In fact, many of the seasoned personnel, both U.N. and NGOs, could and should be assigned to this unit. Finding countries of asylum for noncombatants worries many humanitarians. But perhaps if HUMPROFOR proved successful in its early stages, more countries would have confidence that the "temporary, short-term" status of refugees was truly that, and these countries would be more willing to accommodate the presence of thousands of unexpected guests.

To date, the greatest opponents of military humanitarianism come from many humanitarian workers fearful of losing neutrality and from Third World countries reacting to what they claim are renewed "imperialist" interventions in the guise of humanitarianism. The first set of opponents would not be found in great numbers in the field once HUMPROFOR was set in motion. Concerns of Third World countries could be alleviated by a reconfigured Security Council and by other council decisionmaking pathways that would pursue more consistent or less selective application of international norms.

HUMPROFOR is one idea of how to improve the international humanitarian system with a focus on alleviating the suffering of noncombatants brought on by protracted conflict and targeted populations. New ideas that bring the focus back to the victims are valuable commodities in the field of humanitarian action and are constantly wanting. It is incumbent upon humanitarians, journalists, policymakers, and, yes, readers of this book to struggle and conceptualize alternate organizational forms that would be more effective than the current response mechanisms and structures of the international humanitarian system in assisting victims of war without furthering the aims of the combatants.

FACILITATING COORDINATION
THROUGH A NEW U.N. INSTITUTION

The creation of the DHA in 1992 was but one fledgling step since the end of the Cold War to counter increasing criticism of overlapping institutional mandates and poor coordination and priority-setting, all of which add up to a less-than-optimal impact from the resources supposedly devoted to war victims. Ironically, the threats to reduce U.N. funding by the U.S. Congress are among the few incentives to incite the world organization to get its house in order. In addition to U.N. credibility lost in the former Yugoslavia, Rwanda, and Somalia, budgetary constraints have been the most recent impetus for U.N. self-reflection and reform. If the United Nations cannot police itself, tough choices will be made for it. Either its reform efforts will be effective as judged by its actions in the field and its improved cost-efficiency, or suggestions of replacing the United Nations with a new kind of intergovernmental organization will be taken more seriously.

Danziger, © *Christian Science Monitor.*

The most prominent recent commissions of eminent persons focusing on U.N. reform do not confront directly the possibility of starting anew.[10] But governments are voting with their contributions. In addition to the fact that total debts and arrears have reached about three times the United Nations' annual regular budget, for example, states are also diverting more funds traditionally channeled through the United Nations or their own governmental aid agencies through nongovernmental organizations. Even if the United Nations is partially successful in tightening its belt and implementing reform strategies and member states, such as the United States, meet their treaty obligations, hardly foregone conclusions, there continues to be a widening market for private-sector institutions whose humanitarian action collectively now is more important than the United Nations system.

During U.N. multifunctional operations in complex emergencies, the DHA and the U.N. Departments of Political Affairs and Peace-keeping Operations each oversee their respective mandates. Yet the DHA is severely underfunded and poorly placed to hold up its allotted portion in the division of labor as the representative of humanitarian perspectives within the secretary-general's inner circle. Without better U.N. coordination of activities and their priority in humanitarian action, there will continue to be unnecessary overlap, duplication, and waste. The division of labor approach discussed earlier would seek to identify the strengths and weaknesses of particular U.N. agencies, identifying those that are better at distribution than logistics, better at protection than assessment, and so on. There have been numerous conferences and colloquiums on all aspects of the relief-to-development continuum and coordination. Everyone is interested in U.N. reform and increased U.N. credibility, but few are willing to take the first steps or be coordinated by another agency, to have their funding sources administered through a single source, or to reduce personnel, eliminate subagencies, or streamline functions in the name of greater efficiency in providing sustenance and protection to war victims.

In a sense, St. Augustine's prayer appropriately describes the attitude of many U.N. officials toward coordination and reform: "Lord, make me pure, but not now." In relationship to better multilateral humanitarian action, then, the most crucial problem is a lack of specialization—the failure to ascertain who does what best. Effective international responses to humanitarian crises require a clearer division of labor among humanitarians. It would be gratuitous to denigrate the courage and dedication of individuals assisting victims for all three ethnic groups in the former Yugoslavia, for example. At the same time, humanitarian action there, as elsewhere, has been marred by needless duplication and competition. Like St. Augustine, everyone is for coordination, but no one wishes to be coordinated, not just now.

In December 1991, in response to the visible problems encountered in the Persian Gulf crisis, the General Assembly authorized the secretary-general to appoint a humanitarian coordinator and created the Department of Humanitarian Affairs. However, the DHA has made no appreciable difference in leadership or performance within the major recent tragedies in the former Yugoslavia or Somalia, although information-sharing was improved in Rwanda.[11] This is hardly surprising when the coordinator has no real budgetary authority and does not outrank the heads of the agencies that he is supposed to coordinate. In the words of veteran U.N.-hands Erskine Childers and Brian Urquhart: "The real 'division of labour' that needs concentrated effort is between a unified U.N.-system emergency machinery and the volunteer NGOs upon which it must in any case in the end depend. That need remains seriously neglected in the continued jockeying and jostling of the U.N.-system organizations vis-à-vis each other and the intrinsically weak new DHA 'Coordinator.'"[12]

In spite of seeming unfeasibility and apparent naïveté, the following suggestion nonetheless is a crucial clarion call: It is absolutely essential to consolidate U.N. organizations. Otherwise, unnecessary and unacceptable waste will continue during multilateral humanitarian action in war zones. As the late Fred Cuny lamented: "Too many lives are being lost, too many resources are being wasted, there are too many delays. Operations are poorly planned and . . . there is no accountability within the international humanitarian system."[13] The necessity for rationalizing and refocusing organizational mandates in order to reduce overlap and improve performance as well as address glaring gaps such as responsibility for internally displaced persons has become obvious. In spite of difficulties in overhauling completely extant intergovernmental machinery, Raimo Väyrenen is not alone in coming to the conclusion that "the world community needs a new, long-term, and comprehensive doctrine of humanitarian intervention and a new multifaceted international mechanism to carry it out."[14] Moreover, this notion has moved from the hands of scholars and analysts and into the mainstream of intergovernmental discussion. At the July 1995 session of ECOSOC, Secretary of State Warren Christopher tabled a "nonpaper" that proposed considering "whether and how to consolidate the emergency functions of the U.N. High Commissioner for Refugees (UNHCR), the World Food Programme (WFP), the U.N. Children's Fund (UNICEF), and the Department of Humanitarian Affairs (DHA) into a single agency."[15]

In spite of the obstacles that this and other recommendations encounter, they are based on common business sense. There should be no additional major U.N. conferences on humanitarian issues, from relief to development, until the results of previous conferences have been implemented, monitored, and evaluated. A number of humanitarian functions are performed by a multiplicity of U.N. entities, resulting in unnecessary administrative costs and duplication of efforts in some functions and gaps in others. Consolidation of related functions of different agencies through structural reorganization would be sensible.

The hurdles to the consolidation of the UNHCR, the WFP, UNICEF, and the DHA, however, center primarily on controlling agency resources and extracting power from individual agency heads, who operate more as feudal barons than as members of a confederation. Pending structural changes, certainly an unlikely prospect, cooperation between and among agencies that perform a number of similar tasks in the field can be improved to better meet the needs of noncombatants. The UNHCR and the WFP both work on issues of food distribution. The UNHCR and UNICEF address the needs of unaccompanied and orphaned children, including tracing relatives. In fact, UNICEF, with its focus on children and hence the family, could and does make a claim to be involved in every sector because every sector of both relief and development has an impact on children. Relief supply operations are concurrently performed by the UNHCR, UNICEF, and the WFP; and they all self-contract independently to a handful of large nongovernmental organizations. The health care needs of refugees and internally displaced people are performed by WHO, the UNHCR, and UNICEF. Many U.N. development organizations perform similar functions but do not necessarily communicate or coordinate their actions with each other in a way that both improves the impact of U.N. activities on victim populations and reduces the administrative costs of administrative and resource overlap incurred by the entire U.N. system. The UNDP, the titular "coordinator" of development assistance, is ill-equipped in terms of concepts and personnel to orchestrate efforts in emergencies but is nonetheless competing with the DHA for this role— that is, when a special representative of the secretary-general is also not on the scene to constitute yet a third magnet for coordination. The notion of bureaucratic politics introduced in Chapter 1 provides insights into the inertia and self-interests that inhibit better decisionmaking to meet common objectives.

Closer functional cooperation among U.N. agencies could also produce more accurate data about the number of noncombatants in need and the form and amount of assistance required in various phases, geographical areas, and sectors of a relief operation. U.N. agencies, governments, NGOs, and journalists frequently have different data for the same operation. Discrepancies flow from no agreement upon definitions of populations in desperate need of assistance and no way to clearly distinguish between those suffering from an emergency and those simply trapped in the low swing of a cycle of chronic deprivation. Actors use their own data to determine inputs, frequently without visiting a site firsthand or speaking to local leadership. Through interagency coordination and free exchange of information about anticipated material and personnel inputs, humanitarian operations could become more cost-effective and could thereby reduce criticism leveled at the United Nations and increase its credibility, which has been damaged in the eyes of war victims and of the international public. There is a tendency for all bureaucracies to address problems by forming new committees and new agencies, while shying away from consolidation or complete elimination of various agencies. The creation of the DHA, which included its subsuming the U.N. Disaster Relief Office, was a first step in the right direction, but it was not large enough to overcome those institutions that defy being coordinated.

Accountability and transparency of expenditures and actions are key to recreating a United Nations capable of responding effectively and efficiently to human need long into the future. All U.N. organizations, including the various organs and bodies of the U.N. Secretariat itself, should be subject to periodic outsider reexamination of their cost-effectiveness, efficiency, purpose, and functions. Yet such practices, which are common in the business world, rarely surface within international organizations. Current modifications to U.N. business-as-usual have been an increased use of private contractors with efforts to decrease staff size (to counter the costs of salaries and benefits of permanent U.N. staff); a new performance appraisal system (to counter criticism of unqualified U.N. personnel in highly responsible jobs); professional training programs geared toward problem areas such as timely procurement operations, logistics, and transportation; and ongoing efforts to create a management culture within the U.N. system based on accountability, responsibility, and cost-to-impact ratio. These steps must accelerate. Again, not more resources but their more effective and creative utilization is required.

IMPROVING THE IMPACT OF THE MEDIA

The media are partially responsible for conveying to international society the belief, disguised as fact or news, that a region or a people are beyond hope; that in itself has its own harmful consequences. In 1917, Senator Hiram Johnson commented, "The first casualty when war comes is truth."[16] Disproportionate media attention to some crises and not others may lead to inappropriate humanitarian action. Concerned citizens, if they are not aware of needs, cannot exert influence on their governments to intervene on behalf of noncombatants. The media have been a powerful tool for stirring public opinion, and the media interaction with humanitarians and with policymakers can be improved to better serve the needs of victims.

Danziger, © *Christian Science Monitor.*

Not all vulnerable populations, for reasons of politics or physical inaccessibility, have the benefit of sufficient relief to counter the magnitude of life-threatening suffering. Under such circumstances, the greatest opportunity to mitigate human suffering may lie with humanitarians and members of the media working together to send more appropriate messages across the news wires and into the homes of concerned publics throughout the globe—to shame governments into action. Opportunities to place the concerns of noncombatants into living rooms and classrooms cannot be overlooked or undervalued. Governmental, intergovernmental, and nongovernmental responses to humanitarian crises are often preceded by public outcry stimulated by media coverage, which was itself stimulated and facilitated by humanitarian and media interaction.

Humanitarian and media interaction in recent years has often not reached beyond superficiality and has contributed to a trend, prominent in the United States and elsewhere, that favors sound-bite sensationalism over more thoughtful substance. Why? What are the interests of the media and individual reporters? How do they affect reporting on humanitarian action? And can the media facilitate a broader understanding of complex emergencies and humanitarian efforts?

Television stations and newspapers are concerned with ratings and subscriptions and with the basic bottom line: staying in business. In a limited amount of time and space, the news media first normally address the domestic agenda and move on to the editorial policy, leaving for last world news. Whatever human tragedy finally makes its way to the screen or printed page depends upon which geographical parts of the world interest the audience and where the news media have placed their correspondents and satellites. If the personnel and technology are there, the gatekeepers—owners, producers, editors who control budgets and make decisions about coverage—of the media will use them to justify expenses. In addition, stories must be packaged so as not to run more than a few minutes and not bore the viewer. Sensationalism sells more than substance, giving accounts of human tragedy a virtual-reality feel. The interests of the media as a whole are dependent upon advertising revenue, government information sources (which the media understandably hesitate to offend), and the preferences of the viewing and reading publics of largely Western societies.

A symbiotic relationship exists between Western media, largely U.S., which rely on what has been referred to as "disaster pornography" to boost ratings and readership, and many relief agencies, which rely on such dramatic images to stimulate donations. NGOs are frequently the agencies that guide journalists to the most horrific villages or homes struck by famine or violence. As a BBC correspondent covering the Somalia famine remarked, "Relief agencies depend upon us for pictures and we need them to tell us where the stories are. There's an unspoken understanding between us, a sort of code. We try not to ask the question too bluntly, 'Where will we find the most starving babies?' And they never answer explicitly. We get the pictures all the same."[17]

An additional criticism of the media's search for sensationalism is that much of the historical context leading up to a shooting war is ignored. This approach thereby contributes a great deal to stereotypes of powerless or hopelessly corrupt victims but very little to public education and interest in adopting preventive measures for less noisy emergencies. The media argue that the public itself determines how much substance it would like to hear; a long attention span of the public for human suffering in a war zone is wanting.

John Hammock and Joel Charny, the former president and current director of research at Oxfam-America, respectively, have examined the dilemmas of operational NGOs, which are both helped and hindered by the stereotypical images presented of complex emergencies by the media. The "scripted morality play" includes the victims ("teeming masses or suffering masses of Africans or Asians"), the heroes (usually "angels" from the Red Cross and private relief agencies), and the villains ("U.N. bureaucrats" and "local military authorities"). Most NGOs are happy with this script as it helps with their visibility and fund-raising; but it "is ultimately unsatisfying and works against the long-term interests of the relief agencies."[18]

The media are sometimes viewed as an extension of a public relations office for a government's foreign policy. The media were viewed by a host of analysts and scholars as following Washington's agenda during the Gulf War, never adamantly protesting government censorship of certain media coverage, such as the death of thousands of Iraqi soldiers in their outdated Soviet armor by U.S. "smart" weapons. The media did not fully disclose Iraq's rebutted attempts to open diplomatic talks with Washington, although they did broadcast President Bush's statement prior to bombing Baghdad that all diplomatic efforts to resolve the conflict had been exhausted. Rather than expose the magnitude of civilian suffering after surgical strikes ripped apart much of Baghdad's infrastructure, newsrooms focused on Iraq's refusal to allow the inspection and destruction of its weapons arsenal. Humanitarians would not dispute that this is more or less important news; they would, however, argue that the complete picture of war and its effects on civilians should be accurately presented. The current interaction between the media and humanitarian agencies does favor mobilization of emergency aid, but this yields questionable results in the longer term for the vast pool of war-related victims—refugees, internally displaced persons, returnees, and those who never left a war zone.

The interaction between the media and policymakers is also symbiotic and equally questionable. The media have an interest in not offending public officials whom they rely on for stories; this may conflict with recognizing the interests of noncombatant lives or of simply informing the attentive public of relevant and complete facts. For example, in August 1995 U.S. intelligence produced aerial photos of what were believed to be mass graves possibly concealing the bodies of nearly twenty-seven hundred Muslim men and boys slaughtered by Bosnian Serbs following the fall of Srebrenica. U.S. Permanent Representative to the U.N. Madeleine Albright was seen on the news exposing the alleged atrocities committed by the Bosnian Serbs. According to Ambassador Albright, the perpetrators of this savagery would be brought before the International Tribunal for the Former Yugoslavia. No action to investigate or address the atrocities immediately followed Albright's verbal admonition.

It would have been helpful to the public, war victims, and humanitarianism, and hardly unthinkable in terms of both news hooks or responsible journalism if the media had followed Albright's remarks with commentators describing the difficulties that had been already encountered by the underfunded and understaffed International Tribunal for the Former Yugoslavia. Without the sufficient support of governments, the Commission of Experts had to rely on NGOs, such as Physicians for Human Rights, to conduct field research, and on private contributions from financier George Soros.[19] Even after a peace agreement was signed in December 1995, NATO commanders denied the tribunal the assistance of NATO troops to uncover the mass graves, although the tribunal was permitted access to certain U.S. intelligence reports concerning possible mass gravesites. As mentioned earlier, media and public pressure overcame NATO's initial reluctance to transport two captured war criminals to The Hague and be on the lookout for others. The media's extensions of basic information would be a straightforward step toward the international humanitarian regime. It would also prevent governments from misleading the public into believing that they are responding to an inhumane act when, in fact, they are doing nothing. Clearly there are a variety of ways to improve the media's impact. And it is incumbent upon humanitarians to help. This task requires rethinking information strategies and priorities, not necessarily on securing more resources.

INVENTING PREVENTION AS A NEW WORLDVIEW

At the height of the humanitarian crisis in Somalia, eight hundred to nine hundred people were dying each day. In air-conditioned offices across the ocean, dedicated and well-intentioned people packed up their briefcases and headed home, wondering if tomorrow would bring the political will necessary to stop the suffering. In the morning, they would return to work, check faxes from the field, and begin another day of wondering. Guidelines for political will or won't, judging from current humanitarian crises, do not appear to be guidelines at all but simply streams of thought provoked into improvisation by unexpected, yet expected, human tragedy. There is no substitute for prevention of crises; the best time to plan for emergencies is always yesterday.

What emerges from the history of the humanitarian crises of the post–Cold War is the international community's desperate need for a new guiding concept. Such a concept would stress the prevention of both inter- and intrastate war. As Under-Secretary-General for Administration Dick Thornburgh was leaving office in 1993, he characterized the continuing overextension of U.N. military activities as a "financial bungee jump."[20] Apart from saving money, however, preventing violence is clearly preferable to picking up the pieces of war or conducting humanitarian intervention. If the consequences of civil war are becoming more dire, and if such wars are developing faster than the international community's ability to respond to them, it would be more reasonable to act earlier and head them off. This voice resonates with the Universal Declaration of Human Rights: "It is essential, if man is not to be compelled to have recourse, as a last resort, to rebellion against tyranny and oppression, that human rights should be protected by the rule of law."

Preventive mechanisms include early warning systems, election monitoring, preventive diplomacy, regional or international mediation and conciliation, peace monitoring, and development assistance. These mechanisms are identical to postconflict mechanisms, yet they are less costly given that personal vendettas have not accumulated and infrastructure has yet to be destroyed. Successful preventive mechanisms also circumvent the need for substantial active-conflict mechanisms such as emergency relief, expensive peacekeeping and peace enforcement measures, and the humanitarian consequences of economic sanctions. If institutional memory is capable of affecting rationality in future behavior, then prevention is the most logical focus for increased funding and worldwide attention.

Preventive diplomacy is the latest conceptual fashion. There is, for instance, the Carnegie Commission on the Prevention of Deadly Conflict. The emphasis on prevention has been correctly characterized by one commentator as "an idea in search of a strategy."[21] Such preventive actions as the symbolic deployment of a detachment of U.N. soldiers to Macedonia or the expanded use of fact-finding missions, human rights monitors, and early warning systems are beginning to be implemented. And although ultimately the emphasis will have to be on economic and social development as a necessary, if insufficient, condition to prevent conflict, effective prevention today and tomorrow will necessarily also entail the deployment of troops. If they are to be an effective deterrent, however, such troops must be provided with contingency plans and reserve firepower for immediate retaliation against aggressors. This would amount to extending advance authorization for Chapter VII action in the event that a preventive force was challenged. Although such backup firepower would be no easy matter to assemble—and, for example, the combined forces of the JNA and the Bosnian Serbs would have been hard to intimidate—it is absolutely essential. Otherwise, the currency of the U.N. preventive action will be devalued to such an extent that preventive action should not be attempted.

The problem is that prevention is cost-effective in the long run but cost-intensive in the short run. In the former Yugoslavia, the "long run" lasted over three and a half years, whereas in Rwanda it was reduced to a matter of weeks. The argument that an earlier use of force would have been more economical in the former Yugoslavia runs up against the inability of Security Council governments to look very far into the future to determine the payoff to quick action and their consequent tendency to magnify the disadvantages of immediate expenditures and to discount those of future expenditures. In Rwanda, the costs of at least five hundred thousand dead and 4 million displaced persons along with a ruined economy were soon being borne by the same governments that had refused to respond militarily only a few weeks earlier. The United States and the European Union ended up providing at least $1 billion in emergency aid in 1994 alone. Again, the implementation of a preventive approach requires creativity and political will, not necessarily additional resources, although their allocation would vary.

For those of us who have difficulty filing income tax forms before the deadline in mid-April, the idea of advance planning and timely action, the prerequisites for the adoption of prevention as a worldview, may seem unrealistic for large institutions. Prevention requires a change in the way everyday people view the world and their relation to it. It also requires that governments move beyond immediate concerns, which tend not to extend past the next public opinion poll or scheduled election, and increase transparency and accountability for their actions. In short, prevention necessitates a more comprehensive notion of international society.

Ambassador Albright has declared on several occasions that U.S. men and women thwarted Saddam Hussein's forces, carried out the longest continuous airlift of humanitarian assistance ever to Bosnia's civilians, saved hundreds of thousands of lives in Africa, restored democracy in Haiti, and helped U.N. forces withdraw from Somalia safely. Although such deserved accolades fit nicely into sound bites, they misrepresent reality in order to showcase U.S. resolve and leadership. All the actions mentioned by Albright were carried out by coalitions of forces, not by Washington alone, which the statement implied.

Ambassador Albright's statement was also framed entirely from the perspective of an important external actor that mixes rhetoric of leadership with isolationist actions and has a deserved reputation as the United Nations' biggest deadbeat because Washington's debt is so enormous. The perspective of victims and relief personnel in the field would be less self-congratulatory and no doubt highlight the need for more prevention and rapid response strategies. Paralleling her comments, but from the humanitarian's perspective, could be the following: Thousands of noncombatants suffered in Baghdad from air strikes on nonmilitary infrastructure and economic sanctions; the expensive airlift operations were necessitated by lack of military resolve to address Serb aggression on relief convoys; early warning signs of genocide in Rwanda were ignored; and in the three years that passed between the overthrow of Haiti's first elected president and the restoration of democracy, the Haitian people were subjected to documented torture, arbitrary arrest and detention, and assassination, while many others died trying to reach shores of refuge, where their pleas for temporary asylum were denied.

Showcasing a government's achievements while ignoring the substantial contributions of other external actors represents the absence of an "international identity," or a true "international society," that might facilitate a more consistent and preventive response to human suffering. Although contemporary social science tends to toss those terms about liberally without precise definitions, it is difficult to locate conceptually where international society resides. Perhaps part of what is needed are symbols of an international society that would help stimulate its emergence and loyalty. Monuments to fallen peacekeepers should be more prevalent throughout the world—both within countries where they have fallen and from countries where they have been sent. The United Nations has a flag, but schoolchildren's familiarity with it is hardly universal. The public relations requirements for an international society and humanitarian activities are wanting. To foster prevention of the abuse of noncombatants caught in political struggles, the international society of peoples must challenge some practices of the international society of states; such a society has yet to be grounded in reality or in symbols.

Deterrence—the prevention that results because potential wrongdoers fear plausible retaliation—has been an essential ingredient in world politics for centuries. Preventive measures include addressing economic root causes and using troops to forestall the outbreak of violence as mentioned earlier, but there are other mechanisms by which aggression against noncombatants can be deterred.

Prosecution of those accused of international crime is one potential and ignored means of forcing other would-be offenders at least to think twice before flaunting international norms. Agreements among states regarding extradition, prosecution, and punishment of terrorists are respected because they cover acts of violence against a state that are spelled out in advance of any wrongdoing. Yet acts of violence against people within societies and against humanitarian and peacekeeping personnel at present go without punishment. Security Council Resolution 827 of May 1993 established the International War Crimes Tribunal, whose intent was "to send a clear message to all in former Yugoslavia that they must stop immediately violations of international humanitarian law or face the consequences." More than two years later, the consequences appeared nominal to the perpetrators of war crimes. In spite of the annexes to the agreement initialed in Dayton, Ohio, it is hardly guaranteed that all states, particularly Russia, will cooperate with the extradition of potential Serb war criminals, and it is equally doubtful that Russia's comrades on the Security Council will push the issue. In early 1996, implementation of the Dayton peace agreement became stalled when Bosnian Serb military commander Ratko Mladic, himself listed as a war criminal by the tribunal, protested the detaining of a number of Bosnian Serbs on war crimes charges. Within days, the self-proclaimed Bosnian Serb government declared that the peace process would continue and that the Bosnian Serb military did not have the right to speak on behalf of the Bosnian Serb people. The world has yet to see the success of war crime trials in the absence of an unconditional surrender; it is important that readers pay attention to the issues that continue to emerge in the tribunal's efforts to add justice to the peace process. The history of war crimes prosecution for civil wars has little precedent.

The well-known Nuremberg Trials and the less familiar ones in Tokyo following World War II set precedents for enforcement of laws of war crimes against individuals from the defeated countries after an interstate world war. But these precedents have had no international application since. In 1991, the first draft of the Code of Crimes Against the Peace and Security of Command was completed by the International Law Commission. Building upon the principles of Nuremberg and Tokyo, the code calls for criminal liability against nations as well as individuals and includes crimes such as genocide, aggression, threat of aggression, systematic or mass violations of human rights (including violations involving a state's own nationals); the recruitment, use, financing, and training of mercenaries; international terrorism; illicit traffic in narcotic drugs; and willful and severe damage to the environment. Whether approved as a declaration or convention, the code's ratification would constitute a double-edged sword. Although Saddam Hussein and Iraq could be candidates for violations of the code because of the invasion of Kuwait, so, too, could former President Reagan and the United States for the invasion of Panama.

Deterrence as a preventive measure would require a permanent and standing international criminal court, whose jurisdiction was accepted by all countries, to judge war crimes and enforce punishment within an international penal facility. There would not be any death penalty given the number of countries that have outlawed such punishment. To deter abhorrent behavior, the court and its statutes must exist *before* war crimes are committed so that would-be wrongdoers clearly understand the consequences of committing crimes. Assistant Secretary of State for Democracy, Human Rights, and Labor John Shattuck noted the logic for not sweeping under the historical rug the reprehensible behavior of war criminals: "History demonstrates that impunity breeds anger, anger provokes retaliation, retaliation begets more hatred, hatred spawns more violence—and so the cycle continues." Although such deeds cannot be undone and it may be tempting to turn a page on armed conflicts as quickly as possible, Shattuck also noted the importance of sending a clear signal to deter future criminals against humanity: "Over the long term, the Yugoslavia tribunal and its Rwandan counterpart can create a body of precedent that will remind would-be perpetrators that there are consequences to violating international standards."[22]

In the absence of a permanent judicial mechanism, the more normal recourse is to determine compensation for those who suffered inhumane acts rather than punishment for those who performed them. As such, the deterrence value of war crimes is lost. The Serbs' rape of Muslim women in military brothels is similar to Japanese brothels with Korean women. Genocidal crimes committed in Rwanda bear similarity to inhumane acts against Jews in the Third Reich; and these are comparable, in substance, if not in numbers, to crimes against noncombatants in Latin America's Southern Cone or against civilians in Eastern Europe during the Cold War. National reconciliation demands exposure of those who are guilty of inhumanity; but with procedures and punishment lacking, so, too, is deterrence. Prospective war criminals are not obliged to factor into their evil calculations the risk of punishment.

Measures to prevent humanitarian crises must also take a look at the means by which violence is carried out against noncombatants. In addition to an increase in intrastate conflicts themselves, a correlation exists between the relaxation of arms exports following the Cold War and the arming of combatants in the rising tide of intrastate conflicts. In 1993, the United States recorded its best year yet for export sales of weapons at $32 billion, with 25 percent of the weapons sold to democratic countries, 34 percent to partly democratic countries, and 41 percent to nondemocracies. In 1994, France surpassed the United States in arms exports. Illegal transfer of light weapons has increased in recent years. As trade restrictions among countries are lowered and economic interdependence continues to create new pathways for legal trade, trade of illegal goods such as drugs and weapons rises as well.

Reluctant to dismantle Cold War military complexes and thereby put hundreds of thousands of voters out of jobs, suppliers of light and conventional weapons and inexpensive land mines will continue to find opportunities in civil wars. It is in the interest of weapon producers and belligerents in prolonged conflicts to forestall international efforts to curb arms sales and production. Noncombatants and humanitarians who assist them are the ones who suffer. To prevent future humanitarian crises, the same amount of attention must be given to light and conventional arms proliferation as nuclear weapons.

Until prevention is adopted as a standard strategy for dealing with potential human tragedy before it explodes, causing populations to scatter for safety and sustenance, humanitarians will continue to respond even under the most dangerous circumstances. The harassment, kidnapping, torture, and killing of aid personnel have not dampened the humanitarian impulse. The growth of NGOs in the field of humanitarianism is testament to the increased number of individuals committed to relieving human suffering at home and abroad, regardless of foreign policies and sometimes in spite of them. Whether in combat zones in inner cities or in unfamiliar countries, the humanitarian impulse is strong. The humanitarian idea continues to evolve, with each new generation influenced by ideals of democracy and human rights grounded in written instruments and institutions and buttressed by societal norms.

CONCLUSION

A criticism often leveled against prevention is also applied with even more derision to humanitarian action: Both are fraught with idealism, or the pursuit of high or noble principles. If idealism is characterized by a striving for what ought to be, whereas realism claims to react to what is, it makes sense that a global strategy for dealing with today's and tomorrow's crises requires a healthy combination of both. As the Independent

The positive impact of humanitarian intervention is
reflected in the eyes of this Central American child.
U.N. Photo/134.479.

Commission on International Humanitarian Issues observed, "The problem is not of morality versus politics but rather of the kind of politics
which allow moral restraints to emerge and to be observed."[23] This challenge starkly confronts the authors and the readers of this book.

In essence, the story told here of humanitarianism during war and its
various manifestations throughout history represents the eternal human
struggle between compassion, based on recognition of a common humanity, and self-interest. Neither individuals nor bureaucracies are free from
this philosophical dilemma, which underpins the operational ones ex-
plored in Chapter 3 and the policy debates and recommendations in

Chapters 4 and 5. For victims of war and humanitarian personnel, the cry goes out for compassion to prevail, as revealed in a May 25, 1995, letter to the Security Council from the mayor of the Bosnian safe area of Tuzla. Bosnian Serbs had just shelled the city. Sixty-five children gathered in the center of town were killed. There comes a time in all crises, stressed Mayor Beslagic, when an obvious and timely course of action—of compassion—is required: "Do not expect that I address you in a diplomatic language in this the most painful moment in the history of this town. Tonight parents were collecting parts of their children's bodies on the streets of Tuzla. Their children had left their homes a few hours earlier, with the belief in a better future. You should know, that at this moment when the pain is all over Tuzla, there is no dilemma anymore."[24]

It is to be hoped that this book has demonstrated that lack of compassion is not a sufficient explanation for why the international system does not answer every call for help or why suffering occurs even though there are sufficient financial resources and food to fill the pockets and bellies of the needy. The actors making up the international humanitarian system bring their own set of institutional challenges to the delivery of succor and protection—perhaps the most important being the political will to give aid based purely on need and to cooperate based on common objectives. The actions of belligerents and various contextual factors place additional dilemmas and challenges before those who feel a humanitarian imperative or impulse. However daunting these organizational, ethical, and operational challenges may seem, it is absolutely essential that the new breed of young humanitarians confront and work to resolve the dilemmas of help. This is your world; undoubtedly the solutions will be yours as well.

□ □ □

Discussion Questions

CHAPTER ONE

1. According to international law, do states have a duty to intervene in wars where human atrocities are evident?

2. If international law is to be respected, do humanitarians have an obligation to address local mores that ignore the rights of certain groups, such as women?

3. When is state sovereignty sacrosanct?

4. Can humanitarians be apolitical in a war zone?

5. How do you foresee the future evolution of the humanitarian idea?

CHAPTER TWO

1. What are the difficulties encountered in the coordination of a collective response to humanitarian needs in a war zone? Which flow from within an organizational structure, and which exist across organizational structures?

2. Are the problems outlined in the previous question surmountable? If so, how?

3. What elements should be added to a design for an international humanitarian system that "works" from the perspective of the victims of war?

4. Is there an international humanitarian community? system? regime?

5. Which of the five case studies seemed most and least successful in terms of minimizing life-threatening suffering? Why?

CHAPTER THREE

1. What kinds of solutions can you offer for operational difficulties associated with refugee camps?

2. Should human rights protection be included in an emergency relief effort? Can a single organization effectively satisfy both the provision of food and the protection of rights?

3. What criterion could the international humanitarian system use for determining which war-affected populations are "good candidates" to receive reconstruction and development assistance in addition to emergency relief? Should those completely destitute receive more assistance than those who are marginally destitute?

4. Is triage operationally or ethically acceptable?

CHAPTER FOUR

1. According to the text, and in your opinion, what are the sources of compassion or donor fatigue?

2. Why does the international humanitarian system respond more quickly and generously to loud rather than silent emergencies?

3. Would it be preferable to cordon off wars until belligerents are exhausted and then devote all humanitarian resources to the alleviation of abject poverty?

4. What is the most pressing policy issue facing humanitarians?

5. Is it naive to expect humanitarian actors to aspire to neutrality and impartiality?

6. How can states and aid agencies respond more effectively to large and sudden movements of displaced people?

7. Can a meaningful distinction be made among refugees, internally displaced persons, and other types of voluntary or involuntary migrants?

8. Who should determine when it is safe for refugees to be repatriated?

9. What policies would support distressed communities so that the period of their dependency on external assistance is short and the social, economic, and political recoveries are longer lasting?

CHAPTER FIVE

1. Is geopolitical reality or creativity a large constraint to immediate improvements in the international humanitarian system?

2. Do the media help or hinder the international humanitarian system and the plight of the hungry and fearful?

3. To what extent have your views about humanitarian emergencies been influenced by print or electronic media?

4. Would centralization help or hinder international humanitarian responses?

5. Is humanitarian action principled and pristine? Or is politics dirty, or is "humanitarian politics" inevitable?

6. Is prevention a Pollyannaish pursuit?

□ □ □

Notes

INTRODUCTION

1. Laurence Urdang, ed., *The Random House College Dictionary* (New York: Random House Inc., 1988).

2. Steven Kull, "What the Public Knows That Washington Doesn't," *Foreign Policy* (Winter 1995–1996):102–115.

3. James F. Hoge Jr., "Editor's Note," *Foreign Affairs* 73, no. 6 (November-December 1994):v. For a wide-ranging collection of essays, see Paul A. Winters, ed., *Interventionism: Current Controversies* (San Diego: Greenhaven Press, 1995).

4. Alex de Waal and Rakiya Omaar, "Can Military Intervention Be 'Humanitarian?'" *Middle East Report*, nos. 187–188 (March-April/May-June 1994):7.

5. This term was first used by Thomas G. Weiss and Kurt M. Campbell, "Military Humanitarianism," *Survival*, Vol. 33, No. 5, September/October 1991, pp. 451–465.

6. See Malcolm N. Shaw, *International Law*, 3d ed. (Cambridge: Cambridge University Press, 1991).

7. Adam Roberts, "Humanitarian War: Military Intervention and Human Rights," *International Affairs* 69 (1993):429–449.

8. For these and other gruesome statistics, see United Nations High Commissioner for Refugees, *The State of the World's Refugees 1995: In Search of Solutions* (New York: Oxford University Press, 1995).

9. Commission on Global Governance, *Our Global Neighbourhood* (Oxford: Oxford University Press, 1995), p. 90.

CHAPTER ONE

1. Immanuel Kant, *Perpetual Peace*, edited with an introduction by Lewis White Beck (New York: Liberal Arts Press, 1957).

2. For a more detailed understanding of realism and neorealism, respectively, see Niccolo Machiavelli, *The Prince*, trans. and ed. Harvey C. Mansfield Jr. (Chicago: University of Chicago Press, 1985); and Kenneth Waltz, *Man, the State, and War* (New York: Columbia University Press, 1959).

3. John Ruggie, "Continuity and Transformation in the World Polity: Toward a Neorealist Synthesis," in Robert O. Keohane, ed., *Neorealism and Its Critics* (New York: Columbia University Press, 1986), pp. 131–157, and John Ruggie, ed., *Multilateralism Matters* (New York: Columbia University Press, 1993).

4. See Robert Keohane and Joseph S. Nye, *Power and Interdependence* (Boston: Little, Brown, 1977), p. 19.

5. Jean-Jacques Rousseau, *Selections* (New York: Perennial Library, 1986), p. 162.

6. See Joseph Wronka, *Human Rights and Social Policy in the 21st Century* (Lanham, Md.: University Press of America, 1992).

7. Hersch Lauterpacht, *International Law and Human Rights* (London: Stevens and Son, 1950), p. 84, quoted in Wronka, *Human Rights and Social Policy*, p. 49.

8. Thomas Buergenthal, *International Human Rights Law* (St. Paul, Minn.: West, 1988), p. 3.

9. See Gil Loescher, *Beyond Charity: International Cooperation and the Global Refugee Crisis* (New York: Oxford University Press, 1994).

10. See Ephraim Isaac, "Humanitarianism Across Religions and Cultures," in Thomas G. Weiss and Larry Minear, eds., *Humanitarianism Across Borders: Sustaining Civilians in Times of War* (Boulder: Lynne Rienner, 1993), pp. 16–21.

11. See Benedict Anderson, *Imagined Communities* (London: Verso, 1983).

12. See Craig Murphy, *International Organizations and Industrial Change* (Oxford: Polity Press, 1994).

13. The League of Nations' institutional life span technically stretched from January 1920 to April 1946, although it had been pronounced dead in 1935 and again in 1939 and was mothballed during World War II.

14. José E. Alvarez, "The 'Right to Be Left Alone' and the General Assembly," in *Article 2(7) Revisited*, Reports and Papers 1994, No. 5 (Providence, R.I.: Academic Council on the United Nations System, 1994), p. 9.

15. See Felice Gaer, "Human Rights NGOs Confront Governments at the UN," *Third World Quarterly* 16, no. 3 (September 1995):389–404. For an extended discussion of this issue, see Jack Donnelly, *International Human Rights* (Boulder: Westview Press, 1994).

16. See *The Geneva Conventions of August 12, 1949,* and *Protocols Additional to the Geneva Conventions of 12 August 1949* (Geneva: International Committee of the Red Cross, 1989).

17. Anthony Parsons, *From Cold War to Hot Peace* (London: Michael Joseph, 1995), p. viii.

18. For a discussion of the range of such conflicts, see Ted Robert Gurr and Barbara Harff, *Ethnic Conflict in World Politics* (Boulder: Westview Press, 1994); Michael E. Brown, ed., *Ethnic Conflict and International Security* (Princeton: Princeton University Press, 1993); and a special issue of *Daedalus* 122, no. 3 (Summer 1993), entitled *Reconstructing Nations and States*.

19. Boutros Boutros-Ghali, *An Agenda for Peace* (New York: United Nations, 1992), par. 59.

20. Boutros Boutros-Ghali, *Supplement to an Agenda for Peace: Position Paper of the Secretary-General on the Occasion of the Fiftieth Anniversary of the United Nations* (New York: United Nations, 1995), pars. 4, 77.

21. Ibid., par. 6.

22. International Peace Academy, *The OAU and Conflict Management in Africa* (New York: International Peace Academy, 1993), p. 2.

23. Francis M. Deng, "Sovereignty, Responsibility, and Accountability: A Framework of Protection, Assistance, and Development for the Internally Displaced" (Washington, D.C.: Brookings Institution, 1995), p. 58.

24. Rakiya Omaar and Alex de Waal, *Humanitarianism Unbound?* Discussion Paper 5 (London: African Rights, November 1994), p. 5.

25. International Committee of the Red Cross, *Respect for International Humanitarian Law: ICRC Review of Five Years of Activity (1987–1991)* (Geneva: ICRC, 1991), p. 4.

CHAPTER TWO

1. *Crosslines* 3, No. 4 (December 1995–January 1996).

2. For further analysis, see Marion J. Levy Jr., "Armed Force Organizations," in Henry Bienen, ed., *The Military and Modernizations* (Chicago: Aldine-Atherton, 1971), pp. 41–78.

3. See Laura Miller and Charles Moskos, "Humanitarians or Warriors? Race, Gender, and Combat Status in Operation Restore Hope," *Armed Forces and Society* 21, no. 4 (Summer 1995):624, 631.

4. Gayle Young, "Countries Train Together in Egypt," www.cnn.com, November 14, 1995.

5. Refugee Policy Group, *Somalia: Lives Lost, Lives Saved* (Washington, D.C.: Refugee Policy Group, November 1994), p. 27.

6. U.S. Permanent Mission to the United Nations, *Global Humanitarian Emergencies, 1995* (New York: U.S. Permanent Mission to the United Nations, January 1995), pp. 14–15.

7. Barbara Crossette, "UNICEF Asks Broader Aid for Children," *New York Times,* June 12, 1995, p. A5; and "Aid OECD," *Development Cooperation 1994, 1995, GNP* (World Bank: World Bank Atlas, 1995).

8. Jim Clancy and Jackie Shymanski, "Snow . . . Fog . . . Grumbling Troops," www.cnn.com, December 16, 1995.

9. See UNHCR, *Concept Paper: Humanitarian Emergencies and Refugees* (Geneva: UNHCR, April 3, 1995).

10. U.S. Permanent Mission, *Global Humanitarian Emergencies,* p. 14.

11. *UNDHA Humanitarian Bulletin* 95/2 (October 31, 1995).

12. Graham Allison, "Conceptual Models of the Cuban Missile Crisis," *American Political Science Review* 63, no. 3 (September 1969):689–718. See also Graham Allison, *Essence of Decision: Explaining the Cuban Missile Crisis* (Boston: Little, Brown, 1971).

13. Eric Schmitt, "Troop Move Pits White House Against Pentagon," *New York Times,* June 7, 1995, p. A19.

14. Levy, "Armed Force Organizations," p. 49.

15. Quoted in Miller and Moskos, "Humanitarians or Warriors?" p. 624.

16. Erskine Childers, with Brian Urquhart, *Renewing the United Nations* (Uppsala: Dag Hammarskjöld Foundation, 1994), pp. 28–29.

17. Patricia Weiss-Fagen, *After the Conflict: A Review of Selected Sources on Rebuilding War-Torn Societies* (Geneva: U.N. Research Institute for Social Development, May 1995), p. 2.

18. Peter Macalister-Smith, *International Humanitarian Assistance: Disaster Relief Actions in International Law and Organization* (Dordrecht: Nijhoff, 1985), p. 37.

19. Hugo Slim and Angela Penrose, "U.N. Reform in a Changing World: Responding to Complex Emergencies," in Joanna Macrae and Anthony Zwi, eds., *War and Hunger* (London: Zed Books, 1996), p. 198.

20. See Gayle E. Smith, "Relief Operations and Military Strategy," in Thomas G. Weiss and Larry Minear, eds., *Humanitarianism Across Borders: Sustaining Civilians in Times of War* (Boulder: Lynne Rienner, 1993), pp. 97–116.

21. See James P. Ingram, "The Future Architecture for International Humanitarian Assistance," in ibid., pp. 171–193.

22. See Bernard Kouchner and Mario Bettati, *Le devoir d'ingérence* (Paris: Denoël, 1987); Bernard Kouchner, *Le malheur des autres* (Paris: Odile Jacob, 1991); and Mario Bettati, "Intervention, ingérence ou assistance?" *Revue Trimestrielle des Droits de l'Homme*, no. 19 (July 1994):308–358.

23. Charles Tilly, *From Mobilization to Revolution* (Reading, Mass.: Addison-Wesley, 1978), p. 5.

24. Lars Schoultz, "U.S.–Latin American Relations," in Joel Krieger, ed., *The Oxford Companion to Politics of the World* (New York: Oxford University Press, 1993), p. 948.

25. Cristina Eguizábal, David Lewis, Larry Minear, Peter Sollis, and Thomas G. Weiss, *Humanitarian Challenges in Central America: Learning the Lessons of Recent Armed Conflicts*, Occasional Paper 14 (Providence, R.I.: Thomas J. Watson Jr. Institute for International Studies, 1993), pp. 35–36.

26. Ibid., p. 56.

27. Larry Minear, U.B.P. Chelliah, Jeff Crisp, John Mackinlay, and Thomas G. Weiss, *United Nations Coordination of the International Humanitarian Response to the Gulf Crisis 1990–92*, Occasional Paper 13 (Providence, R.I.: Thomas J. Watson Jr. Institute for International Studies, 1992), p. 1.

28. Ibid., p. 17.

29. Jeffrey Clark, "Debacle in Somalia: Failure of the Collective Response," in Lori Fisler Damrosch, ed., *Enforcing Restraint: Collective Intervention in Internal Conflicts* (New York: Council on Foreign Relations Press, 1993), pp. 205–239.

30. Enrico Augelli and Craig N. Murphy, "Lessons of Somalia for Future Multilateral Humanitarian Assistance Operations," *Global Governance* 1, no. 3 (September-December 1995):341–368.

31. Mohamed Sahnoun, *Somalia: The Missed Opportunities* (Washington, D.C.: U.S. Institute of Peace, 1994).

32. Clark, "Debacle in Somalia," pp. 220, 229.

33. Lawrence Freedman, "Why the West Failed," *Foreign Policy* 97 (Winter 1994–1995):59.

34. Quoted in Stanley Meiser, "U.N. Relief Hopes Turn to Despair," *Washington Post*, October 25, 1993, p. A1.

35. Quoted in Roger Cohen, "Allied Resolve to Bolster U.N. Peacekeeping in Bosnia; US Weighs a Combat Role," *New York Times*, May 30, 1995, p. A1.

36. Quoted in Barbara Crossette, "At the U.N., Thoughts About Bosnia but No Action," *New York Times*, December 9, 1994, p. A12.

37. Quoted in Larry Minear, Jeffrey Clark, Roberta Cohen, Dennis Gallagher, Iain Guest, and Thomas G. Weiss, *Humanitarian Action in the Former Yugoslavia: The U.N.'s Role, 1991–1993*, Occasional Paper 18 (Providence, R.I.: Thomas J. Watson Jr. Institute for International Studies, 1994), p. 1.

38. "Rwanda Appeals for Halt of Arms Flow to Rebels," *New York Times*, May 31, 1995, p. A6.

39. See Holly J. Burkhalter, "The Question of Genocide: The Clinton Administration and Rwanda," *World Policy Journal* 9, no. 4 (Winter 1994–1995):45.

40. Ibid.

41. Antonio Donini and Norah Niland, *Rwanda: Lessons Learned: A Report on the Coordination of Humanitarian Activities* (Geneva: U.N. Department of Humanitarian Affairs, 1994), pp. 11, 2–3.

42. Ibid., p. 8.

43. "Tribunal Readies Case in Rwandan Massacres," www.cnn.com, November 14, 1995.

44. Gordon Adam, "A Dramatic Treatment . . . ," *Crosslines* 3, no. 2 (April-May 1995):42.

CHAPTER THREE

1. Situation Report no. 5, www.ifrc.org, July 27, 1995.

2. Alain Destexhe, "A Border Without Doctors," *New York Times*, February 9, 1995, p. A7.

3. Ian Smillie, *The Alms Bazaar: Altruism Under Fire—Non-Profit Organizations and International Development* (London: Intermediate Technology Publications, 1995), p. 111.

4. Quoted in United Nations High Commissioner for Refugees, *The State of the World's Refugees, 1995* (New York, Oxford University Press, 1995), p. 37.

5. Antonio Donini, *The Policies of Mercy: U.N. Coordination in Afghanistan, Mozambique, and Rwanda*, Occasional Paper 22 (Providence, R.I.: Thomas J. Watson Jr. Institute for International Studies, 1996).

6. Human Rights Watch, *The Lost Agenda: Human Rights and U.N. Field Operations* (New York: Human Rights Watch, 1993).

7. Gayle E. Smith, "Emerging from Crisis: From Relief to Development," *Humanitarian Monitor*, no. 2 (February 1995):28.

8. These issues are discussed in a series of essays in Robert I. Rotberg and Thomas G. Weiss, eds., *From Massacres to Genocide: The Media, Public Policy, and Humanitarian Crises* (Washington, D.C.: Brookings Institution, 1996); and in Larry Minear, Colin Scott, and Thomas G. Weiss, *The News Media, Civil War, and Humanitarian Action* (Boulder: Lynne Rienner, 1996).

9. Larry Minear, U.B.P. Chelliah, Jeff Crisp, John Mackinlay, and Thomas G. Weiss, *United Nations Coordination of the International Humanitarian Response to the Gulf Crisis 1990–1992*, Occasional Paper 13 (Providence, R.I.: Thomas J. Watson Jr. Institute for International Studies, 1992), pp. 15–16.

10. International Federation of Red Cross and Red Crescent Societies, *World Disasters Report 1995* (Geneva: IFRC, 1995), p. 42.

11. John Seaman, "Relief, Rehabilitation, and Development," *IDS Bulletin* 25, No. 4 (October 1994), pp. 34–35.

12. Shashi Tharoor, "The Changing Face of Peace-Keeping and Peace-Enforcement" (Speech presented at the International Institute for Strategic Studies meeting, Vienna, Austria, September 9, 1995), p. 10.

13. Boutros Boutros-Ghali, *Supplement to an Agenda for Peace: Position Paper of the Secretary-General on the Occasion of the Fiftieth Anniversary of the United Nations* (New York: United Nations, 1995), par. 70.

14. Cristina Eguizábal, David Lewis, Larry Minear, Peter Sollis, and Thomas G. Weiss, *Humanitarian Challenges in Central America: Learning the Lessons of Recent Armed Conflicts*, Occasional Paper 14 (Providence, R.I.: Thomas J. Watson Jr. Institute for International Studies, 1993), p. 13.

15. Giandomenico Picco, "The U.N. and the Use of Force," *Foreign Affairs* 73, no. 5 (September-October 1994):15.

16. Larry Minear and Philippe Guillot, *Soldiers to the Rescue: Humanitarian Lessons from Rwanda* (Paris: OECD, 1996).

17. Congressional Research Service, *Peacekeeping: Issues of U.S. Military Involvement*, Issue Brief IB94040 (Washington, D.C.: Congressional Research Service, updated September 28, 1995).

18. Charles G. Boyd, "Making Peace with the Guilty," *Foreign Affairs* 74, no. 5 (September-October 1995):23.

19. Sadako Ogata, "Statement to the Economic and Social Council on Humanitarian Assistance, July 1, 1993," p. 4.

20. "Going In," *Boston Globe*, September 18, 1994, p. 74.

21. Quoted in *Humanitarian Monitor*, no. 2 (February 1995):5.

22. International Institute for Strategic Studies, "Military Support for Humanitarian Operations," *Strategic Comments*, no. 2 (February 22, 1995), p. 2. The ICRC is increasingly preoccupied by this subject. See Umesh Palwankar, ed., *Symposium on Humanitarian Action and Peace-Keeping: Report* (Geneva: ICRC, 1994).

23. John G. Sommer, *Hope Restored? Humanitarian Aid in Somalia, 1990–1994* (Washington, D.C.: Refugee Policy Group, 1994), p. 116.

24. For a discussion, see Carol Bellamy, *The State of the World's Children 1996* (Oxford: Oxford University Press, 1996), pp. 34–36.

25. See Francis M. Deng and Larry Minear, *The Challenges of Famine Relief: Emergency Operations in the Sudan* (Washington, D.C.: Brookings Institution, 1992).

CHAPTER FOUR

1. Congressional Research Service, *Bosnian Brierpatch: Military Options, Mid-1995*, Report for Congress 95/732A (Washington, D.C.: Congressional Research Service, June 20, 1995), p. 2.

2. "America's Least-Wanted," *The Economist* 332, no. 7872 (July 16, 1994), pp. 23–24.

3. UNHCR, *A UNHCR Handbook for the Military on Humanitarian Operations* (UNHCR: Geneva, January 1995), p. 33.

4. Javier Solana, Speech at the Wehrkunde Conference, Munich, Germany, February 3–4, 1996.

5. See Peter Uvin, "Rwanda and Burundi: Challenging Current Development Practice," *Brown Journal on Third World Affairs* (Spring 1995):3–7.

6. Alvaro de Soto and Graciana del Castillo, "Obstacles to Peacebuilding," *Foreign Policy* 94 (Spring 1994):70.

7. Mary B. Anderson and Peter J. Woodrow, *Rising from the Ashes: Development Strategies in Times of Disaster* (Boulder: Westview Press, 1989).

8. Matthias Stiefel, *UNDP in Conflicts and Disasters: An Overview of the "Continuum Project"* (Geneva: Graduate Institute of International Studies, May 1994), p. 3.

9. United Nations Development Programme, *Human Development Report 1995* (New York: Oxford University Press, 1995), p. 12.

10. Roberta Cohen, "Put Refugee Women in Charge of Food Distribution," *Hunger 1996, Countries in Crisis: Sixth Annual Report on the State of World Hunger* (Silver Springs, Md.: Bread for the World Institute, 1996), p. 35.

11. Larry Minear and Thomas G. Weiss, *Humanitarian Action in Times of War: A Handbook for Practitioners* (Boulder: Lynne Rienner, 1993), p. 33.

12. Stephen John Stedman, "The New Interventionists," *Foreign Affairs* 72, no. 1 (1993):9, 14.

13. Stephen John Stedman, "Alchemy for a New World Order," *Foreign Affairs* 74, no. 3 (May-June 1995):16.

14. Evelyn Waugh, *Scoop* (Boston: Little, Brown, 1938).

15. Quoted in Phillip Knightley, *The First Casualty: From the Crimea to Vietnam: The War Correspondent as Hero, Propagandist, and Myth Maker* (New York: Harcourt Brace Jovanovich, 1975), p. 171.

16. Nik Gowing, *Real-Time Television Coverage of Armed Conflicts and Diplomatic Crises: Does It Pressure or Distort Foreign Policy Decisions?* Press Politics, Public Policy Working Papers 94-1 (Cambridge: Harvard University Press, 1994), p. 86.

17. David Reiff, *Slaughterhouse: Bosnia and the Failure of the West* (New York: Simon and Schuster, 1995), p. 41.

18. Rony Brauman, "When Suffering Makes a Good Story," in Médecins Sans Frontières Report on World Crisis Intervention, *Life, Death, and Aid*, ed. François Jean (London: Routledge, 1993), p. 154.

19. UNHCR, *A UNHCR Handbook*, p. 21.

20. John Clark, "Policy Influence, Lobbying, and Advocacy," in Michael Edwards and David Hulme, eds., *Making a Difference: NGOs and Development in a Changing World* (London: Earthscan, 1992), p. 199.

21. Michael Edwards and David Hulme, "Introduction," in ibid., p. 20.

22. Lawrence Susskind, *Environmental Diplomacy: Negotiating More Effective Global Agreements* (New York: Oxford University Press, 1994), p. 51.

CHAPTER FIVE

1. Advertisement of the International Rescue Committee, *New York Times*, July 18, 1995, p. A9.

2. Quoted in Roger Cohen, "NATO Demands Serbs Withdraw Guns from Sarajevo," *New York Times*, September 4, 1995, p. A3.

3. Ian Smillie, *The Alms Bazaar: Altruism Under Fire—Non-Profit Organizations and International Development* (London: Intermediate Technology Publications, 1995), p. 240.

4. Catholic Relief Services, *Catholic Relief Services Guidelines for Humanitarian Assistance in Conflict Situations* (Baltimore, Md.: CRS, 1992); ICRC, *Implementation of International Humanitarian Law Protection of the Civilian Population and Persons Hors*

de Combat (Geneva: ICRC, 1991); and UNHCR, *UNHCR: Coping with Stress in Crisis Situations* (Geneva: UNHCR, 1992).

5. Larry Minear and Thomas G. Weiss, *Humanitarian Action in Times of War: A Handbook for Practitioners* (Boulder: Lynne Rienner, 1993), chap. 2.

6. See Larry Minear and Thomas G. Weiss, "Evolving Humanitarian Standards: Toward a Code of Conflict for Armed Conflicts," in ibid., pp. 83–91.

7. Citizens Conference on NGO-U.N. Relations, "Declaration of Accountability for Global Governance," June 24, 1995.

8. See Antonio Donini, *The Policies of Mercy: U.N. Coordination in Afghanistan, Mozambique, and Rwanda,* Occasional Paper 22 (Providence, R.I.: Thomas J. Watson Jr. Institute for International Studies, 1996).

9. See the series of papers for the PVO Conference on Disaster Response, organized by InterAction and the Carnegie Endowment for International Peace, Carnegie Endowment for International Peace, Washington, D.C., September 17–18, 1995.

10. See Commission on Global Governance, *Our Global Neighbourhood* (Oxford: Oxford University Press, 1995); and Independent Working Group on the Future of the United Nations, *The United Nations in Its Second Half-Century* (New York: Ford Foundation, 1995).

11. For discussions, see Larry Minear, Jeffrey Clark, Roberta Cohen, Dennis Gallagher, Iain Guest, and Thomas G. Weiss, *Humanitarian Action in the Former Yugoslavia: The U.N.'s Role, 1991–1993,* Occasional Paper 18 (Providence, R.I., Thomas J. Watson Jr. Institute for International Studies, 1994); and Jarat Chopra, Åge Eknes, and Tralv Nordb, *Fighting for Hope in Somalia* (Oslo: Norwegian Institute of International Affairs, 1995). Antonio Donini and Nora Niland, *Rwanda: Lessons Learned: A Report on the Coordination of Humanitarian Activities* (New York: United Nations, 1994). Less sanguine judgments about the overall impact are found in Rakiya Omaar and Alex de Waal, *Rwanda: Death, Despair, and Destruction* (London: African Rights, 1994); Alain Destexhe, *Rwanda: Essai sur le génocide* (Brussels: Editions Complexe, 1994); and Rony Brauman, *Devant le Mal: Rwanda, un génocide en direct* (Paris: Arléa, 1994).

12. Erskine Childers, with Brian Urquhart, *Renewing the United Nations System* (Uppsala: Dag Hammarskjöld Foundation, 1994), p. 114.

13. Quoted in William Shawcross, "A Hero for Our Time," *New York Review of Books* 42, no. 19 (November 30, 1995), p. 38.

14. Raimo Väyrenen, *Enforcement and Humanitarian Intervention* (South Bend, Ind.: Kroc Institute, 1994), p. 29.

15. U.S. Permanent Mission to the United Nations, "Readying the United Nations for the Twenty-First Century: Some 'U.N.–21' Proposals for Consideration" (New York: U.S. Permanent Mission to the United Nations, July 1995, undated nonpaper).

16. Quoted in Phillip Knightley, *The First Casualty: From the Crimea to Vietnam: The War Correspondent as Hero, Propagandist, and Myth Maker* (New York: Harcourt Brace Jovanovich, 1975), p. vii.

17. Rakiya Omaar and Alex de Waal, "Doing Harm, Doing Good? The International Relief Effort in Somalia," *Current History* 92, no. 574 (May 1993):202.

18. John C. Hammock and Joel R. Charny, "Emergency Response as Morality Play: The Media, the Relief Agencies, and the Need for Capacity Building," in Robert I. Rotberg and Thomas G. Weiss, eds., *From Massacres to Genocide: The Media, Public Policy, and Humanitarian Crises* (Washington, D.C.: Brookings Institution, 1996), pp. 115–135.

19. David P. Forsythe, "Politics and the International Tribunal for the Former Yugoslavia," *Criminal Law Forum*, no. 2–3 (1994):406–407.

20. Dick Thornburgh, *Reform and Restructuring at the United Nations: A Progress Report* (Hanover, N.H.: Rockefeller Center, 1993).

21. Michael S. Lund, *Preventive Diplomacy and American Foreign Policy* (Washington, D.C.: U.S. Institute of Peace Press, 1994), p. 27.

22. John Shattuck, "Pursuing Justice in Bosnia," *Boston Globe*, September 1, 1995, p. A23.

23. Independent Commission on International Humanitarian Issues, *Winning the Human Race* (London: Zed Books, 1988), p. 11.

24. www.cnn.com.

□ □ □

Additional Reading
and Related Web Locations

ADDITIONAL READING

American Academy of Arts and Sciences. *Reconstructing Nations and States*. Special issue of *Daedalus* 122, no. 3 (1993).

Amnesty International. *Peace Keeping and Human Rights*. IOR 40/01/94. London: Amnesty International, January 1994.

Anderson, Mary B., and Peter J. Woodrow. *Rising from the Ashes: Development Strategies in Times of Disaster*. Boulder: Westview Press, 1989.

Appleyard, Reginald. *International Migration: Challenges for the Nineties*. Geneva: International Organization for Migration, 1991.

Benthall, Jonathan. *Disasters, Relief, and the Media*. London: Tauris, 1993.

Boutros-Ghali, Boutros. *An Agenda for Peace 1995*. New York: United Nations, 1995.

Bread for the World Institute. *Countries in Conflict*. Silver Springs, Md.: Bread for the World, 1995.

Brown, Michael E., ed. *Ethnic Conflict and International Security*. Princeton: Princeton University Press, 1993.

_____. *International Implications of Internal Conflict*. Cambridge, Mass.: MIT Press, 1996.

Cahill, Kevin M., M.D., ed. *A Framework for Survival: Health, Human Rights, and Humanitarian Assistance in Conflicts and Disasters*. New York: Basic Books, 1993.

Childers, Erskine, with Brian Urquhart. *Renewing the United Nations System*. Uppsala: Dag Hammarskjöld Foundation, 1994.

Claude, Richard P., and Burns H. Weston, eds. *Human Rights in the International Community*. Rev. 2d ed. Philadelphia: University of Pennsylvania Press, 1992.

Cohn, Ilene, and Guy S. Goodwin-Gill. *The Role of Children in Armed Conflict*. Oxford: Clarendon Press, 1994.

Commission on Global Governance. *Our Global Neighbourhood*. Oxford: Oxford University Press, 1995.

Cortright, David, and George A. Lopez. *Economic Sanctions: Panacea or Peacebuilding in a Post–Cold War World*. Boulder: Westview Press, 1995.

Cuny, Frederick. *Disasters and Development*. New York: Oxford University Press, 1984.

Cuny, Frederick, Barry N. Stein, and Pat Reed, eds. *Repatriation During Conflict in Africa and Asia*. Dallas: Center for the Study of Societies in Crisis, 1992.

Damrosch, Lori Fisler, ed. *Enforcing Restraint: Collective Intervention in Internal Conflicts.* New York: Council on Foreign Relations, 1993.

Damrosch, Lori Fisler, and David J. Scheffer. *Law and Force in the New International Order.* Boulder: Westview Press, 1991.

Deng, Francis M. *Protecting the Dispossessed: A Challenge for the International Community.* Washington, D.C.: Brookings Institution, 1993.

Deng, Francis M., and Larry Minear. *The Challenges of Famine Relief.* Washington, D.C.: Brookings Institution, 1992.

Diehl, Paul. *International Peacekeeping.* Baltimore: Johns Hopkins University Press, 1993.

Donnelly, Jack. *Human Rights and International Relations.* Boulder: Westview Press, 1993.

Duffield, Mark, and John Prendergast. *Without Troops and Tanks: Humanitarian Intervention in Ethiopia and Eritrea.* Trenton, N.J.: Red Sea Press, 1994.

Durch, William J., ed. *The Evolution of U.N. Peacekeeping: Case Studies and Comparative Analysis.* New York: St. Martin's Press, 1993.

Edwards, Michael, and David Hulme, eds. *Beyond the Magic Bullet: NGO Performance and Accountability in the Post–Cold War World.* West Hartford, Conn.: Kumarian Press, 1996.

Ferris, Elizabeth G., ed. *The Challenge to Intervene: A New Role for the United Nations?* Uppsala: Life and Peace Institute, 1992.

Field, John Osgood, ed. *The Challenge of Famine: Recent Experience, Lessons Learned.* West Hartford, Conn.: Kumarian Press, 1993.

Forsythe, David P. *Human Rights and Peace: International and National Dimensions.* Lincoln: University of Nebraska Press, 1992.

_____. *Humanitarian Politics.* Baltimore: Johns Hopkins University Press, 1977.

_____. *The Internationalization of Human Rights.* Lexington, Mass.: Lexington Books for the Free Press, 1991.

Girardet, Ed, ed. *Somalia, Rwanda, and Beyond: The Role of the Informational Media in Wars and Humanitarian Crises.* Dublin: Crosslines Global Report, 1995.

Gordenker, Leon. *Refugees in International Politics.* London: Croom Helm, 1987.

Gordenker, Leon, and Thomas G. Weiss, eds. *Soldiers, Peacekeepers, and Disasters.* London: Macmillan, 1991.

Gottlieb, Gidon. *Nation Against State: New Approaches to Ethnic Conflicts and the Decline of Sovereignty.* New York: Council on Foreign Relations, 1993.

Gowing, Nik. *Real-Time Television Coverage of Armed Conflicts and Diplomatic Crises: Does It Pressure or Distort Foreign Policy Decisions?* Cambridge, Mass.: Harvard University Press, 1994.

Gurr, Ted Robert, and Barbara Harff. *Ethnic Conflict in World Politics.* Boulder: Westview Press, 1994.

Halperin, Morton H., and David J. Scheffer. *Self-Determination in the New World Order.* Washington, D.C.: Carnegie Endowment, 1992.

Hannum, Hurst. *Autonomy, Sovereignty, and Self-Determination.* Philadelphia: University of Pennsylvania Press, 1990.

Henkin, Alice H., ed. *Honoring Human Rights and Keeping the Peace.* Washington, D.C.: Aspen Institute, 1995.

Henkin, Louis. *Right v. Might.* New York: Council on Foreign Relations, 1991.

Henkin, Louis, and John Lawrence Grove, eds. *Human Rights: An Agenda for the Next Century.* Washington, D.C.: American Society of International Law, 1995.

Hoffman, Stanley. *Duties Beyond Borders: On the Limits and Possibilities of Ethnic International Politics.* Syracuse, N.Y.: Syracuse University Press, 1981.

Human Rights Watch. *The Lost Agenda: Human Rights and the U.N. Field Operations.* New York: Human Rights Watch, 1993.

Independent Commission on International Humanitarian Issues. *The Dynamics of Displacement.* London: Zed Books, 1987.

_____. *Famine: A Man-Made Disaster?* New York: Random House, 1985.

_____. *Modern War: The Humanitarian Challenge.* London: Zed Books, 1986.

_____. *Winning the Human Race?* London: Zed Books, 1998.

International Committee of the Red Cross. *Geneva Conventions of August 12, 1949* and *Protocols Additional to the Geneva Conventions of August 12, 1949.* Geneva: ICRC, 1989.

Johnstone, Ian. *Aftermath of the Gulf War: An Assessment of UN Action.* Boulder: Lynne Rienner, 1994.

Kalshoven, Frits, ed. *Assisting the Victims of Armed Conflict and Other Disasters.* Dordrecht: Nijhoff, 1989.

Kent, Randolph. *Anatomy of Disaster Relief: The International Network in Action.* London: Pinter, 1987.

Lake, Anthony, ed. *After the Wars: Reconstruction in Afghanistan, Indochina, Central America, Southern Africa, and the Horn of Africa.* Washington, D.C.: Overseas Development Council, 1990.

Larkin, Mary Ann, Frederick Cuny, and Barry Stein, eds. *Repatriating Under Conflict in Central America.* Washington, D.C.: Georgetown University and CIPRA, 1991.

Loescher, Gil. *Beyond Charity: Interventional Cooperation and the Global Refugee Crisis.* New York: Oxford University Press, 1994.

Louise, Christopher. *The Social Impacts of Light Weapons Availability and Proliferation.* Discussion Paper 59. Geneva: United Nations Research Institute for Social Development with International Alert, March 1995.

Lyons, Gene M., and Michael Mastanduno, eds. *Beyond Westphalia? National Sovereignty and International Intervention.* Baltimore: Johns Hopkins University Press, 1995.

MacAlister-Smith, Peter. *International Humanitarian Assistance: Disaster Relief Organizations in International Law and Organization.* Dordrecht: Nijhoff, 1985.

Macrae, Joanna, and Anthony Zwi. *War and Hunger: Rethinking International Responses to Complex Emergencies.* London: Zed Books, 1995.

Makinda, Samuel. *Seeking Peace from Chaos: Humanitarian Intervention in Somalia.* Boulder: Lynne Rienner, 1992.

Martin, Lisa. *Coercive Cooperation: Explaining Multilateral Economic Sanctions.* Princeton: Princeton University Press, 1992.

Minear, Larry, and Philippe Guillot. *Soldiers to the Rescue: Humanitarian Lessons from Rwanda.* Paris: Organization for Economic Cooperation and Development, 1996.

Minear, Larry, Colin Scott, and Thomas G. Weiss. *The News Media, Civil Wars, and Humanitarian Action.* Boulder: Lynne Rienner, 1996.

Minear, Larry, and Thomas G. Weiss. *Humanitarian Action in Times of War: A Handbook for Practitioners.* Boulder: Lynne Rienner, 1993.

_____. *Humanitarian Politics.* New York: Foreign Policy Association, 1995.

_____. *Mercy Under Fire: War and the Global Humanitarian Community.* Boulder: Westview Press, 1995.

Mingst, Karen A., and Margaret P. Karns. *The United Nations in the Post–Cold War Era.* Boulder: Westview Press, 1995.

Moynihan, Daniel Patrick. *Pandaemonium: Ethnicity in International Politics.* New York: Oxford University Press, 1993.

Norwegian Refugee Council. *The Protection of Internally Displaced Persons by NRC.* Oslo: NRC, January 1994.

Omaar, Rakiya, and Alex de Waal. *Somalia: Death, Destruction, and Despair.* London: African Rights, 1994.

_____. *Humanitarianism Unbound? Current Dilemmas Facing Multi-Mandate Relief Operations in Political Exercises.* Discussion Paper 5. London: African Rights, November 1994.

Ramcharan, B. G. *The International Law and Practice of Early Warning and Preventive Diplomacy: The Emerging Global Watch.* Dordrecht: Nijhoff, 1991.

Reed, Laura W., and Carl Kaysen, eds. *Emerging Norms of Justified Intervention.* Cambridge, Mass.: American Academy of Arts and Sciences, 1993.

Rieff, David. *Slaughterhouse: Bosnia and the Failure of the West.* New York: Simon and Schuster, 1995.

Roberts, Adam, and Benedict Kingsbury, eds. *United Nations, Divided World: The U.N.'s Role in International Relations.* 2d ed. Oxford: Clarendon Press, 1994.

Rodley, Nigel, ed. *To Loose the Bands of Wickedness.* London: Brassey, 1992.

Rosenau, James N. *The United Nations in a Turbulent World.* Boulder: Lynne Rienner, 1992.

Rotberg, Robert I., and Thomas G. Weiss, eds. *From Massacres to Genocide: The Media, Public Policy, and Humanitarian Crises.* Washington, D.C.: Brookings Institution, 1996.

Sahnoun, Mohamed. *Somalia: The Missed Opportunities.* Washington, D.C.: United Nations Institute of Peace, 1994.

Salomon, Kim. *Refugees in the Cold War: Toward a New International Refugee Regime in the Early Postwar Era.* Lund, Sweden: Lund University Press, 1991.

Sen, Amartya. *Poverty and Famines.* New York: Oxford University Press, 1981.

Shawcross, William. *The Quality of Mercy: Cambodia, the Holocaust, and Modern Conscience.* New York: Simon and Schuster, 1984.

Shepherd, Jack. *The Politics of Starvation.* Washington, D.C.: Carnegie Endowment for International Peace, 1975.

Slim, Hugo, ed. "Children and Childhood in Emergency Policy and Practice, 1919–1994." Special issue of *Disasters: The Journal of Disaster Studies and Management* 18, no. 3 (September 1994).

Smillie, Ian. *The Alms Bazaar: Altruism Under Fire—Non-Profit Organizations and International Development.* London: Intermediate Technology Publications, 1995.

Smillie, Ian, and Henny Helmich. *Non-Governmental Organisations and Governments: Stakeholders for Development.* Paris: Organization for Economic Cooperation and Development, 1994.

Sommer, John G. *Hope Restored? Humanitarian Aid in Somalia, 1990–1994.* Washington, D.C.: Refugee Policy Group, November 1994.

UNDP. *Human Development Report.* New York: Oxford University Press, 1995.

UNESCO. *International Dimensions of Humanitarian Law.* Dordrecht: Nijhoff, 1988.

UNHCR. *The State of the World's Refugees 1995: In Search of Solutions.* New York: Oxford University Press, 1995.

UNHCR. Division of Programmes and Operational Support. *Policy and Methodological Framework for Quick Impact Projects.* Geneva: United Nations High Commissioner for Refugees, June 30, 1994.

Weiss, Thomas G., David P. Forsythe, and Roger A. Coate. *The United Nations and Changing World Politics.* Boulder: Westview Press, 1994.

Weiss, Thomas G., ed. *The United Nations and Civil Wars.* Boulder: Lynne Rienner, 1995.

Weiss, Thomas G., and Leon Gordenker, eds. *NGOs, the UN, and Global Governance.* Boulder: Lynne Rienner, 1996.

Weiss, Thomas G., and Larry Minear, eds. *Humanitarianism Across Borders: Sustaining Civilians in Times of War.* Boulder: Lynne Rienner, 1993.

World Bank. *Governance: The World Bank's Experience.* Washington, D.C.: World Bank, 1994.

Zartman, I. William, ed. *Elusive Peace: Negotiating an End to Civil Wars.* Washington, D.C.: The Brookings Institution, 1996.

WEB LOCATIONS

ACUNS (Academic Council on the U.N. System)—www.netspace.org/acuns—addresses current issues related to U.N. reform and activities and provides related web sites to various U.N. agencies.

CNN—www.cnn.com—offers brief profile of current events and provides related web sites with more detailed analysis of conflicts in progress, such as Croatian Radio Broadcast, which is updated daily, and the weekly Bosnian newspaper.

Hunger Web—www.netspace.org/hungerweb—addresses a variety of issues related to hunger, provides situation updates and reference materials, and does excellent research.

International Federation of the Red Cross—www.ifrc.org—updates the activities of international and national Red Cross organizations, offers detailed description of relief activities and resource demands, and states code of conduct.

Journal of Humanitarian Affairs—www.gsp.cam.ac.uk/jha.html—offers in-depth articles on humanitarian issues updated monthly and lists job postings.

One World Organization—www.oneworld.org—acts as server for "globally minded broadcasters and NGOs" on a variety of issues, such as conflict, aid, health, human rights; provides related web sites of NGOs, including CARE, Oxfam, and Amnesty International; and is updated daily.

USAID—www.info.usaid—is a resource for country statistics upon which U.S. aid policy is based and provides related web sites for the State Department, the Peace Corps, and other U.S. agencies.

Volunteers in Technical Assistance—www.vita.org—an information resource service active in international development issues, provides related web sites to NGOs and is updated regularly.

□ □ □

Glossary

Anarchy carries two distinct meanings. When applied to international relations, anarchy refers to the absence of authoritative institutions or norms above sovereign states. In an international system of anarchy, states must employ self-help methods to survive. Anarchy and chaos are synonymous in more popular usage and often refer to general disorder.

Asylum is temporary refuge granted by one state to those fleeing their country of origin because of reasonable fear of persecution or harm.

Bilateral (or foreign) aid (to be distinguished from multilateral aid) is financial, material, or technical assistance provided to an individual country by another donor country. Such aid can be used to maintain the political influence of donor countries in recipient countries. Bilateral aid may be tied, meaning that recipient governments are required to purchase a certain percentage of goods and services from the donor government, or it may be conditional, meaning the recipient government is required to change certain of its current policies to receive aid.

Chapter VI of the U.N. Charter outlines the means used for the pacific settlement of disputes. Legitimate action includes diplomatic efforts, such as the use of good offices, mediation, and fact-finding.

Chapter VII of the U.N. Charter outlines coercive action with respect to threats to the peace, breaches of the peace, and acts of aggression. Legitimate action includes economic and military sanctions to enforce international decisions.

A **charter** is a written instrument executed in due form that creates and defines the signatories' rights and responsibilities and procedures for signatories' interaction.

A **civil war** is an intrastate armed conflict generally fought between the regime in power and its challengers. Conflicts within failed states, where there is no recognized state authority, are also described as civil war.

The **CNN effect** is the presumed causal phenomenon, coming to light especially during the Gulf War, in which the media (CNN in particular) demonstrate their power to inform and sway public opinion, which in turn affects international responses to humanitarian emergencies.

The **Cold War** is a concept used to imply the ideological standoff between the United States and the Soviet Union following World War II and ending with the demise of the Soviet Union in 1991. The Cold War was characterized by East-West conflicts by proxy, usually in developing countries.

Comparative advantage refers to a group of actors, each with specific and unique contributions to a common objective, that exploit their differences in order to produce together more effectively than they could separately, thereby providing the motivation for cooperation and coordination of tasks. Tasks are assigned in a way that recognizes the differences among actors and reflects who does what best.

Compassion (or donor) fatigue is a notion used to explain a decrease in resources or interest in humanitarian activities in complex emergencies or in related development activities designed to foster growth. It implies that donors have become overwhelmed by the increase in humanitarian needs and the rise in conflicts in recent years, along with the lack of success in development efforts, and have reduced their contributions because of personal or institutional resignation to the inevitability of conflict and the inability of past efforts to produce measurable or meaningful successes.

A **complex emergency** is a crisis characterized by political, economic, and social destabilization. A complex emergency might also include natural disasters, such as famine, and massive population movements.

Consent of political authorities within a conflict area means that some humanitarian actors, such as the ICRC, will withhold assistance to suffering populations until internal political authorities agree to the presence of external humanitarian workers and the conditions under which they will operate.

A **contact group** is a coalition of states that use their collective diplomatic, and sometimes economic, power to foster or negotiate peace among belligerents in a conflict.

The **continuum from relief to rehabilitation** (short-term, transitional projects designed to facilitate the restoration of a community's social, economic, judicial, and political infrastructure) **to development** (long-term projects designed to improve living standards) is an analytical concept that describes an approach to addressing comprehensively complex emergencies.

A **convention** is a legally binding international agreement among states on a particular matter of common concern.

A **corridor of tranquillity** is an access road used to deliver humanitarian assistance during active fighting. Theoretically, warring parties agree not to impede the transport of humanitarian aid through designated corridors of tranquillity.

A **declaration** is a nonbinding international document that embodies states' individual and collective intention to uphold the ideals contained in this joint proclamation.

Dependency is the condition of relying upon external sources for aid or support. Dependency can be created when victims are not capable of providing for themselves and may linger long after the initial stages of crisis have passed, which was the original justification for short-term aid.

Distributive justice is a process in which gross disparities in ownership of and control over resources and funds are remedied through a process of more equitable redistribution.

The **division of labor** is a classic economic theory stipulating that if an actor has a comparative advantage performing a particular activity, there will be an efficiency gain from allowing that actor to specialize in that task.

The **domino theory**, coined by President Dwight Eisenhower in 1954, hypothesized that if one country fell to communism, that would produce a domino effect whereby other countries would begin to fall as well.

Donor fatigue—see **compassion fatigue.**

Empowerment is a process by which those previously without the means to provide certain benefits (physical or psychological) for themselves are given the means and opportunities to do so.

Enforcement/coercion strategies, as outlined in Chapter VII of the U.N. Charter, represent the forceful means by which the international community applies pressure to belligerents to insist upon a change in behavior that violates international law or norms. This is a synonym for intervention.

Ethnic cleansing is the systemized elimination of a targeted ethnic group for political purposes. Ethnic cleansing can be carried out through genocidal acts or forced migration.

Ethnicity is the perceived or actual identifying characteristics showed by a group of people based on language, culture, history, race, or religion.

A **failed state** is one in which there is no clear legitimate sovereign or governing authority.

Genocide is the deliberate, planned, and systematic extermination of a national, ethnic, religious, political, or racial group.

Human rights, the rights that one has simply because one is a human being, are held equally and inalienably. They are the social and political guarantees necessary to protect individuals from the standard threats to human dignity posed by the modern state and modern markets.

Humanitarian action covers a range of activities, such as diplomacy, emergency relief, and rehabilitation and development projects, designed to alleviate human suffering both in the short and long term and to protect human rights.

The **humanitarian imperative** refers to an individual belief that wherever there is human suffering the international humanitarian system must respond, regardless of political considerations.

Humanitarian intervention consists of efforts by outside parties to ensure the delivery of emergency aid and accompanying efforts to protect the rights of local peoples without the consent of local political authorities.

Humanitarian space is a concept that refers to the range of operational freedom within which humanitarian actors can provide assistance.

Idealism is a perspective that was adopted by many political leaders following World War I. Idealism claims that humankind is perfectible, that war is not inevitable, and that a harmony of interests among states is possible; it is a theoretical tradition in international relations that focuses on international cooperation and international law.

Impartiality is the requirement that humanitarian aid be provided to noncombatants solely on the basis of need.

Imperialism is a policy of extending a country's influence over other territories and peoples.

Import substitution is the economic process through which local production displaces or substitutes for previously imported goods.

Intergovernmental organizations (IGOs) are associations whose members are composed of states and whose functions, in theory, are to reflect the common concerns of members.

Internally displaced persons (IDPs) are those who have fled their homes as a result of a conflict but have not crossed over internationally recognized borders into another state.

International humanitarian law (or international law of armed conflicts) is the body of legal standards, procedures, and institutions governing the social intercourse of sovereign states with respect to war. The principles of humanitarian law, which are found primarily in the four Geneva conventions of 1949 and the Additional Protocols of 1977, state that armed forces are not free to pursue their objectives by any means they consider necessary or convenient, that only military personnel and property can be targeted, and that it is unlawful for an armed force to engage in any attack or operation if the anticipated suffering of either soldiers or civilians is disproportionate to the military gains that might be made.

International law governs relations between states and other legal persons in the international system. The sources of international law include international conventions, international custom, and general principles of the laws of states.

Jus ad bellum is the humanitarian law governing resort to war whereby self-defense is deemed the only legitimate cause for declaring war.

Jus in bello is the humanitarian law of war by which states must discriminate between combatants and noncombatants and must demonstrate proportionality with regard to the means of war.

A **lead agency** is a U.N. organization designated by the secretary-general to assume a leadership position in a particular relief operation. Its functions are to coordinate relief activities among a multitude of humanitarian actors within and outside of the U.N. system and to serve as a focal point for information dissemination.

Liberal institutionalism is the school of thought among international relations theorists that recognizes that states are indeed the most important actors in international relations but also claims that cooperation among them is achievable through involvement in transnational institutions, where common interests merge, transparency of others' actions is revealed, and transaction costs are reduced.

Liberation theology, as it emerged in Latin America in the 1960s, is the argument that the special duty of the believing Christian is to work for the liberation of the poor and oppressed through, among other avenues, active opposition to existing power structures.

Loud and silent emergencies are two types of humanitarian crises and the degree of international responses that each tends to generate. Loud emergencies are those represented by active physical violence between warring parties, and they tend to receive attention—from the media and humanitarians. Silent emergencies, which can contribute to the eventual emergence of a loud emergency, are best characterized by structural violence—that is, conditions arising from social, economic, and political structures that increase the vulnerability of various groupings of people to many forms of harm, such as hunger, poverty, and disease. The latter emergencies are considered to be less newsworthy.

Multilateral aid (to be distinguished from bilateral aid) is financial, material, or technical assistance channeled to countries by other countries via such international organizations as U.N. agencies or the European Union.

Neutrality is the requirement that humanitarian aid be provided regardless of the origins, beliefs, or ideology of the beneficiaries.

A **no-fly zone** is a demarcated territory determined to be off limits to antagonistic aircraft. No-fly zones require effective individual or collective security measures to enforce the integrity of the territory and its protected population.

Nongovernmental organizations (NGOs) are typically nonprofit, nonofficial organizations that are actively involved in processes of humanitarian assistance, human rights advocacy, or socioeconomic development. NGOs can be local, national, or international in scope, and they rely on donations, grants, or contract fees for their operations.

Réfoulement occurs when countries of asylum forcefully expel or return a refugee to the frontiers of territories where his or her life or freedom would be threatened. *Réfoulement* is a violation of Article 33 of the Refugee Convention.

A **norm** is a standard, model, or pattern of behavior in a certain issue area to which actors adhere with a certain degree of predictability.

Official development assistance is aid provided by governments, through their own bilateral agency or intergovernmental and nongovernmental organizations, with the provision that at least 25 percent is a grant and not a loan.

A **paramilitary** group is an association of combatants that operates in place of or as a supplement to a regular military force. It is often indeterminable who controls the actions of paramilitary groups.

Peace-building refers to rehabilitation strategies applied to a war-torn society once a peace agreement has been signed. Peace-building includes activities such as demobilization programs and community building.

Peacekeeping is the deployment of a U.N.-sanctioned troop presence in the field, hitherto with the consent of all the parties concerned and normally involving U.N. military and/or police personnel and frequently civilians as well. Military force is used only in self-defense and as a last resort.

Peacemaking traditionally is action to bring hostile parties to agreement, essentially through such pacific means as those foreseen in Chapter VI of the Charter of the United Nations.

Populations at risk are those dependent on outside aid to avoid malnutrition or death as a result of a complex humanitarian emergency.

Preventive deployment refers to efforts by the international community to stabilize a region affected by progressively escalating political and military conflict. Preventive deployment requires consent of a host government and can include early posting of civilian, police, and/or military personnel to maintain order within a country, along both sides of a border in dispute, or on one side of a border.

Protection in the context of humanitarian action refers to ensuring respect for the human rights of vulnerable populations.

Realism (and neorealism) is the dominant approach to international relations. It assumes that people are self-interested and seek to dominate others; that the state is a rational, unitary actor pursuing its perceived self-interest within an anarchic international system; and that cooperation among states is determined by a state's narrow and immediate interest in doing so.

A **refugee** is a person who has fearfully fled his or her home as a result of political conflict and has crossed an internationally recognized border in search of asylum.

A **regime** is a set of principles, norms, rules, and decisionmaking procedures influencing state behavior (and other relevant international actors) in an issue area. The notion of a regime points to patterns of international governance that are not necessarily limited to a single treaty or organization.

Relief is the delivery of emergency goods and services that ameliorate hunger, pain, anxiety, and other forms of human vulnerability.

Repatriation is the sending of refugees or other economic migrants back to their countries of origin.

Resettlement consists of permanently permitting refugees to remain in a country of asylum or establishing a new community for internally displaced persons within their own country.

A **safe haven or safe area** is an internationally protected area within a conflict zone that is reserved for the care and safeguarding of civilians, who are generally dependent upon outside humanitarian assistance for day-to-day survival. The reality of safe havens has not always matched the theory.

Sanctions are nonforcible, economic measures, as outlined in Chapter VII of the U.N. Charter, by one or more states to force another state to comply with legal obligations or international norms. Sanctions include the cessation of economic transactions, the freezing of assets abroad, and the suspension of travel and communication links.

Sister-city programs, in the context of Central American humanitarian crises, were advocacy projects designed to educate those in developed countries with the material resources and political clout to apply pressure on U.S. decisionmakers to alter what was deemed aggressive U.S. foreign intervention in the political affairs of Central America.

Sovereignty, narrowly defined, is a state's claim to supreme political authority in a defined territory, particularly to the rights of self-determination and noninterference from other states.

A **treaty** is a contract in writing between two or more states.

Triage is the process by which treatment of vulnerable populations at various levels of need is prioritized in situations where there are multiple demands for attention and limited human and material resources.

The **Vietnam syndrome** is the resistance to U.S. military engagement in overseas conflicts that grew out of the substantial public opposition to U.S. involvement in Vietnam, where over fifty thousand Americans lost their lives. Conflict situations that stimulate the appearance of the Vietnam syndrome are those that are perceived to require substantial military ground-troops in a civil war environment and in which the possibilities of protracted involvement in the conflict and substantial U.S. deaths are high, while the chances of success are low. The alternative is the "Powell Doctrine," named after the former chairman of the Joint Chiefs of Staff Colin Powell, which requires a clear definition of policy goals and the ability to use all available firepower and moral resolution to overwhelm an enemy as quickly as possible.

About the Book and Authors

There are two distinct contemporary challenges to the relief of war-induced human suffering: one that occurs within the institutions that make up the international humanitarian system, the other in war zones. Varied interests, resources, and organizational structures within institutions hamper the efficiency and effectiveness of humanitarian operations. At the same time—on the ground—ethical, legal, and operational challenges and dilemmas continually arise that require humanitarian actors to choose a course of action with associated necessary evils.

Humanitarian Challenges and Intervention shows how institutional concerns—combined with the domestic context of armed conflicts—often yield policies that do not serve the immediate requirements of victims for relief, stabilization, and community reconstruction. Based on case studies of the post–Cold War experience in Central America, northern Iraq, Somalia, the former Yugoslavia, and Rwanda, the authors make recommendations for a more effective and efficient humanitarian system.

Thomas G. Weiss is associate director of Brown University's Thomas J. Watson Jr. Institute for International Studies and executive director of the Academic Council on the United Nations System. **Cindy Collins** is a graduate student in the Department of Political Science at Brown University.

Books in This Series

□ □ □

Kenneth W. Grundy
South Africa: Domestic Crisis and Global Challenge
□ □ □

David S. Mason
**Revolution in East-Central Europe
and World Politics, Second Edition**
□ □ □

Georg Sørensen
**Democracy and Democratization:
Processes and Prospects in a Changing World**
□ □ □

Steve Chan
**East Asian Dynamism: Growth, Order, and
Security in the Pacific Region, Second Edition**
□ □ □

Jack Donnelly
International Human Rights
□ □ □

V. Spike Peterson and Anne Sisson Runyan
Global Gender Issues
□ □ □

Sarah J. Tisch and Michael B. Wallace
**Dilemmas of Development Assistance:
The What, Why, and Who of Foreign Aid**
□ □ □

Ted Robert Gurr and Barbara Harff
Ethnic Conflict in World Politics
□ □ □

Frederic S. Pearson
**The Global Spread of Arms:
Political Economy of International Security**
□ □ □

Deborah J. Gerner
**One Lane, Two Peoples:
The Conflict over Palestine, Second Edition**
□ □ □

225

Karen Mingst and Margaret P. Karns
The United Nations in the Post–Cold War Era

□   □   □

Gareth Porter and Janet Welsh Brown
Global Environmental Politics, Second Edition

□   □   □

Bruce E. Moon
Dilemmas of International Trade

□   □   □

Barry B. Hughes
**International Futures: Choices in the
Creation of a New World Order, Second Edition**

□   □   □

Thomas G. Weiss and Cindy Collins
**Humanitarian Challenges and Intervention:
World Politics and the Dilemmas of Help**

Index